C000156229

THE LIFE
JAMES J. HILL

BY

JOSEPH GILPIN PYLE

AUTHORIZED

ILLUSTRATED

VOLUME
II

GARDEN CITY   NEW YORK

DOUBLEDAY, PAGE & COMPANY

1917

JAMES JEROME HILL
1838-1916

CONTENTS

VOLUME II

CONTENTS

LIST OF ILLUSTRATIONS

THE LIFE OF
JAMES J. HILL
VOLUME
II

CHAPTER   TWENTY–TWO

REORGANIZATION OF NORTHERN PACIFIC

JANUARY, 1893, saw the Great Northern opened for business through to the Pacific coast. August 15, 1893, an application for the appointment of receivers was made by creditors of the Northern Pacific, who alleged that the company was insolvent. Receivers were appointed; and in October of the same year the Farmers' Loan and Trust Company, as trustees for the mortgagees, filed a bill for the foreclosure of the mortgages securing its second, third, and consolidated mortgage bonds. This was more than coincidence. The financing of one system had been as reckless as that of the other was prudent. The operation of the one was lacking where that of the other was strong. The competition for business between the two had for some time made its consequences felt. Not alone in the stock market is the money value of coming events discounted by a rise or fall based on calculations of what is about to happen. People who cared to know it knew now that the Great Northern could, if it wished, by virtue of its low capitalization, method of construction and system of management and operation, control through competitive business. If the Northern

Pacific had been a solvent concern, its owners and creditors must still have dreaded a doubtful future. Staggering as it was under accumulated indebtedness, this last touch of hard fact toppled it over. The financial condition of the country as a whole had seldom been worse. With comparatively few exceptions its railroads were trying to keep away from the sharp edge of bankruptcy. There was no possibility of any arrangement with the creditors of this system which could prevent or even postpone disaster. So it was added to the long list of transportation companies in the hands of receivers. Such a situation could not fail to be of deep moment to those interested in the Great Northern, above all to Mr. Hill.

He had, of course, foreseen the event. In fact, he was almost as well informed about the resources and liabilities of the Northern Pacific as its own officers and and directors. Some references of his to the state of its affairs have been given in preceding chapters. He was always quietly on the watch. In May, 1893, he wrote to Lord Mount Stephen: "I cabled you a few words about the Northern Pacific. That company has run its length and will have to be entirely reorganized, wiping out all present and preferred shares. There are two very strong parties, including the very strongest financial concerns here, who will take up the reorganization provided we will name half the new board and find men to manage the prop-

4

erty. . . . We will not invest money in it, but our position in traffic matters is so well recognized that the parties feel safer with our coöperation than in any other position." This shows that, before any announcement of the bankruptcy of the Northern Pacific, those on the inside of its affairs had been sending out distress signals and looking about; and had seen only one way in which the property could be saved. The largest holders of Northern Pacific securities, by whom they must be rehabilitated, were by this time well acquainted with Mr. Hill and his methods. The Deutsche Bank knew that it had to deal with a supremely able and successful man. In this country, the Northern Pacific people had turned to Mr. J. P. Morgan, a colossus of finance and a master hand in reorganizing properties that had gone to pieces. Mr. Morgan and Mr. Hill had long known each other and were personal friends. They had not been so closely connected in business interests as they now became. "Community of interest" was beginning to mean something in the upper circles of the railroad and financial world.

Mr. Morgan never was, pretended or desired to be a practical railroad manager. He was a financier. If he discovered a workable plan for financing the Northern Pacific, it would be as worthless as a watch without a mainspring unless two conditions were satisfied. First, the property must be efficiently managed, or it would again complete the cycle of a few years of artificial prosperity ending in another fall. Second, there must be an understanding by which that superdreadnought, the Great Northern, would not be found in a hostile fleet. In a word, it was no clearer to Mr. Hill that the interest of his property would be served by his participation in the future of the Northern Pacific than it was to Mr. Morgan that any reorganization without some such understanding would be time wasted and money thrown away. So, while the receivers did what they could with the property—and they made no shining success of it—in the next two years plans and arrangements matured for the greatest railroad combination that had yet appeared in American history.

Mr. Hill canvassed the situation with characteristic thoroughness. He was chary of glittering possibilities. Always he scrutinized them and, as soon as he saw the remotest chance that his own great property, the work of his life, might even suffer chance of loss, drew away. But control—actual or essential—of the Northern Pacific was no common temptation. It would mean railroad harmony throughout the territory from the Great Lakes to the Pacific, including seven states. Yet in Mr. Hill's mind such a power was desirable principally because it conduced to the certainty of economical operation. He saw how, with rate wars abolished, offices consolidated, reckless building stopped, freight shipped by the shortest line from point to point regardless of systems—

6

rates might be steadily lowered while millions were added to profits on both lines. The business side of the proposition appealed to him powerfully. For that reason, he was especially careful not to let himself be carried away by a sudden impulse. He studied this question to the bottom, as he had that of the St. Paul & Pacific before its bonds were bought. He trusted greatly the judgment of Lord Mount Stephen, a born financier and now an influential personage in foreign financial circles. His letters to this friend tell pretty nearly the whole story of the part which the Great Northern was to play in the reorganization of the Northern Pacific. When such letters exist they make authentic history. In October, 1894, while negotiations went on with Mr. Morgan and the others who were working out a plan, he wrote:

"If the Northern Pacific could be handled as we handle our property and all the wild and uncalled-for rate cutting stopped, it could be made a great property. Its capacity to earn money is good, and with all unnecessary expenses, commissions, and train service abolished, it would, I think, astonish even its friends.

"You will recall how often it has been said that when the Northern Pacific, Union Pacific and other competitors failed, or went into the hands of receivers, our company would not be able to stand; and that they, having nothing but expenses to pay, would destroy our business. Now we have had them all in bankruptcy

7

and in the hands of receivers for more than a year; and while the Northern Pacific has been forced to issue $5,000,000 receivers' debentures, we have gone along and met not only their competition but that of the 'Soo' line and the Canadian Pacific Railroad on coast traffic, which is really more destructive than Northern Pacific if we followed it down, and in addition we have had the worst conditions of business and other matters affecting our company, and still we hold our own. I hope you will not consider this as self praise, for it is not so intended. The quality is in the property, and careful management and constant effort will bring it out.

"The treasury situation on Nov. 1 will show a balance of nearly half a million dollars in the treasury over and above the amount necessary to pay all coupons due the first of January following. Of course, the above leaves a small margin for a large company like ours—too small—but in view of what we have come through in the way of panics, strikes, floods, storm, and fire, I think it shows the real strength of the company more than anything else could."

Five days later he sent to the same correspondent a very long letter. After analyzing in detail the property and liabilities of the Northern Pacific with the precision and thoroughness of an expert who might have been examining it for a report to the owners, he said:

"To handle the property in the courts and hasten a

reorganization would require actual control and a strong party. The amount of work to be done would be very great, and the men who could be of use are very few. The advantages to our company would mainly come from the freedom from competition and needless friction and expense in operation, all of which I think would be worth to us about $600,000 or possibly $750,000. When they went into the hands of receivers a year ago, timid people said, 'Now the Great Northern meets its Waterloo, with its competitors in hands of receivers and released from fixed charges, etc.'; but you will bear in mind our difficulties from serious floods, strikes, fires, etc., during the past year, and still we are prosperous and in good financial condition, while they are asking the court to pay their shortages. I speak of this to show that we can get along without them and against their operating at an enormous loss. At the same time the control of an empire such as lies between Lake Superior and the Pacific Ocean, which is served by the lines of both companies, would render the future reasonably secure for both properties, and its value should not be overlooked. . . . There are many other matters of detail of which I could write, but unless there is a probability of our doing something it is hardly worth while taking your time. However, I am reasonably satisfied that if the Berlin people or any other holders of Northern Pacific securities do not realize how much more we can do with the property than any other organization without exception, they will surely realize this before they are done."

The people by whom the future of these hundreds of millions of dollars' worth of property was to be decided must reach a common understanding. They all looked to Mr. Hill for knowledge of detail and for future assurance. There were the bankers in Berlin, and, below them, the many investors in other European countries. There were the American banking houses. While all of them had relied on Mr. Morgan to outline a financial scheme and to find the necessary capital or credit to float it, they knew that Mr. Hill must not only be a part of this scheme, but that he must declare the project practicable as to operation and profits. How very cautious he was about this may be read in a letter to Mr. Schiff, January 4, 1895, as the time for a final decision approached:

"I think I fully appreciate the situation as it affects both companies. A very large saving could be made in (Northern Pacific) operating expenses and waste of revenue, and further by reducing all unnecessary train mileage. The net result would be so great as to astonish you.

"The work of looking after all this could not be done anywhere else than on the ground, and it would require an organization which could not be made in a day. I am sure you feel in our own case that we are doing our work with fair economy, and that we are improving

10

from month to month; still no one knows better than I do how far we are from doing as well as could be done. A difference of ten cents in the average cost of moving one ton of freight one hundred miles on any line will make a difference in our net revenue of $1,000,000; and I think the difference in our average cost per ton per mile and that of the Northern Pacific last year would have given them over $3,000,000 more net revenue than they earned.

"I have gone over their mortgages carefully and spent what time I could spare evenings on their reports, but I am not clear as to many of their worthless branches.

"It is beyond doubt a very desirable thing to do, and at the same time one that calls for the greatest caution and wise forethought in making a plan of campaign, and after the work of reorganization was carried out, the real hard drudgery would begin in order to secure an organization that would get the results which should be had to justify the work."

At the last moment, March 19, 1895, just before the die was to be cast, he reported to Lord Mount Stephen the results of his conferences with Mr. E. D. Adams, the American representative of the Deutsche Bank, who later was to become Chairman of the Board of Directors for the reorganized Northern Pacific:

"Since our arrival in New York, which will be two weeks to-morrow evening, I have spent most of my time on Northern Pacific matters and have had several interviews with Mr. Adams, during which I have gone over the entire situation with him as it was discussed in London and also covering about all the ground relating to the property, its value as a railway, present and prospective. I also made up a comparative statement from the Railroad Commissioners' reports, showing the results on the basis of operating cost of the Milwaukee & St. Paul, the Chicago & Northwestern and the Great Northern. Applied to the business of the Northern Pacific, the result shows that it would be necessary to get better results than either of these in order to place the Northern Pacific where it could pay the obligations necessary to an acceptable reorganization and at the same time leave the new company on a basis of net earnings which would enable it to pay its interest charges beyond question, even if a failure of crops or other temporary cause reduced its income.

"I have urged on Mr. Adams, and I am sure that he agrees with me, that the market price of the bonds of the reorganized company will be the measure of the company's credit, and the importance of having the bonds so good that the holders will not be at all anxious to sell them. There would be much difficulty in building up the credit of the new company in the face of so many bondholders watching the market with a view to selling on every little rise.

"Mr. Adams has evidently worked very hard since

12

he went into the committee, and I find he has acquired a great deal of information which is more or less valuable and which must really have taken a great deal of time and labour to work out. At the same time the whole question comes down to, first, a determination of what the company can be made to earn *net;* and, then, the best and the most practicable distribution of these earnings to the new bonds and stocks by an equitable merging of the several classes into the new company's securities. I think I have shown Mr. Adams to his satisfaction that the Northern Pacific can be made to do better work than it has ever done in the past. . . . and a reorganization made on these lines will be creditable to the makers and profitable to all who receive the securities.

"I may be mistaken, but I think I could see in Mr. Adams's mind a somewhat remote desire toward a *unification* of the two corporations. However, with the past experience of the Northern Pacific in operation of its lines, and the small proportion of net to gross earnings, it was not easy to devise any plan of reorganization that would meet the expectations of the bondholders and at the same time be on a really safe basis looking to the future credit of the company.

"The Adams committee seem to have made a really good plan for that company, if they can get some *good men* to handle the property on a basis of good economy. It makes little difference what else is done if a property

13

is not handled with close regard to expenses and income."

In the period between the order for a receivership and the announcement of a definite plan of reorganization, the course which must be adopted to save the Northern Pacific and restore to it the financial and business standing worthy of so great a property was studied and discussed by all the parties interested. There were goings and comings across the Atlantic. Mr. Hill and his friends were ready to contribute money support, and their still more necessary knowledge and advice about the practical management of the system. The three principal parties to the agreement to be reached were the Deutsche Bank of Berlin, J. P. Morgan, and James J. Hill. Finally a plan was matured and defined in a memorandum which constituted the first "London Agreement." It was drawn up at Mr. Morgan's house in London, and in its terms all the parties at last found common ground. The following is the text of this important document:

London, May 10th, 1895.

To Edward D. Adams, Esq.,
   Chairman of the Reorganization Committee,
    Northern Pacific R. R. Co.

The undersigned, on behalf of a majority of the capital stock of the Great Northern Railway Company, hereby propose that the Great Northern Co. shall guarantee the payment of the principal and interest of new Gold Bonds, secured by a mortgage lien upon the Land Grant and Railway of the Northern Pacific R. R. Co., of such an amount as you may require in your reorganization,

14

provided the principal sum shall not exceed the amount of $175,000,000, and that the annual interest thereon shall not exceed $6,200,000, and further provided as follows:

1. The new Company shall not have any other fixed interest charges than those now existing upon the present outstanding bonds of the St. Paul and Northern Pacific R. Co. ($509,760) and the Northern Pacific Terminal Co. of Oregon ($70,000), and such as may hereafter be assumed with our aproval.

$8,423,000 of the new 4% Bonds shall be set aside in trust to provide for the same amount of Saint Paul & Northern Pacific Bonds at their maturity. The mortgage shall provide for further issues upon additional mileage, at the rate of not exceeding $20,000 per mile of road, limited in total amount to 200 millions, and restricted in method of issue, with or without the guarantee of the Great Northern Railway Company, to the cash value of the property acquired, and to the action of a majority of the Board of Directors of the new Company.

The $15,249,000 of Branch Companies' Bonds held by the public to be offered the privilege of conversion into such an amount of the above mentioned additional issue as the interest upon which will not exceed an average of $400 per mile per annum.

The form of the Mortgage to be approved by our Counsel as well as by yours.

2. One half of the entire capital stock of the new Company, succeeding to the present property of the Northern Pacific Railroad Company, shall be delivered to the Great Northern Railway Co.

3. A majority of one, in a Board of Directors of nine, shall be nominated by us. The minority capital shall be entitled to four of nine Directors, and to elect the Chairman of the Board of Directors, so long as the majority capital remains en bloc, in the interest of the Great Northern R. Co., but not after Dividends at the rate of five per cent. per annum shall have been paid for two consecutive years upon the entire Capital Stock of the new Company, and not in any event for more than five years.

4. The treasury of the new Company shall contain, when the control of the property and shares are delivered to us, not less than

$3,500,000 cash assets, or $4,000,000 of new 4% Bonds, in addition to whatever stocks and bonds now among the assets of the Northern Pacific Railroad Co., may not be required by you in perfecting your reorganization.

5. The unconditional guarantee of the principal and interest of the new bonds, by the Great Northern Railway Company, shall be executed upon each bond, to the extent of $175,000,000.

6. The $6,200,000 guaranteed per annum shall be payable as required by the service of the debt, and shall accrue from the date of transfer of the property from the Receivers to our control of its operations.

7. The details of the reorganization, and the methods for carrying out the purpose of this proposal, are to be under your control, and such only as your Counsel approve.

Should your Committee and your bankers, Messrs. J. P. Morgan & Co., and the Deutsche Bank, approve this proposal, and undertake in good faith to carry the same into effect, with the least possible delay, we pledge to you our loyal and active coöperation.

(Signed)   JAS. J. HILL

MOUNT STEPHEN

EDWARD TUCK.

Referring to the above, as well as the letter of Mr. Adams to James J. Hill, dated London, May 9, 1895, we hereby approve of the terms expressed in the correspondence, and pledge our best endeavour in good faith to carry the same into effect.

(Signed)   Deutsche Bank.

G. SIEMENS. A. GWINNER.

The within proposal is hereby accepted, subject to the formal ratification of the Reorganization Committee.

(Signed) EDWARD D. ADAMS,

Chairman.

This agreement contemplated not only a gigantic financial operation, but something new in the relation of the transcontinental lines. It provided that the bondholders should obtain a decree of foreclosure and have the property bid in by a committee of their own. The outstanding stock of the Northern Pacific was upward of $80,000,000. Besides its floating debt, it had outstanding bonds to a total of more than $121,000,000, on most of which no interest had been paid for two years. It was to be reorganized as a new company, with new bonds to the total of $100,000,000 or over, and the same amount of capital stock. The assignment of these to holders of the old securities is of no interest here. What is of interest is that the Great Northern Company guaranteed the payment of the principal of the bonds, and interest on them not to exceed $6,200,000 a year. In return, the reorganized company was to turn over one half its capital stock to the Great Northern or to its trustee. Provision was made for joint use of certain tracks and terminals, and for an amicable and equitable interchange of traffic. It was not looked upon as a final but a tentative affair. It was an advantageous deal for both sides; but was certain to rouse both public and private remonstrance.

Trouble began at once when the details of the arrangement were noised about. It was an especially trying time for Mr. Hill. The people who feared or professed to fear the consequences of such a consolidation emptied their vials of wrath on him and his railroad. The Northern Pacific was down; why kick it? The Great Northern was represented as

17

the octopus which was trying to take that property from its owners and fasten the grip of a mighty traffic monopoly on the Northwest.   A wave of public excitement swept over all that section.   An alleged railroad combination to dominate the business of the Northwestern states raised an issue too well adapted to political controversy to be neglected.   A legal test of the validity of the agreement was inevitable, and was desired by both its friends and its enemies.   Thomas W. Pearsall, a stockholder of the Great Northern, brought suit in the Federal Court to prevent the carrying out of the arrangement, alleging that it would depreciate the value of his holding, by making the Great Northern the guarantor of a financially unstable system.   The basis of the legal attack may be stated simply.

The charter of the Minneapolis & St. Cloud Company, which was that of the Great Northern with only a change of name, as amended by subsequent legislation, was extremely liberal.   It gave to the company a right to consolidate with others at pleasure.   But in 1874 the Minnesota legislature had passed an act forbidding the consolidation of parallel and competing lines.   And in 1881 it enacted another law strengthening the prohibition in these positive terms: "No railroad corporation shall consolidate with, lease or purchase, or in any way become owner of or control, any other railroad corporation, or any stock, franchises, rights, or property thereof, which owns or controls

18

a parallel or competing line." Two questions only called for decision. Were the Great Northern and the Northern Pacific parallel and competing? Was the Great Northern, by the terms of its original charter, exempt from the operation of these later statutes? The Circuit Court held for the company's contention. The Supreme Court of the United States, on appeal, reversed the decision, March 30, 1896. So the project of a reorganization by joint ownership and guarantee of securities came to grief on one of the scores of legal reefs which line the course of every large railway corporation, and of which the pilot of the Great Northern seems to have encountered his full share.

During this litigation the burden of the battle had fallen on the Great Northern, that is to say on Mr. Hill. His letters in 1895 are full of it. The highest court had not yet spoken its final word. September 3, he wrote to a confidential friend in Seattle; "My time has been so taken up with this Northern Pacific matter that I have been unable to do much else. It seems very unfortunate that the affairs of that company have become so badly involved. The bondholders, scattered through Switzerland, France, Belgium, Holland, Austria, Germany, England and Scotland, are so discouraged with American transcontinental railway securities that they absolutely refuse to take the independent, unsupported bonds of any reorganizing company. Their first choice is to sell the property outright and get rid of it and, as they

19

say, 'Wipe its name from the face of the earth,' if not
from their own recollections. To find a company to buy
the Northern Pacific would be practically impossible.
Therefore, their next, and what they consider the most
feasible plan, is to have the company reorganized by
the security holders and placed in charge of some existing company with a well established credit, which will
guarantee the bonds, and this guarantee will enable
the old Northern Pacific bondholders to dispose of their
new securities at a price. Our company, although a
young one in years, has excellent credit abroad, and I
think it would not be difficult to start the market of
the new securities in Europe on a basis that would incline the holders to retain their bonds rather than to sell
them."

He had at least the comfort of knowing his plans
to be the best, and his own property impregnable in
either event. With proper pride he made this re-
trospective summary and sent it to Lord Mount
Stephen at the end of the year: "Our company is
the only Pacific line paying a dividend on its shares,
while three out of five lines other than our own are in
process of reorganization, which must wipe out many
millions of the capital invested in those enterprises. Every
other Pacific line except our own received enormous
sums of money or lands or both as subsidies, while
our line, or rather our company, has gone on steadily
paying dividends to its shareholders for fifteen years,

and all this time the dividend has been earned during the year in which it was paid except in 1889 and 1894, the deficiency for these two years being made up from former surpluses, without materially reducing such surplus."

The following extracts from the same review show that he had considered and computed every item connected with the Northern Pacific system as closely as he had the details of his own: "The Northern Pacific has had large earnings during the fall months. Their car equipment, while not such large cars as our own, is greater in number and they have rushed everything to market, while we have encouraged holding in country elevators and have advanced money to help carry the wheat so held, to ensure a steady winter traffic. I think we will have on the line and in farmers' hands to come forward on January first fully 25,000,000 bushels, while the Northern Pacific will not have over 5,000,000 bushels. I think, therefore, that our earnings will hold up longer, while those of the Northern Pacific relatively will fall off after the holidays, and next year the parties who are now shouting huzzas for independent reorganization will have another song to sing. At any rate, there will be a more solemn note in their music long before they reach a reorganization on any basis. . . . The Northern Pacific, for the year ended June 30, 1895, shows an average cost per train mile of $1.10, and an average load hauled of 163 tons per train mile run.

This would make their average cost for the year .68 of a cent per train mile against our .41 for the same time and .34 for the first half of the present fiscal year. . . . . From the above I estimate that with such changes as we could make in from twelve to eighteen months on the Northern Pacific, we could rely with reasonable safety on earning a good dividend on the preferred shares at the end of the first year."

All of these facts and calculations were of service in another kind of reorganization to which the parties interested were soon compelled to turn. The order of the highest tribunal in the country, March 30, 1896, put a final end to the negotiations which they had contemplated. It forbade a combination which, in its judgment, was forbidden by the law. Joint ownership, in the form proposed, ran up against the blank wall of a decree of the Supreme Court. Opposite the scheme so carefully matured, which later events were to show devoid of any unfortunate consequences for either the corporations directly concerned or the people of the country they served, was written a final *non possumus*.

The owners of the Northern Pacific, together with those who were prepared to furnish the new capital necessary to any reorganization, had planned to rebuild its property. The courts had built a wall across their path. But this scheme was not merely a device of men looking after their own comfort or profit. It was the true offspring of the business evolution of the country.

22

Nevermore were the owners of great railroads to be either persuaded or coerced into cutting each other's throats for anybody's pleasure or benefit. They had seen their way clearly. As they could not climb over the court's wall, they walked around it. After the decision was announced, other plans which had been considered tentatively while it was in abeyance, in case it should be adverse, were carried out. The same parties and no others were to be consulted. The principal owners of the Northern Pacific had placed their interests in the hands of Mr. Morgan. They had felt it prudent to consider and prepare for a possibly unfavourable decision of the Supreme Court. Mr. Hill had a complete plan of reorganization for the Northern Pacific on new lines worked out by the beginning of 1896. He sent it in detail to Lord Mount Stephen for his judgment, February 15. It need not be quoted at length, for the essential features are those that were later adopted. His letter concluded with the following paragraph: "Bearing in mind the opposition to the consolidation of the interests of the two companies which has grown out of the public discussion, lawsuits, etc., during the past summer, I think it would be well to avoid for the present any discussion of the proposed unification of interests. My plan would be for a party of the friends and large shareholders of the Great Northern to buy all the consolidated bonds of the Northern Pacific to be had in the market. We should secure one-half the issue if possible. . . . I think I could make up a party to take the whole transaction in America, but as it would be very profitable, I would prefer to distribute it among some of our good friends abroad." He and his friends were ready now to act promptly after the court had spoken.

The new plan settled upon, by the same parties that had joined in the old, after conferences in London and New York, simply substituted the principle of joint ownership by individuals for that by corporations. What the companies could not do legally was entirely lawful for their stockholders in a private capacity. Mr. Hill and his friends had bought a large block of Northern Pacific stock. Mr. Morgan acted for the body of the old stockholders and for associates of his own who were putting new money into the enterprise. March 16, 1896, a plan of reorganization was announced, and declared operative April 24. It provided for the sale of the property at foreclosure, and the organization of a new company with $80,000,000 common and $75,000,000 preferred stock, and the issue of not to exceed $130,000,000 prior lien 4 per cent. bonds and not to exceed $60,000,000 3 per cents. These bonds were issued only in part, and from time to time, as necessity required. A syndicate consisting of Mr. Morgan and representatives and friends of the Deutsche Bank subscribed $45,000,000 to underwrite the scheme, and $5,000,000 to make improvements in the property immediately. Mr. Hill was not a member of the syndicate. But by an agreement reached in London between him and Mr. Morgan, he and his friends were to have the right to take such portions of the stock as were not subscribed for by the old stockholders under the plan of reorganization. This amount turned out to be about $16,000,000; and gave them a large interest and the usual stockholders' voice, to the extent of that holding, and such additional stock as they purchased from time to time, in the management of the company. The right to retire the preferred stock at par on any first of January during the next twenty years was reserved; a provision whose importance, soon to be tested, was not then foreseen. Both classes of stock were vested in five voting trustees for the first five years, the voting power of the trust expiring November 1, 1901. Mr. Morgan was placed at the head of it.

This reorganization was an event of the first magnitude for several reasons. It put the Northern Pacific on its feet again, permanently this time, and gave Mr. Hill and his friends a substantial stock interest. A more important factor was the effect of his personality; the qualities of the man, his record as the builder and manager of the Great Northern and his friendly relations with many of those who held large interests in the Northern Pacific. In this way was established the sort of community of interest which is all the more real and lasting because it rests on mutual understanding and confidence

25

rather than on any formal stipulation. It gave practical effect to natural laws of railroad growth and development, in a shape that did not run counter to laws or court decisions. It was a long step forward in the adjustment of traffic facilities for the Northwest according to economic necessities. It prepared the way for the purchase of the Burlington system, soon to follow, and for the formation of the Northern Securities Company. It drew closer the relations between Mr. Hill and Mr. Morgan, which were to remain unbroken the rest of their lives.

Seldom have two men so powerful in their way and time, and yet so different in many things, been more closely united in so great an undertaking. Each understood and appreciated the strength of the other. Both were pledged by their very natures to that loyalty to any obligation which shines starlike wherever it exists in the business world. It was presently to be put to the uttermost test; when unimagined profits and willing millions should be the price ready for a breach of trust. Shoulder to shoulder they stood then; and each had only scorn and wonder for one who could dream it possible that either should, for gain, be false to his plighted faith. On the practical side, this interest gave to the Northern Pacific the advantage, when desired, of consultation with a man whose genius for operation, given anything more than a scrap heap to work on, could turn a deficit into a dividend. Matat the time. To it were devoted more of the thought and activity of Mr. Hill than any one except those immediately associated with him and familiar with his plans would believe. Here, in fact, the knot must be tied which would unite the three great railway systems of the West in permanent harmony and coöperation; or else here war would begin and continue until somebody was beaten or a truce had to be declared. To determine beyond future controversy the status of the property usually spoken of as the Oregon Railway & Navigation Company was more imperative at this time than to open new territory. There could be no peace or security until its relation to the northern transcontinental systems had been definitely fixed. The place which this occupies in the correspondence of Mr. Hill in the years down to the end of the century proves that study of the problem was a considerable factor in the work he was labouring to bring to completion. There was no use in beating about the bush. So Mr. Hill took up the matter directly with Mr. Harriman. It had, of course, been the subject already of some negotiations and many tentative suggestions. Now Mr. Hill set out his views in detail and in writing, so that there could be no question of what he would prefer and what he was prepared to do. This personal letter to Mr. Harriman is immensely interesting, not only as giving the results of his study of the whole situation, but as an illustration of his power of condensed

41

and luminous statement. It was sent first to Mr. Schiff with this advisory note:

"I am sending you under cover a letter which I have written to Mr. Harriman in regard to O. R. &. N. matters, which, after reading, please hand to Mr. Harriman. I have endeavoured to give him a plain statement of the case as it appears to me. You will see why I want to include Northern Pacific. I do not think they should be left out, to build lines as they might find occasion to, while we would be bound up under the Navigation Company's load of $50,000 per mile for an old road, poorly laid out, and upon which a large expenditure of money will have to be made. It costs the Navigation Company about the same per ton mile now as the Great Northern receives from the public as its entire freight revenue."

The letter to Mr. Harriman, complete, dated September 12, 1899, follows:

"The change in plan of operation made necessary by the sale of the Northern Pacific's holdings of Navigation Company preferred shares, and that Company's withdrawal from the agreement, leaves the situation as regards the relations of the Great Northern and the Navigation Company in a position of too great uncertainty to be allowed to continue for any length of time beyond what is necessary to re-arrange a basis for jointly operating the Navigation Company's lines. As you are well aware, I have always considered it to fast, faster than the merchandise trade of the people of Washington, even with the addition of Alaska and Honolulu. The result was that we had more cars of lumber to carry east than we had full cars going west. To make them equal again we had to look for more tonnage from the East."

He had not waited until this emergency confronted him to look about for sources of more traffic. He believed that a great business could be built up with the Orient. This is what he had already done about it: "I sent men to Japan and China and kept them there, one man for more than a year. His business was to get a manifest of every ship that entered or left a Chinese or Japanese port, if he could; to find what the exports and imports of those countries consisted of and where they went." The low rates on lumber. required a heavy tonnage, and loaded cars in both directions, if it were to pay anything more than cost of carriage. He was convinced that the Orient would supply a vast amount of west-bound freight for his railroad, if markets could be established there. He went into the matter with his usual thoroughness. He sent agents to China to study the food problem; and to India to investigate not only that but also the possibility of increased production there, and the danger of India's wheat supply as a possible competitor in the Chinese market, assuming that such a market could be built up. The manifests of ships carrying traffic to and from the

53

Orient were studied and tabulated. Agents in this country quietly visited home sources of production from which the Japanese and Chinese could obtain as advantageously the things they were buying elsewhere. He felt sure that the people of China and Japan could be made good customers for the wheat and flour of the United States. "I found," he said, "that if the people of a single province of China should consume an ounce a day of our flour, they would need 50,000,000 bushels of wheat per annum, or twice the Western surplus." These people were poor, but if only a small fraction of them could be brought to substitute wheat flour for rice, it would mean the creation of a great, new market. He intended to make such freight rates that they would get it cheap enough. Always prominent in his mind was the idea of what this would mean to the farmers of the country along his lines. Like most of the bows that he drew, this one had two strings to it. To send a surplus of 70,000,000 bushels of wheat to the Orient at that date would, according to his calculation, raise the price in Minnesota and Dakota twenty cents a bushel.

In a year or two the situation resolved itself to his satisfaction; and measures were taken for what, if left unimpeded, might have become one of the greatest steps in the commercial development of the United States. In 1896 a contract was concluded with the principal steamship company of the Japanese empire, the Nippon

Yusen Kaisha, fixing such rates between Seattle and the Orient as would enable the Great Northern to gather up freight from all parts of the United States as far east as Pittsburg. Again let Mr. Hill tell how it was done. Some influential business men of Japan were in this country and he met them:

"They were interested in securing rails for their railways. I asked them where they were going to get their rails. They thought they would get them either in England or in Belgium. The Belgian rails would come from Antwerp, the English rails from Middlesborough. I asked them, as they were going to stay here a day or two, to let me see what could be done for American rails. I immediately cabled to my friends in London and got quotations for Antwerp and Middlesborough rails and the best charters to Yokohama. I remember that they could be laid down at about $29. I telegraphed to Chicago. I told them that if they would make a rate of $19.50, we would give them a rate of $8 a ton—forty cents a hundred—from Chicago to Yokohama, which would be $1.50 a ton lower than the English or Belgian quotations. After some hesitation they made the rate and got the contract for 15,000 tons.

"Some Japanese interested in the cotton trade were passing through. Our men in the field had reported the amount of cotton spun in Japan, and the fact that the raw cotton came mostly from India. This was a short staple cotton which made an inferior yarn and

55

sold at a low price. I got these gentlemen to try a small shipment of American cotton, with the guarantee that, if it did not prove profitable to mix our long staple with the short staple of India, I would pay for the cotton. The result was satisfactory, and the cotton trade grew very fast. We made a rate from Minneapolis to Hong Kong that would enable the Chinese to ship flour. We found the necessity of permanent rates. We could not build up a great permanent business, extending across the continent and even across the ocean, on the basis that to-morrow the rate might be changed or the party with whom we were working to reach the different points of production or consumption had some other interest or some greater interest elsewhere. It was necessary that we should have some reasonable expectation that we could control the permanency of the rate and be able to reach the markets."

To read this is to be present at the birth of a great idea; to watch the evolution of a world-wide plan. Mr. Hill started originally to get business for the Great Northern. First, he needed east-bound freight, and created a new market for Washington and Oregon lumber. That grew so fast that he needed west-bound freight, and created a market for American products in China and Japan. To distribute the lumber widely where it was needed, and to gather up the cotton and the steel that the Orient wanted, he had to go far afield through the interior and southern sections of the United

States. All this business depended on low and settled through rates. He must be in a position to maintain joint rates, as well as rates on the Great Northern alone. Therefore he must have an ally with lines which would give access to Chicago and St. Louis, and also cover the immense central region. The Chicago, Burlington & Quincy would best answer his purpose. A glance at the map will show that the territory served by that system, added to the section traversed by the northern transcontinentals, forms a giant cornucopia whose body extends from the Great Lakes to the Ohio River, contracts as it stretches west and northwest, and pours its contents through the relatively narrow orifice of Puget Sound and Portland.

This shows as by a mathematical diagram the practical necessity of the purchase of the Burlington system, to be described in a succeeding chapter. The idea itself had been germinating for a long time in the mind of Mr. Hill. The practical benefits, the real urgency of it as a matter of business, came to the surface with startling distinctness through the scientific effort to create new traffic for the new transcontinental line. Although it was to be some years before an actual crisis should reveal the desirability of binding all the agencies engaged in a common work into one corporate unity, the intelligent observer of events will not fail to see here another root of the plan that afterward developed into the Northern Securities Company. So true is it that the genesis of conceptions and acts which are explained in their day as the outgrowth of some Machiavellian scheme for seizing power and wealth can often be traced far back through the years to the honest paternity of a wise business policy.   Events bear most great men at some time in their lives to a port where at first they never dreamed of casting anchor.

Mr. Hill's ideas carried far.   His venture in taking rails from Chicago to Yokohama, in competition with the mills of Belgium and Great Britain, meant more than getting business for the Great Northern.   It was the casting down of a gage of battle.   The established trade route from Antwerp and Liverpool to the Orient was through the Suez Canal.   From earliest time such commerce from Europe to Asia as could not be carried on by land had sought the water route around the Cape of Good Hope.   To shorten this the Suez Isthmus had been cut through.   The Suez route now met a bold challenge.   Mr. Hill had demonstrated the possibility of taking this business away from Europe by reversing the direction of the needle on the trade compass.   It would be almost like changing the course of one of the mighty ocean currents, if human invention and enterprise should succeed in reversing an immemorial trade movement of the world; if the sea route between Orient and Occident should slowly rotate from the Eastern to the Western Hemisphere.

This possibility lay at the back of Mr. Hill's mind

when he conceived the idea of building steamers larger than the world's merchant marine had ever seen, to ply between Seattle and China and Japan. By these he could lower the rate across the Pacific at his will. They were to be the first of a fleet called into existence to answer the needs of a new commerce. With a promising business already started between the United States and the Orient, a powerful bid could be made for a considerable share of the trade that had gone hitherto by way of Suez. No one can could tell to what dimensions this new venture might swell, or what changes it might bring about in the business relations and transactions of the world. Anticipating a little the chronological order of events, the history of this assault on the trade of the Orient and the movement of world commerce may be completed here. In 1900 the Great Northern Steamship Company was formed, with a capital of $6,000,000, and contracts were let for two mammoth steamships, the *Minnesota* and the *Dakota*, to ply between Seattle and Yokohama and Hong Kong. They were to cost $2,500,000 each, and to be the greatest freight carriers ever floated. The *Minnesota* was launched in 1903. Her length was 630 feet, beam 73.4, displacement 38,000 tons, and capacity 28,000 tons. The following year saw the launching of the *Dakota*. The mayor of St. Paul, in a telegram of congratulation, emphasized again one feature of all Mr. Hill's big enterprises: "Our pride in your great achieve-

59

ment is rendered more complete by the reflection that it is entirely the product of individual genius, unsupported either in promise or performance by the aid of government subsidy."

So long as business was left unshackled, it did not disappoint expectation or refute calculation. In the ten years from 1893, when the Great Northern reached the Pacific Coast, to 1903, the exports of the customs district of Puget Sound increased 540 per cent. In a single year the exports of cotton piece goods multiplied by nearly five, and those of raw cotton by more than three. The hard work had been done. The market was opened. The machinery had been set in motion. Intelligent public coöperation would do the rest. Mr. Hill said at the time: "The future of this business remains to some extent a matter of conjecture. If all the railroad forces, the Government, and the laws unite to help this traffic, Puget Sound will be the greatest seaport of the Pacific. It will be the clearing point for the biggest volume of tonnage going to the Orient and coming from it. Presuming that Japan will come to be a great commercial nation, American trade on the Pacific Ocean should soon rival that on the Atlantic." Had this definite and practical plan for trade development been carried out without change or interruption, the effect upon the business of the United States would have been beyond calculation. It never met its final test. Legislative enactments and official interferences

60

by the political authority of the Government doomed it to substantial failure almost as soon as it had begun to show its promise and its power. The business must be taken away or kept away from European competitors. Low prices alone could do it; and low prices were conditioned on extremely low rates of carriage. Mr. Hill had foreseen that and provided for it. His plan rested upon it as a fundamental postulate. What he had not foreseen and could not meet was the conditions imposed subsequently by laws regulating domestic transportation, but applying as well to joint through rail and ocean rates. The following statement of the practical embargo put upon his work is from his "Highways of Progress":

"If an American line meets a low rate, because its competitor is free to make a cut and has done so, the joint steamship and rail lines that do the work between them must dispose of the reduction somehow. If the steamship bears it all, then it will have to run at a loss and soon go out of business. Freight cannot be carried eight thousand miles at a comparatively low rate without spreading that rate over the whole distance. But if a portion of it is allotted to the railroad end, then, first, there is great delay before it can become effective; and, second, since this reduced rate is published and under supervision, it cannot be raised for another thirty days; and, third, if it is lower than the rate charged to the same destination on freight consigned to local mer-

61

chants, the Interstate Commerce Commission will be appealed to, and eventually the railroad will be ordered to give to local shippers the same rate that it has accepted to that point as its share of the transportation charge on export business. The minimum rate invariably becomes the maximum rate. And then the railroad will go out of business. So the application of domestic regulation to export rates amounts to just this: that one partner or the other must work at a continuing loss. Naturally, Oriental business does not expand."

Against the regulations laid down by law for fixing rates, and against other regulations which increased, from time to time, the cost of operating ships, even Mr. Hill could not contend successfully. He could and did calculate the natural elements of his problem. His solution met their conditions to a nicety. Against the political element, against hampering legislation and the certainty that it would grow rather than decrease in volume and stringency, no wisdom and no preparation would avail. So Oriental trade, as he had conceived it, languished. He built no more ships for trans-Pacific service. But in the conception and the scheme just described two elements were united. Mr. Hill was the promoter and captain of commerce, eager to extend her agencies and her services to every corner of the world; the traffic man whose empire aimed to include sea as well as land in its imperial sweep. He was also the sincere American, whose pride took the bit in its teeth when he saw the shameful decadence of the nation's merchant marine. He had an ambition to restore it to the high estate of those glorious days when our clipper ships rode proudly in all the harbours of the world. At the launching of the *Minnesota,* he used the following words,—no idle boast, coming from his lips: "With that great vessel out there riding at anchor, I don't want to be told to drop any bundle. Moreover, I now give notice to all comers that I will not drop it. Once the American merchant marine was the envy of the nations, and with progression and liberal treatment at the hands of the Government our flag shall again be supreme on the high seas." He would not and did not "drop the bundle" for any competitor; but in all his undertakings the mandate of his country, whether he thought it wise or foolish, just or unjust, he never hesitated to obey.

In his last years he was consulted constantly and wrote and spoke many times on the best methods of building up our foreign trade. Less than three months before his life ended he made the following lucid and succinct statement, which sums up the conclusions of a lifetime of study and experience upon the relation of a country's railways to its export trade:

"The railroads do not own the trade of the country, or in any sense control it. They transport the commodities of which a commerce already established is made up. Their representatives solicit business, of course, but business already agreed upon between the principal parties to it. To create new business, which is what extending our foreign trade means, is a different function. Under existing conditions, the railroads can do little toward that. The things which they might do are forbidden by law.

"It is well-known that the wonderful extension of the foreign markets of Germany in the years preceding the war was brought about largely by coöperation between the Government, the business interests, and the railroads. These being either actually or virtually in partnership with the State, their interests were treated as identical. It was desirable to build up Germany's exports, so the railroads were asked to help. Whatever rate might be necessary to lay down German products in outside markets at a price lower than competitors asked was not only approved but required. The State gave its authority and, if needed, its material aid to the transportation companies in creating and maintaining markets abroad.

"In the United States, important lines of foreign trade that were once established have been cut off by exactly the opposite policy. The railroads are forbidden to make competitive export rates. It was long ago made impossible for them, under the law, to give any assistance through cheaper transportation in selling American goods abroad. It would be possible for them to build or acquire steamship lines to be run in connection with their systems; but this also has been made illegal.

"At present, therefore, the laws of the country offer an effectual barrier to any activity of importance or value on the part of the railroads to build up American foreign trade. That trade is strictly competitive, and cannot be persuaded or cajoled. It must be captured by offering it better terms than it can obtain elsewhere. The experience of other countries seems to show that community of effort between the Government and the railroads can go a long way toward securing it. Until some such understanding is reached or permitted here, the influence of the railroad companies on the growth of foreign commerce cannot be made of much importance."

His plan for new alignments in world's commerce and its routes was one of the few visions of Mr. Hill on a grand scale which he did not live to see accomplished. At the beginning and at the close of his active life the Orient receded and eluded him. Yet the thought was worthy of the man. Like all his plans, it was constructive. His ideas centred less on rivalry with existing instruments of commerce in this country than on the making of new markets and the opening of rivers of trade where before only a few rivulets trickled through the arid soil. All were fecund. They had within them the creative impulse. The progression from each to the next is as natural and the connection as close as that between the trunk of a tree and its branches. No matter what the hindrance, how deep the disappointment, so far as his own work was concerned, the impersonal and patriotic dream of an American control of the world's commerce never left him. He believed that, with free ships and freedom from onerous regulations, we might again rule the seas commercially. In view of the place which this thought occupied in his mind, it is an interesting and significant fact that the last book he read, finished but a few days before his death, was "The Heritage of Tyre."

CHAPTER TWENTY–FIVE

MASTER OF METHODS AND MEN

THE wide scope of Mr. Hill's action and influence during these years having been outlined in the preceding chapters, many details of the picture remain to be filled in. One of the essential elements of his greatness was that he never let the wood obscure his clear sight of the trees. These plans might work out well or ill; but there was nothing doubtful or passing about the fact that the two thousand miles of railroad line between St. Paul, Duluth, and Seattle, with its other thousands of miles of branches and feeders, must be taken care of. He laboured to build up local business as tirelessly as to create through business. The country must be settled. Farms must be tilled. New enterprises must be encouraged. Much more of his untiring energy and his capacity for sustained effort were devoted to this than to more ambitious projects. This railroad system was his child; and while he might project for it splendid alliances and a shining future, he took endless pains that it should be well fed and cared for in the immediate present.

It had been common belief that the construction of the Great Northern to the Pacific Coast, like the earlier building of the Northern Pacific and the Central and the Union Pacific, was the fulfillment of a personal ambition and a theoretical estimate of the future, without any basis in existing business conditions to justify it. The powerful help of the Federal Government had not saved those undertakings from the inevitable misfortunes of one born out of due season. Some of the best friends of Mr. Hill saw only a country whose development had hardly yet begun, and a traffic from coast to coast which was still a bagatelle. Its railroad revenue must now be divided between two rivals, when the whole of it seemed insufficient to support either. That way, they said sorrowfully among themselves, bankruptcy lies. No doubt bankruptcy would have been the fate of the Great Northern if it had been built and handled as were the other transcontinentals; or if after reaching the Pacific, it had been dismissed with the paternal blessing and told to do the best it could in a cold and selfish world. Mr. Hill did not do things that way. As resolutely as he had set himself to cover the gap between the end of his line, when it stopped in North Dakota and the waters of Puget Sound, as shrewdly as he had built up a long haul business, he now proceeded to assure volume and permanence for the entire traffic of the Great Northern.

In a single year eighteen thousand settlers were located along its line—a great influx for those days—and that work of filling up the country with farmers never slackened. Standing squarely on its own merits, before the creation of new sources and the expansion of old forms of traffic, it appeared that the Great Northern, including the new through line, was no weakling. The terrible year 1893 swept down railroad properties like a tornado. Panic, bankruptcy, labour unrest, loss in all its protean forms, were everywhere. Yet the report of the Great Northern for the year ending June 30, 1894, after enumerating these handicaps, continued: "Notwithstanding these conditions and a general reduction of the average rate per ton per mile from .01232 in 1893 to .01096 in 1894, or 11 per cent. of the former rate, your company has been able, from its income from all sources, to pay its interest and guaranteed obligations and its usual dividend, with a deficiency of $104,153." One year later the company was out of the woods. The report for June 30, 1895, showed gross earnings of $13,109,939, as compared with $11,345,356 for the preceding twelve months, and an increase in net of more than a million dollars. One year later still the progress had been so great as to invite a comparison for the fifteen-year period since 1881, when the old Manitoba system may be said to have got into its stride. The following, from the annual report of June 30, 1896, all of these reports being the personal work of Mr. Hill, is an admirably concise statement of conditions both present and relative:

The articles carried by the Great Northern system, while considerably more diversified in 1896 than in 1881, are substantially of the same description as then; yet in 1880-81 the average charge per ton mile was 2.88 cents, while in 1895-96 it had fallen to .976 of a cent; or to only a little more than one third of the former rate. Has the price of any other commodity, or the rate of pay for any other class of service fallen equally?

In 1895-96 the revenue ton mileage was 1,622,877,423, and the cost of it to the public $15,833,090.47. Had the rate per ton per mile of the year 1880-81 been charged, the earnings would have amounted to $46,738,869.78, or $30,905,779.31 more than the companies actually collected, and during the same time the rate of wage paid by this company has advanced to an average of 45 per cent. higher than the average of 1880-81.

Machine and men must work together to produce such results. Mr. Hill often repeated that "you cannot do good work anywhere with poor tools." For years the Great Northern was operated at from 49 to 51 per cent. of the gross earnings—a remarkable record at that time. Grades which were originally low had been so cut down that, while other transcontinental lines, in crossing the mountains, required double-header engines on 10 per cent. of their grades, the Great Northern used them on but one per cent. His policy was always to make rates low on the staple products of the farm. The farmer must get his wealth to market and receive a good return for it, or he would not remain on the land. If he went away, or if others had no encouragement to come, everything would collapse. Mr. Hill had little patience with the stress laid by shippers and authorities on ordinary merchandise rates, or with their failure to recognize the breadth and fundamental soundness of his policy. His theory and his practice are expressed in the following clear demonstration contained in" Highways of Progress."

"The most important thing to the farmers of the Northwest is a low rate on wheat. Take the case of a farmer with one hundred acres of wheat yielding, say, twenty bushels to the acre; a total of 2,000 bushels or 60 tons. A reduction of five cents a hundred, or a dollar a ton, in his transportation charge would amount to him to $60 per annum. If he visits the country store once a week for fifty-two weeks and takes away from the store each week fifty pounds of merchandise, in a year he will have taken 2,600 pounds, the entire freight on which would not have averaged more than forty cents a hundred, or $10.40; so that, if the railroad carried the merchandise for nothing and charged an additional five cents a hundred on his grain, the farmer would be worse off by nearly $50 a year. Consequently wheat rates have been made relatively lower there than in other parts of the country, and relatively lower than those on merchandise." This policy undoubtedly contributed much to the rapid growth and great prosperity of the Northwest. Again and again the Great Northern voluntarily lowered rates on staple farm products. It expected no increased returns on capital. It planned to make good the lower rate by larger traffic, coming from the growth of the country, and by economies in operation.

"I think," said Mr. Hill in a letter written to Mr.

Forbes in 1896, "in the future it will be difficult to raise rates beyond what the companies have voluntarily made by the usual methods. The only real relief we can look for is in the reduction of the cost of doing the work." This latter item, from the beginning of his career to the end of it, he watched with unrelaxing alertness. If there was waste anywhere, if box cars were seen travelling empty, if men fell into slack methods on any part of the line, presently a sharp message came from headquarters. Every day reports were laid before him. He would put an unerring finger on the weak spot, and nobody was exempt from censure. No matter how highly placed the official, no matter how close his personal relation to Mr. Hill, if he was deficient in this respect he received a warning in terms which, while courteous and sometimes even sympathetic, were so severe that no repetition would be desired. Unless improvement were instant and satisfactory, there was a vacant place and a job for a new man. Efficiency reigned from one end of the Great Northern to the other by virtue of one man's oversight and will.

Few have realized how great a part this played in keeping its finances in good condition when other systems were dying. He made satisfactory operation a part of finance. "I note," said he, in another letter of 1896, "the work of your locomotives, which is certainly very good. It is largely in this direction that we must look for our profit in handling the tonnage of our lines. The public have become so accustomed to low rates that I do not see how under the present conditions, with commissioners, courts, and others, it will be possible to materially advance the rates which have been voluntarily in effect for so long a time." The fight for economical operation was never relaxed. The eye of the master was always watching. Six years later he wrote to another high official on his system: "My instructions were that we should not haul empty cars. We get an average of $160 a car for hauling lumber east, and to haul the car west costs $100 and to haul it east costs at least $100, so that we would be out anywhere from $40 to $60 on every car we hauled west empty. The company has no money to spend that way. We have a large number of box cars, most of which are of recent construction and large capacity. Six round trips of our car equipment will carry 100,000,000 bushels of grain, so that there should be no difficulty in providing cars for the hauling of the grain out west. We want, in place of more cars, a better movement of the cars we already have, and cannot allow shippers to make warehouses of the cars, nor can we furnish warehouses to store other people's business. There is no occasion for it as matters exist in the Northwest, and it should come to an end. In any event, we want it to come to an end on our road." So, whenever any unusual condition arose, a labour difficulty, a bad crop season, a financial panic, the

73

Great Northern never dropped into the hole. Other managements sought different remedies. Mr. Hill had only one, but it never failed. As soon as the unfavourable circumstance declared itself, usually long before, because he was wonderfully weatherwise about these storms, an order went out to cut operating expenses to the full total of the loss of revenue, realized or expected. Everybody knew that orders were to be obeyed to the letter. Everybody knew also that retrenchment would not be accepted as an excuse for inefficient operation. New economies were made, forces were reduced, and when the time for striking a balance arrived, the Great Northern showed a decrease in operating expenses oftener above than below the loss in revenue. Mr. Hill was branded a pessimist more than once because of this prudent policy. He was a pessimist in exactly the same sense as the skipper who orders all hands aloft to shorten sail, because his trained senses have given him sure warning of an approaching gale.

Next after the railroad, the farm was the fulcrum from which he applied his effort. His work to improve agricultural conditions will be dealt with fully in its proper place. Coincident in its rise with his appearance as a railroad manager, it never ceased to hold a prominent place in his thought and work. A preceding chapter described his early efforts to raise the quality of live stock in the Northwest. The story of the upbuilding of the vast new country traversed by his lines would be incomplete without another passing reference to this allied activity. Notwithstanding his somewhat disappointing experience, he did not cease to introduce improved breeds of cattle, whenever he found men who could understand and carry out his ideas. On his five-thousand-acre farm ten miles outside of St. Paul he experimented with strains, with feed, with plants, with fertilizers, with everything that might raise the net product of the farm. The following extracts are from an address made by him before the Minnesota State Historical Society. He himself considered these experiences worthy of a prominent place in his own account of his years and work:

"For many years I fed stock on my farm and exhibited the stock at the Fat Stock Show at Chicago. I think for six or seven years I was always able to carry off a full representation of the top prizes; and I think that for half the time I carried off the actual first prizes for the animals on foot and for the quality of meat of the slaughtered animal. I have probably a dozen and a half or two dozen gold medals which I have taken for fat stock, fed on my farm. I have never failed to take my full share of premiums. I say my full share, but I really took twenty times my share of prizes. Sixteen sheep can be fed on one acre of my ground and cannot eat the products of that acre; or five or six cows on one acre, without eating down the forage on that acre. Yet this is poor land; if you put a spade into it, before the spade is driven home the edge of it is in the sand. I think for the last ten years I have averaged more than 800 bushels of rutabaga turnips to the acre. An excellent good fodder they make. This year I put sixty acres of corn into ensilage, about 300 tons of ensilage. Any farmer who will be careful and try to do his work intelligently, with diversity of crops, stock raising and dairying, can and will make his land worth as much as any in the state." All of this was new gospel at the time and place.

Some of this interest was the passion of the country-bred boy, which he rarely loses, for the land and the actual management of it. Some of it was the love of the man whose life is passed in cities and the offices of great affairs for the clean, wholesome breath of the country, and the relaxation of an interest so different from his ordinary avocation as to be a diversion and a restorative. But his fundamental thought was the improvement of farming and the multiplication of farms and farm products throughout the Northwest. He saw more potential business for his railroad, to put it on the lowest plane, in a section of land than another man would have seen in a factory. Nothing that could promote the agricultural interest left him uninterested. He was a strong advocate of good roads, and favoured every plan for highway improvement that was not based on big bond issues. People generally had given little thought to drainage as early as 1885. In the Northwest, where the best land could be had for a song, the subject had scarcely been considered. But the old Manitoba Company's lines in the Red River Valley were as good as a gold mine. That is a flat country, liable to crop loss from excessive moisture in a wet season. The railroad company agreed to pay half the cost of a drainage survey of the valley, if the counties interested would furnish the rest. It has been related that when the state, later on, made its first drainage appropriation, the railroad gave $25,000 to aid the work. That was the beginning of what became a highly developed and important function of the state. It owes much to the initial impulse given by Mr. Hill.

Disturbed, as most patriotic and sober-minded people were by the clamours preceding the war with Spain, he saw the situation and its needs clearly. He wrote the following letter to one of the Minnesota delegation in Congress early in 1898: "From a national standpoint our blunder was first in bringing foreign matters, like Cuba and Venezuela, or the interests of any other outside people who have no interest or sympathy with us, national or otherwise, into our political contentions and making their conditions a part of our national platforms. Both parties have been guilty of the sin, and both parties ought to suffer the consequences. If we could learn to mind our own business it would save us a great deal of trouble. On the other hand, we have gone so far as to commit the Government

THE LIFE OF JAMES J. HILL

to a policy, and there should be no halting or doubt as
to the loyal support of the Government in whatever
direction Congress and the President may find best.
The destruction of the *Maine* will always remain charge-
able to the duplicity of the Spanish Government in
Cuba, or to that of the Spanish officers in Cuba; and
while there may be a distinction, there is but little
difference between the two. We must now put on a
bold front and bring the matter to a definite close. The
country cannot afford to have the Government take any
step backward. I firmly believe that, in case of war,
with prompt and bold action we should have every
Spaniard bearing arms on the island of Cuba a prisoner
of war within six weeks and have the whole matter
thoroughly in hand. No good end will be served by our
public men losing their heads and firing off political
rockets to show what big men they are. They do not
deceive anybody except themselves. All that sort of
action is short-lived, and the sooner the men in public
life realize that the public school has accomplished
something in the last half century, the nearer they will
be able to estimate their own position. I am going
away for four or five weeks, and by taking passage
under the Union Jack of Great Britain I expect to be
able to make the trip in both directions safely. I hope
that time will come when the Stars and Stripes will
afford equal protection. It ought to now, and it is not
the fault of the flag that it does not." This is the note

of "preparedness," strongly sounded, seventeen years before the country heard and heeded it.

By no means least of the difficulties that beset the newly completed railroad was its share of the labour troubles of the time. The year 1894 was a black date. Unrest swept over the country. The railroads of the West were tied up. Senator C. K. Davis, of Minnesota, was asked by labour organizations to support a resolution offered in the United States Senate forbidding the Government to prevent interference by the strikers with the running of mail trains. To this he telegraphed a reply ending with the famous words, "You might as well ask me to vote to dissolve the United States Government." This, as Mr. Hill wrote to a friend, "made him a hero." It strengthened his national reputation without injuring him at home. But it did not settle the labour troubles. Mr. Hill wrote to President Cleveland in April, urging firm action by the Department of Justice to prevent and quell disorders. It was the time of the American Railway Union, of Coxey armies and marches on Washington. "There are," said Mr. Hill's letter for the president's information, "between four and five thousand men between here and the Pacific Coast in parties of from two to six hundred, desiring to go to Washington. They are mainly of the worst class— men who do not want to work for a living. If they can be prevented from starting and dealt with in small squads, the matter can be settled sooner and more safely than if they are allowed to go as far east as St. Paul or Chicago."

Of course, the Great Northern had its share of the general strike, a full and interesting account of which was given in a letter from Mr. Hill to Mr. Kennedy. Some extracts show the policy of the company in dealing with its first big labour dispute; a policy that was the basis of all its future action. "The order to strike," he said, "was given on three hours' notice, without any consultation or agreement between the different branches along the line. The general condition of unrest, growing out of the large number of unemployed people who passed through the winter with more or less charitable help, feeling that when spring opened they would find something to do, added to those who never do an honest day's work, but prefer beating their way through the world, made, altogether, between Helena, Butte, Spokane, Seattle, Tacoma, and Portland, about 3,500 people who were gathered or gathering together as 'Coxeyites' about this time. It would have been a relatively easy matter for us to have opened the line by force from St. Paul to the Pacific Coast, although we would have run great risk of having costly bridges destroyed. While presenting a firm front to the strikers, I felt that our position was strong enough to leave any question between the company and its men to arbitration." The men at first refused this, and the

80

MRS. JAMES J. HILL

company went resolutely to work to open its lines. Then the strikers agreed to arbitrate; and the company, which might now have refused, consented. The award was accepted, and Mr. Hill concluded his letter thus: "The newspaper reports have indicated that the men won a great victory, and this we have been careful not to contradict."

From this time forward the Great Northern had rather less than its normal share of labour troubles. There were many differences, and many times it seemed that these must lead to a break. When they did, it was of short continuance. The management was known to be a hard fighter, but one that preferred peace on any equitable terms. Generally such disputes were amicably adjusted between the officials of the company and those of the labour organizations, or by arbitration when conciliation failed. Mr. Hill's own position always was that he did not mean to be imposed upon, but that he desired and intended to be just. Partly to create and foster a feeling of loyalty, but also to encourage thrift, the Great Northern Employees' Investment Company was founded in 1900. It is one of the early and successful profit-sharing schemes of this country. Ten thousand shares of the company's stock, at the par value of $1,000,000, were issued for its use. The Investment Company was authorized to receive, from employees named in a list furnished by the Railway Company, sums of ten dollars

81

or multiples thereof, not to exceed $5,000 for any one person.   Length and quality of service were the sole conditions of a place on the list.   The investor received an investment certificate, and for each $100 turned in the Investment Company received one share of stock to be held in trust.   So the employee purchased a high-priced stock at par, and received the regular 7 per cent. dividend.   He was authorized to surrender his certificate and receive principal and interest at 6 per cent. at any time.   On the other hand, he could not transfer or assign a certificate to any other party.

This remained a favourite investment for the thrifty, and a successful form of profit sharing.   It aided in the creation of a feeling of loyalty that amelio-rated labour differences.   By June 30, 1915, regular certificates to the amount of $1,185,450 had been dis-tributed among 578 employees; 95 held $5,000, the maxi-mum allowed.   One hundred and eighty employees were on the waiting list, February 24, 1916, prepared to in-vest about $1,134,750.   Mr. Hill said of this plan and its work, after it had been in operation for a dozen years: "I am as well satisfied with that institution as with anything I have ever had to do with.   I think that its greatest value is teaching the men to save.   The first two or three hundred dollars is the hardest to save, but when you have once started you all know it comes easy." The personal feeling of the men for Mr. Hill minimized labour differences.   To them and with them he was one of the "old timers." He had come up with the railroad, he knew every inch of it, he was familiar with the duties of each man, he could call all those old in the service by their names, and when there was trouble abroad he refused indignantly to accept any protection when going over the line and talking with the men. "I need no other protection," he said scornfully to those who suggested the presence of a secret service man, "when I am among employees of the Great Northern." The result warranted his confidence. Of the scores of banquets and receptions and anniversary dinners at which he was the guest of honour, none was inspired by more genuine feeling, none more enthusiastic or more enjoyed by both parties to it than that which was tendered annually on his birthday by the old employees who swapped jokes and stories as familiarly with this man of world-wide renown, certainly as much to his delight as to their own, as they once did with the young manager of their early recollection.

The public feels a natural interest in the relations between a man like Mr. Hill, occupying such a position as employer, and the men who work for him. Some light was thrown upon that in an earlier portion of this history, and more by the facts just stated. Full illumination will come from two documents now to be quoted, which place in a warm and steady light the feeling that existed between him and his men. His seventy-fifth birthday, in 1913, was celebrated, at

Glacier Park, by a meeting of the Veteran Employees' Association. He and Mrs. Hill were the honoured guests of the occasion. Some extracts follow from his response to the addresses made by others on that occasion:

"Some of you started before I did, but most of you have followed step by step, keeping in step with the forward movement of the company. Now, it has not been the easiest thing in the world to play first violin in the Great Northern Band. Sometimes there might have been a strain that began to show the want of harmony, but that was very seldom; but behind it all I have always felt that I was squarely at home on the old Manitoba or on the Great Northern, and I feel so to-day and expect to feel that way as long as I am living.

"You know, some of you do, that the 'old man' has a temper if he gets started. But I want to confide to you now that when I use discipline I never for a moment want to use it unfairly to anybody, high or low. At the same time you must, if you are going to have progress, if you are going to go on with a great big machine such as we have here, have order; and somebody must lead the band, or there won't be harmony.

"I have always tried to give everybody, no matter what position he is in, opportunity to rise and take a step forward and upward in his own behalf; and it is one of the pleasant things in connection with the road that old-timers everywhere are occupying prominent positions.

84

"No matter who he may be or where his lot may be cast, no man ever won his victory by his own arm. No, no, the successful man always is the one who has made a wise selection of his assistants. Both the old men who have been in service for a great many years and those who have been in service for only a few years may bear in mind that the company is a piece of paper with a state seal on it. It has no life, it has no action except such as the men behind it give it; and whatever it does, whatever success it may have or whatever failures it may have, will be due to the work of the men who carry the flag and the men who follow the flag."

So much for his conception of the relation between employer and employed. Few employers so understood it even at the time when these words were spoken. It was still more unusual in a man of the old school, of the preceding generation, a man whose business apprenticeship was served and whose business methods were formed in the stern days of the middle of the nineteenth century. Not much sentiment was wasted in that epoch on labour. There is much sentiment, a pure and true feeling without any tinge of sentimentality, in these words of Mr. Hill.

The employees showed their attitude not only by what was said and done on occasions like the above, but by their tributes to Mr. Hill when he was no longer there to hear. The Veterans' Association held its meeting on the usual anniversary in 1916. Three and a half months be-

fore, Mr. Hill had gone to his rest. The members adopted
and spread upon their records a memorial whose declared
purpose was not to outline his life, but to express their
own feeling toward him. The extracts which follow are
no more significant than the title under which this
matter appears: "James J. Hill; Our Chief for a Generation, Our Friend Always."

"To the men of this Association, every one of whom
had been tried and taught by not less than twenty-five
years of work under him, Mr. Hill was far less the
official chief or the enterprising leader than the kind
and sympathetic friend. As the lives of greatly successful men recede and are bared to the pitiless light
of history, it has always added something to their glory
if they had the sincere attachment of those who followed their leadership. He had it. Because he valued
it, we dare to think that to his memory it may have
worth. Dearly we shall cherish the thought of years
of association, labour, and recompense. Proudly we shall
remember the tribute of friendship that he paid us in
our past. But what we most wish to express, what will
endure while we live and what we hope may attach itself to his remembered name, is that, while we re-
spected and admired him, first and before all and every
year more and more, we loved him. Many works and
words and thoughts that found high expression through
him will perpetuate his memory. In our hearts, so
long as life beats there, will be his monument."

He was especially severe upon any attempt to use the company or its employees for an outside or ulterior purpose. Back in 1890 he received complaints that an employee had been running political caucuses and otherwise displaying what Mr. Cleveland called "pernicious activity." Instantly a personal order went from headquarters to the General Manager of the system, in these words: "While every man has a right to vote as he pleases and do as he pleases with his own vote, it is a rule of the Company that no foreman will be permitted to use his position for a moment for any political purpose." He dealt as severely with attempts to use a connection with the company for personal financial advantage. The following order, to the Chief Engineer, also given in 1890, covers this phase of the relation between employer, employed, and the public interest: "Since my return from the West I have understood that a number of men—some of whom have been in our employ—have gone into prospective town-siting on the line of the road. I wish you would instruct all your engineers, and through them your men, that no man will be permitted to remain in the company's service who is mixed up with anything of the kind. And further, to avoid their making a success of any such ventures, let me now instruct you that no stations are to be located where they have bought ground. We do not desire that our employees shall in any manner take advantage of any information gotten through their service with the company. On receipt of this I wish that you would examine your own office and see if any one, either typewriter, operators, or clerks, has had access to copies of your reports to me, and find if they are in any manner mixed up in any of these deals. *If there is a shadow of suspicion attached to them, discharge them at once.* That will be the only safe course for us all and will set a good example to others in the future."

Here appears the busy man, attending to the multifarious duties of his post, watching every detail of operation, building up a country and creating traffic from and to it over the whole seven states from Minnesota to Washington and Oregon, while at the same time his brain was weaving mightier plans for the consolidation of interests, the economical conduct of a nation's business, and the possible reversal of relations between world markets, and the movement of a world's commerce. The same principles rule throughout the little and the great. Severity with fairness, efficiency with intelligence, a stern sense of honour, immense pride in genuine achievement, and the courage of a leader of armies when he felt that right was invaded or imperilled— these are the distinguishing traits of the man who walked through the stirring times of the last years of the last century. He had broadened immensely, in mind and sympathy, justified his wonderful self-confidence, but he had not changed radically in any respect. He is precisely the same man, grown to the stature of his years and crowned by great achievements, who had dreamed of ventures on the Ganges and the Indus, spent his days and nights in study of informing books, made himself a force in river transportation, and turned into a master machine the bankrupt old railroad —his supreme touch of daring.

Those elementary qualities which marked the man, his sense of honour and his fearlessness before anything that he felt to be a personal duty, inspired a letter with which this chapter may well conclude. A conductor on the railroad had been discharged for violation of the company's rules. The man had a powerful pull. The organization behind him controlled votes. So it came to pass that a certain United States senator from a Northwestern state, backed up by two members of the bench, addressed to Mr. Hill a request for his re-instatement. In view of the relation of legislative and judicial authority to railroad control at the time, it was a petition to be granted if possible; and if not, to be handled most tenderly and apologetically. Mr. Hill's reply follows:

"I desire to say that we are charged with the responsibility for lives and property committed to our care. The responsibility is a heavy one and we cannot discharge it by retaining undesirable trainmen in our employ. I am surprised that these judges should so far lower themselves as to make their request. They certainly should know better. We have been compelled to make it a rule that where a trainman, who is discharged for cause, seeks re-instatement through any judicial, political, or other pull, he has destroyed all chance for re-employment with this company.

"I would be glad to do anything for you personally, as you well know, but you would be the last one to ask me to destroy the discipline in our organization. You are at liberty to send this to either or both of the judges, and I hope they will know better next time. We have difficulty enough in securing good men, and this difficulty would be greatly increased if we paid any attention to such requests, even from the Bench."

CHAPTER TWENTY–SIX

A TRILOGY

THE year 1901 was big with destiny for Mr. Hill. Upon this date converge, like the sun's rays upon the focus of a lens, the activity of his past and the consummate plan of his future as a creator and master of transportation. Three striking events in the story of his life, in the development of the Northwest, in the planning and segregation of railroad systems into spheres of control, and in the rise and determination of legal questions and principles affecting this whole development, were crowded within the limits of a few months. The tale of the purchase of the Burlington system, of the titanic struggle for control of the Northern Pacific, and of the formation of the Northern Securities Company involves a trilogy. These are distinct but inseparable parts of a connected whole. They are interrelated and interacting members of one organism; while the stirring events connected with each are worthy of an independent history. Each contributed its individual share to the work of Mr. Hill's life. Each can be made wholly intelligible only if the common relations of all are first clearly and logically set out.

In several of the preceding chapters, events and tendencies clearly foreshadowed the substance, though not the form, of what must follow. In the first year of the twentieth century the growth of our trade with the Orient, already discussed, had become pronounced. The agencies which Mr. Hill intended to apply to extending and cheapening it were in process of preparation; and the restrictions of the federal power upon export rates had not yet been so exercised as to threaten any fatal interference. He was full of this plan. What he thought about it and hoped from it has been stated in connection with the launching of his ships for the trans-Pacific trade. That scheme had been fully worked out, and he had written in September, 1899, this summary of it to Mr. Higginson, of Boston: "In order to secure this tonnage to Puget Sound (coming Oriental trade) I may say to you, in confidence, that steps are being taken actively to provide a merchant marine that will be able to carry ocean-going freight at lower rates than it has ever been caried, either by sail or steam. This contemplates ships of much greater carrying capacity than anything afloat on the Atlantic or elsewhere. Our docks and other facilities are convenient, giving low cost of handling, and admitting the largest ships, drawing thirty feet or more of water."

The railroad end was in admirable shape, physically and financially. On September 12, 1899, he wrote to Mr. Farrer, of Baring & Co.: "The present year we are rebuilding practically the line from Williston to the

92

summit of the Rocky Mountains, and 42 miles of the line between Great Falls and Havre. This will enable us to materially reduce the cost of operation on both these divisions. The wooden bridges are either replaced by permanent culverts or steel spans, and the embankments on the entire line are being brought to grade and widened to 16 feet at sub-grade, or two feet wider than when the line was built. The whole is being covered with a heavy coat of good ballast, from eight to eighteen inches, according to the previous condition of the track. Our work next year and thereafter will not be as heavy as this year; at the same time, it will take us from two to three years longer to complete this work on all lines. When it is finished, our operating expenses per train mile will be largely reduced and our train mile tonnage will be increased, so that I look for the cost of transportation on the whole system to be ultimately reduced to one quarter of a cent per ton per mile. This may seem extravagant, but it is not by any means impossible. It would make, as compared with the cost during the past year, on the tonnage hauled, a difference of nearly two million dollars." For the fiscal year, 1899, the net revenue of the Great Northern was more than nine and a half millions, and of its subsidiary companies more than four million dollars additional.

The possible leadership in world-wide traffic appealed to his patriotism and his pride quite as much as to his concern for the financial interests of his railroad. Speaking before a convention of grain growers of Minnesota and the two Dakotas, January 26, 1900, he said: "The market may be expanded. This country has expanded from the beginning. I don't want to take anybody's country away from him. I don't want to play the Arab and camel in his tent. I don't want to put my head in for shelter from the storm and drive everybody else out. But the world will go on and people will improve. They always have and they always will. We must at least keep up with the procession. We are responsible for our own people and to find a way to make them broad, intelligent, and prosperous, and to enable them to live as intelligent citizens of a free country ought to live."

The creation of an eastbound traffic in Pacific lumber had made it necessary to reach with that product a wider range of interior markets than the Great Northern, even working in harmony with the Northern Pacific as it now was, could control. Westbound traffic directed the same enlargement of facilities. For a time, at least, a considerable part of any exports destined for Japan would consist of the raw materials of manufacture. These, with certain lines of machinery, were what Japan needed. China might be expected to join later in a similar demand. All of the raw cotton to be taken to the Orient must be gathered from the South; with St. Louis, Kansas City, and other cities similarly situated with reference to the producing country, as depots of collection. In the South also a great

94

iron industry was expanding every day and seeking new markets. Such machinery and materials as were brought from Pittsburg and other eastern centres must be carried, if they went by rail, to Chicago and thence to St. Paul before they reached the Great Northern. The country was too big for the net. The idea required the addition to the northern transcontinentals of a system of railroad which should provide these two prime essentials: a connection that could pick up and bring to them commodities from the markets of the Middle West and South, and a line between St. Paul and Chicago. The birth of traffic on the Great Northern, the development and promise of transcontinental and trans-Pacific trade, the new relations coming into being in the railroad world between different systems, all demonstrated the necessity of so adding to the land factor of the transportation machine as to make it as capable as the big ships would make the water factor. Toward this the events of the last ten years inevitably tended. In this the Great Northern and the Northern Pacific had a common interest.

The occasion was so new, the events that flowed from it were so momentous, and the man himself was so uncommon that it is necessary once more to pause here and reiterate his fundamental thought. The word "monopoly" was in everyone's mouth. The idea of monopoly was in the air. The national Congress and all the state legislatures were largely occupied with measures designed to prevent, curb, or overthrow monopoly. Nor will any candid historian of the industrial situation of the time assert that the attitude was unreasonable or the apprehension unfounded. Views about the desirability of industrial combination, of the economic value and finality of competition, will always differ. That industrial interests were everywhere increasing their scope and power was undeniable. The anxiety of the time—whether wisely or unwisely is of no consequence in this narrative—was centred on the event. It was bitterly hostile to the new idea. And, singularly and illogically enough, it was more concerned, on the whole, with the operation of the tendency in the field of transportation than in that of production.

The Interstate Commerce Act, though not so intended, made some form of common action between railroads imperative. How else, to name but one instance, could the provision against a larger charge for a short haul than for a long one over the same line and in the same direction, be literally enforced without driving every line but one, of those between competitive points, out of business, or making the local traffic of the longer route unprofitable? But while the consolidation of many little industries into a few big ones went merrily on, the railroads, from whose union least was now to be feared, were watched with the keenest eye and the fiercest spirit of apprehension. This is the less intelligible because every railroad in the country was subject to the orders of federal or state legislative authority, prescribing rates. No legal limitation on the prices of manufactured products was possible. A new rate law or an order from the Interstate Commerce Commission or a state commission could prescribe the reduction of a railroad rate whenever it should appear excessive. Only one familiar with the vagaries of political psychology in the mass of voters can find intelligible the greater vigilance exercised against railroad monopoly.

The people of the Northwest had been from the beginning the sharpest censors of railroads. From there and the Middle West the "Granger" legislation drew its name. They preserved the attitude. They "held the thought." With what quick resentment they sprang at the throat of anything that looked like a unification of large railroad interests was seen in the proceedings by which the first plan for reorganizing the Northern Pacific through participation by the Great Northern was nullified. The mass of them did not know what was in the mind of Mr. Hill. They could not have understood it if they had known. Some of them believed him to be at heart a monopolist; meaning by that, a man who was bent on ever and ever wider control of wealth-bringing agencies, in order that they might be used to wring larger profits from the people, with greater power for himself. Even his helpful offices were used to add weight to the presumption. His preëminently skilful and successful handling of his own system, the belief that the interest held by him and his friends in the Northern Pacific had had its part in placing that company firmly in the way of prosperity, made him a man whose advice was sought. He had helped to reorganize the Erie, and sensation-lovers declared that he had bought it to make a through line across the continent. As a matter of fact, he wrote to President Cassatt, of the Pennsylvania: "In regard to my connection with the Erie, allow me to say that my only object is to try to get that property fairly established on its feet, and that it would no longer be a financial derelict, reflecting no credit on American management." In the same letter he reiterated the conclusion from which he never varied: "I do not believe it is possible to make a strong combination covering the country between the Atlantic and the Pacific." His counsel and support contributed to the making of that then-demoralized but great old property, the Baltimore & Ohio, a solvent and prosperous system; and the same cry went up. From the use of those talents, with which he was gifted for seeing clearly the plight of a railroad system and its remedy, was woven the reproach of an ambition to monopolize the transportation systems of the country.

What was the fact? This is one of the most interesting questions that confront the student of his life. An impartial biographer should answer it frankly and fairly. In attempting this, one psychological principle must be

borne in mind.   Mankind, from greatest to least, is under
the sway of the mixed motive.   Outside of insane asy-
lums, and the minds of people who ought to be in them
—those under the sway of the *idée fixe*—acts are determined by composite influences.   Both consciously and
unconsciously, the acting will is formed or swayed by a
complex of considerations in whose obscure mass it is not
always easy to discern even what was the controlling impulse.   Few men have excelled Mr. Hill in singleness of
purpose and directness of movement toward an end.   But
he was no exception to the laws of mental action.   He was
and he was not a monopolist.   Perhaps the thing can
be explained best by saying that monopoly, within
certain limits and with certain restrictions and conditions, was a logical sequence of the main work of his life.

To make this clear and simple, go back to that early
ambition of his to amass a fortune of one hundred thousand dollars and then cease from acquiring wealth.   It
was sincere.   But before the hour of achievement, the
process of acquisition had set in motion life forces; had
brought the man face to face with facts and conditions
which he found himself fitted to conquer, and in conquering which he found not merely growing power and fortune, but also delight, inspiration, and the satisfaction of
one of the elemental longings of his nature—love of public service.   He could no more pause at a point mechani-
cally predetermined than a man could stop loving or
hating another when the sphygmograph said that his

99

blood pressure had reached a degree arbitrarily fixed in advance. Mr. Hill's wealth went on growing as a necessary adjunct of his labours. It would be foolish to say that he did not appreciate it, value the larger constructive ability it conferred, strive to add to it by shrewd bargaining, by taking advantage of opportunity, by all reasonable and honourable means that presented themselves. It would be just as foolish to deny that his swelling fortune was incidental to his work. "The play's the thing." To him the endlessly varied, unfolding, and captivating procession of life and work was the reality. To speak of him either as a man who despised and rejected wealth, or as a man who lived mainly to accumulate million after million, would be untrue.

The analogy between his relation to wealth and his relation to influence in the transportation world is perfect. So far as the element of monopoly, limited of course both territorially and economically, was bound up with his plans, monopoly was a by-product. He could not easily brook opposition. When he had determined upon an end, he went after the means to that end. He was scrupulous in his methods, but unrelenting in his purpose. Circle beyond circle from a common centre, his influence and his achievements widened with the years. The area grew so great that it could not be extended, could not be maintained, without including something of the monopolistic element. Monopoly was implied in the mere fact of re-

100

maining a competitor in a field where opposition had attained eminence and power like his own. Wherever, then, the carrying out of his ideas involved a control of subordinate interests sufficient to deserve the name of monopoly, he did not hesitate to take that control and exercise it unflinchingly. But he cared no more for power, merely as power, than he did for wealth merely as wealth.

He was a man who did things. He wanted always to do more and greater things. The kind of thing he wanted to do was absolutely determined by his vision of its consequences; his deep conviction that these would be for the public good, for the development of the country, for the increase of American prosperity, and the strengthening of the American idea. When he was opposed, he put out his enormous strength. If any one hit him, he hit back. But he fought fair. Like all the geniuses the world has seen—for it is a necessary attribute of genius—he was tremendously sufficient unto himself. Woe to those who blocked his path. But he would never consciously wrong any man. He would no more have used his wealth and power just to breed more wealth and power; no more have sought control of men and territory and systems for the sake of control alone, than he would have had himself confined for the remainder of his life in his own big vault, to spend his best years in fingering cash or counting securities. A thousand facts of his life, a thousand comments that

101

came from his lips on men and events of his own time, tell that he felt, for this foible of so many of the great, only scorn and contempt.

This analysis of one aspect of the man finds its place here because, without it, his policies about to be described would be misconstrued or not understood at all. It is required by the charge of the will to monopoly brought against him at the time. His words denied that charge. His life contradicted it. The very foundation principles of the transportation business as he grasped and explained them were hostile to the possibility. But a large portion of the public would not believe, because it could not understand. It would have had to be Mr. Hill himself in order to do so. Therefore, one must not be surprised, neither should he judge too severely the people who were using such eyes and brains as nature had endowed them with, such arguments as many experiences with others had furnished them, if he finds Mr. Hill's acts brought at this time to the touchstone of their relation to a traffic monopoly, asserted by many and believed by some to be colossal in its comprehensiveness and its peril to the public. Before such an audience the first part of the trilogy, the purchase of the Burlington system, was about to be put upon the boards.

Before the curtain rises, however, clearness of understanding and just judgment will be aided by letting the author have his say. There exists an authentic "argument" of the play. In it the whole action of the three separate parts of the trilogy is condensed into a few paragraphs of wonderful clarity of statement, imbued with deep feeling. Just before Christmas, 1901, Mr. Hill returned from New York, where stirring events had been taking place, to find himself bitterly attacked in his own state in the discussion of the Northern Securities. For the only time in his life, so far as is known, he prepared and signed a statement for publication dealing with his own acts and purposes. It covers the ground of all the transactions briefly. No one can read it to-day without feeling a sincerity and an outraged public spirit that breathe from every line. Like the syllabus of a great case, it sets out the main points of the findings which are to be reached in the following chapters. The copy published here is taken from the St. Paul *Globe* of December 22, 1901. The fact that Mr. Hill owned at that time all the stock of this newspaper is a guarantee that the statement appeared exactly as he wrote it:

"I have been absent from Minnesota for more than two months and during that time there has arisen a wide discussion throughout the State of what has been generally called a consolidation or a merger of the Northern Pacific and Great Northern Railways, and in this discussion statements have been made which are so widely different from the facts that I feel called upon to make a conservative statement of just what has been done in the past and what will be done in the future.

"When the Northern Pacific failed and the Banking House of J. P. Morgan & Co reorganized it, myself and friends were holders of a large amount of that Company's securities. After the reorganization was completed we bought about twenty-six millions of Northern Pacific stock, both common and preferred. Some of this stock was afterward sold by individuals, but a large amount has been held from that time to the present.

"About a year ago the Union Pacific Company bought the Huntington and other interests in the Northern Pacific and at the same time made an effort to buy the control of the Chicago, Burlington & Quincy.

"With these lines in the hands of the Union Pacific interests, both the Northern Pacific and Great Northern would be largely shut out of the states of Nebraska, Kansas, Missouri, South Dakota, Iowa, Illinois, and Wisconsin, except by using other lines of railway, some of which were in the market for sale and might at any time pass under the control of or be combined with the Union Pacific interests. We then, with the Northern Pacific, made proposals to the Directors of the Burlington to buy their entire property. When this transaction was about being closed the people who represented the Union Pacific Company, and who had previously tried to buy the Burlington, asked to be allowed to share with us in the purchase of that Company; this
104

proposal we refused for the reason that it would defeat our object in buying the Burlington, and, further, it was against the law of several of the States in which the largest mileage of the Burlington was located.

"At that time, against the opposition of the more southerly lines, both the Northern Pacific and Great Northern had put into effect a low colonization rate and were carrying daily thousands of people into the Northwest, many of whom were coming from Kansas and Nebraska along the lines of the Union Pacific. This movement was at its height in the month of April, and after we had closed the purchase of the Burlington, the Union Pacific people undertook the boldest effort that ever was made in this country and bought more than sixty millions of the stock of the Northern Pacific in the markets of Europe and the United States. I was in New York at the time, and after Messrs. Morgan & Co. were aware of the action of the Union Pacific people, it was found that together we held about twenty-six millions of Northern Pacific common stock; and, inasmuch as the common stock, by right of a contract made with the preferred stockholders when the Company was reorganized and the stock issued, had the privilege of paying off the preferred stock at par on the first day of January in any year until 1917, Messrs. Morgan & Co. then bought in London and New York about sixteen millions of the common stock of the Northern Pacific; at the same time the Union Pacific interests, having already so large an investment, bid the stock up until there was the largest stock corner ever known; the common stock in three or four days went up to one thousand dollars per share.

"I explained to my friends how that, with control of the Northern Pacific, the Union Pacific would control the entire Northwest and of the West from Mexico to the Canadian line, except for the Great Northern. So great was the effort to get this control that one of my friends in London, who owned two millions of Northern Pacific common, was offered and refused fourteen million dollars for his stock. The result was that Messrs. Morgan & Co. and ourselves owned forty-two out of eighty millions of the Northern Pacific common, with the privilege of paying off the seventy-five millions of Northern Pacific preferred. The Union Pacific people owned thirty-seven millions of the common and about forty-two millions of the preferred, which was a clear majority of all the stock of the Northern Pacific, and claimed the exclusive control of the Northern Pacific Railway and through that ownership a control of one half the Burlington. When it was known that these preferred shares could and would be paid off and before the annual election, mutual negotiations resulted in Mr. Morgan giving them a representative in the Northern Pacific Board. At the same time I was elected a member of the Northern Pacific Board. When I was advised of my election I notified them that I could not legally act as a Director of the Northern Pacific and Great Northern at the same time, and I resigned after the first meeting of the Board.

"Several of the gentlemen who have long been interested in the Great Northern Railway and its predecessor, the St. Paul, Minneapolis & Manitoba Company, and who have always been among its largest shareholders, but not the holders of a majority of its stock, whose ages are from seventy to eighty-six years, have desired to combine their individual holdings in corporate form and in that way secure permanent protection for their interests and a continuation of the policy and management which had done so much for the development of the Nor hwest and the enhancement of their own property in the Northwest and elsewhere. Out of this desire has grown the Northern Securities Company.

"It became necessary (in order to prevent the Northern Pacific from passing under the control of the Union Pacific interests and with it the joint control of the Burlington) to pay off the seventy-five millions of Northern Pacific preferred. The enormous amount of cash required for this purpose from a comparatively small number of men made it necessary for them to act together in a large and permanent manner, through the medium of a corporation, and the Northern Securities Company afforded them the means of accomplishing this object without the necessity of creating a separate company to finance the transaction for the Northern Pacific; while, at the same time, the credit of the Northern Securities Company would be much stronger, as it would also hold a considerable amount of Great Northern and other securities.

"The Northern Securities Company is organized to deal in high-class securities, to hold the same for the benefit of its shareholders, and to advance the interests of the corporations whose securities it owns. Its powers do not include the operation of railways, banking, mining, nor the buying or selling of securities or properties for others on commission; it is purely an investment company and the object of its creation was simply to enable those who hold its stock to continue their respective interests in association together, and to prevent such interests from being scattered by death or otherwise; to provide against such attacks as had been made upon the Northern Pacific by a rival and competing interest, whose main investment was hundreds of miles from the Northwest and whose only object in buying control of the Northern Pacific was to benefit their southern properties by restraining the growth of the country between Lake Superior and Puget Sound, and by turning away from the Northern lines the enormous Oriental traffic which must follow placing on the Pacific Ocean of the largest ships in the world.

"The foregoing is a brief and absolutely correct statement of the whole subject and its truth can easily.

108

be verified by the State of Minnesota or any other State or person having sufficient interest to investigate the facts which are all matters of record.

"Now as to the effect of what has been done upon public interests of the country, let me ask a few questions which I want every candid and honest man to answer for himself:

"Did the Union Pacific people, with their railway lines extending from Omaha and New Orleans to California and Oregon through the several States in the Middle West and South, purchase a majority of the stock of the Northern Pacific Company for the purpose of aiding that Company and increasing the growth and prosperity of the Northern country, or was it for the purpose of restricting such growth and aiding the development of their enormous interests hundreds of miles to the south?

"Did they purchase the Northern Pacific and with it an equal share in the Burlington for the purpose of building up the Asiatic trade between the Northern zone, lying between St. Paul and Minneapolis and the Pacific Coast, or to prevent such building up and control the Oriental trade for their own railway lines through their own seaports and over their own ships?

"In defeating their control of the Northern Pacific and Burlington, and retaining it in the hands of those who had built it up and with it the entire Northwest, did we injure or benefit the people of the Northwest?

109

"Did I, by inducing my friends to hold their Northern Pacific common stock and act jointly with Messrs. Morgan & Co. when this stock was selling at five hundred and one thousand dollars a share, and thus prevent the Union Pacific from controlling the Northwest, injure or benefit every interest—agricultural, business, and otherwise—of the entire country between Lake Superior and the Pacific Ocean?

"Had we sold our twenty millions of Northern Pacific even at three hundred dollars a share, amounting to sixty million dollars, or forty millions more than its present value, and transferred to the Union Pacific control the entire country between Canada and Mexico, what law of Minnesota would we have violated? Could we not have legally put the money in our pockets and let the country learn what it was to be dominated by a parallel and competing railroad?

"Why did Governor Van Sant sit still from May until November, while a majority of the stock of the Northern Pacific Company was controlled by a parallel and competing railroad company, to which the law is clearly opposed, and wait until myself and friends have by our efforts and with our own money relieved the Northwest, not as a rival parallel or competing railroad, but doing what we clearly have the right to do as individuals or working together for greater permanency and security as a financial corporation?

"Has there ever been a case in the history of this

country when men have dropped their money profit and stood firmly by the interest of the communities which had grown up with their own and largely by their own efforts and capital?

"The public is interested in having a good railway service and at fair and reasonable rates. The past is gone and speaks for itself. I can speak for the future, and I have no hesitation whatever in saying that the increased volume of traffic, both through and local, will enable the companies to reduce their rates in proportion to the volume of such traffic, and that in the near future the public will have a chance to see for itself this feature of what I have said. The development of the country will increase with greater increase in population between Minnesota and the Pacific.

"No merger or consolidation of the Northern Pacific and Great Northern is contemplated. Each company will be operated separately in the future, as in the past.

"I greatly dislike to discuss my business in the newspapers, but during my absence an attack has been made upon myself and friends which has been persistently supported by both political and rival interests. All I ask is fair play, and let time determine whether the public will be benefited or injured by what we have done and will continue to do."

JAMES J. HILL.

CHAPTER TWENTY-SEVEN
THE BURLINGTON PURCHASE

IT WAS now definitely agreed between Mr. Hill and Mr. Morgan, representing the two sets of stockholders, and each largely interested in both companies, that some railroad system must be acquired by the Great Northern and the Northern Pacific, which should answer the double purpose of furnishing them with their own through line to Chicago and admitting them to the markets of the Middle West and a portion of the South and the Southwest. This would link them up over their own tracks with the eastern trunk lines. It would round out the territory to and from which a great body of transcontinental trade was to be carried. It would complete the eastern abutment of that mighty railroad bridge, spanning the country from the Great Lakes to the Pacific, to which the Great Northern system has been aptly compared. It would also be protective in an important sense. The Union Pacific was bold, energetic, and a dangerous rival. Its mind was already set upon obtaining a foothold in the northern country. It was strong in Oregon and looked toward the primacy of the whole Pacific Coast with a longing eye. It, too, could make good use of one of the large systems centred

112

in Chicago. To any one as familiar with railroad strategy and the minds of the railroad men of the time as was Mr. Hill, the need of quick action was obvious. What had been in his thought for some years was to become accomplished fact early in 1901.

Any one of three systems, the Chicago & Northwestern, the Chicago, Milwaukee & St. Paul, and the Chicago, Burlington & Quincy, might serve his purpose. The Chicago & Northwestern in 1901 had a length of 5,576 operated miles. It was spread over Wisconsin, Michigan, Illinois, Minnesota, Iowa, and the two Dakotas. Its Minnesota and Dakota Division alone was 1,256 miles, with a line of 486 miles running west from Winona, Minnesota, to Pierre, South Dakota. It was an old property, organized in 1859, and would be a powerful ally in some ways. Its total common and preferred stock was nearly $64,000,000 and its bonded debt $145,000,000. It was perhaps the least desirable of the three possibilities. It did not have the desired ramifications south or southwest. By reason of its affiliations with the New York Central, it would be the least easy to obtain.

The Chicago, Milwaukee & St. Paul was even more distinctively a Northwestern system. Organized in 1863, it had grown and spread until its total length of miles operated in 1901 was 6,746. It had a network of lines over Wisconsin, Minnesota, northern Iowa, and eastern Illinois. It was reaching out in all directions

113

over South Dakota, with lines in operation to Aberdeen, Mitchell, Woonsocket, and Chamberlain. It went down into Missouri to Kansas City, and up to Edgley, North Dakota. In the early days its managers had themselves aspired to the ownership of the St. Paul & Pacific, and were greatly disappointed when it escaped from their hands. It understood, better than most others, the value and possibilities of the new country to the west and northwest. As a subsequent chapter in its history showed, it also meant to get through to the Pacific by one means or another. Its total common and preferred stock, in 1901, was in excess of $100,000,000 and its funded debt almost $127,000,000.

The Chicago, Burlington & Quincy, the third possibility, was one of the best-constructed, best-managed, and most profitably operated systems in the West. A glance at the map instantly confirms the opinion that it would be the one best suited to the particular purposes in the minds of Mr. Hill and those who were to join with him in this project. It had its own line from Chicago to St. Paul, well built, well handled, and with good terminal facilities and connections. It had a network of lines in northwestern Illinois, reached Peoria and Quincy, and ran thence to St. Louis. It covered southern Iowa and northern Missouri, from Burlington to Omaha and from Omaha to St. Joseph, Kansas City, and St. Louis. Across southern Nebraska its lines stretched, with termini at Denver and Cheyenne.

114

Northwest it had a line straight up to and through the Black Hills to Billings, in Montana. To add this system to the Great Northern and the Northern Pacific would be almost like clasping tight together and making homogeneous the two slightly separated parts of one great transportation whole. The total length of lines operated by it in 1901, exclusive of systems leased or otherwise controlled, was 7,911. The Burlington, or "Q," as it was called, had been organized under another name as early as 1849. It absorbed one line after another and built steadily, growing rich and powerful because it ran through one of the best traffic countries in the West. Tributary to it were the fertile lands of northern Illinois, Iowa, and Nebraska, the coal mines of Illinois and Iowa, the river valleys of the Mississippi and its tributaries, and now the mining industries of Colorado and the Black Hills. During its existence it had paid out, up to 1901, regular cash dividends of more than $127,000,000 besides $6,700,000 in stock distributed. Its capital stock in 1901 was, in round numbers $110,500,000 and its funded debt a little more than $145,000,000.

Mr. Hill and Mr. Morgan, who were working with a friendly understanding, as they did so long as they both lived, held different views as to the best system to add to their own. Mr. Morgan, because of his many eastern affiliations, preferred to take up the possible purchase of the Chicago, Milwaukee & St. Paul.

He described the situation as he saw it, on the stand as a witness in the Northern Securities case. He said: "I think it was in 1899 that I made up my mind that it was essential that the Northern Pacific Railway should have its eastern terminus practically in Chicago. I talked it over with a great many people interested in the Northern Pacific and I found that all agreed with me, and the question came up as to how it best could be done. I came to the conclusion that there were but three lines available, the St. Paul, the Chicago, Burlington & Quincy, and the Wisconsin Central. I made up my mind that I would rather have the St. Paul. Soon after that I met Mr. Hill and I said: 'Mr. Hill, I think that the best thing we could do—I think your line perhaps is in the same condition—I think we had better go to work and secure the St. Paul road or a road to Chicago and if you will share with us we will do it together'; and he said, 'All right.' So he said; 'Who would take it up?' I said: 'I will. I think we had better take the St. Paul.' He said he thought we had better take the Burlington. I said I would rather have the St. Paul because the financial responsibility would be less. He did not agree with me but he acquiesced with my decision, and I took it up with the directors of the road." The gist of Mr. Morgan's testimony is that Mr. Hill preferred the Burlington because he thought it was better situated than the St. Paul for handling interior freight business destined for the

116

Pacific. After some negotiations the directors of the St. Paul refused to sell the road on any terms; "they would not even name terms; so," says Mr. Morgan, "I went to Mr. Hill and told him: 'You can go ahead and see what you can do with the Burlington.'"

The idea of using the Burlington as a Chicago connection and a line to the south had been in Mr. Hill's mind for some time. He said that the earliest consideration of it as a practical possibility was in 1897. He had talked the matter over with some London friends, but it was a larger undertaking than they cared to assume for the Great Northern alone. It would be equally available for the Northern Pacific, but at that time the latter had too many troubles of its own to be looking for a new one. The matter slumbered until the failure of negotiations with the St. Paul brought Mr. Morgan over to Mr. Hill's point of view. The latter's main reasons for preferring the Burlington were given in the published statement with which the preceding chapter concluded. He had studied the question—country, products, markets, lines of development—until he saw it all as a geometrician sees a diagram in a book. "In relation to the Great Northern and Northern Pacific," said another authority, "the Burlington is like the point and moldboard of a plough, the beam and handles of which are constituted by the former systems." Its acquisition had become another of Mr. Hill's enthusiasms. His argu-

117

ment had a dozen postulates before it, and as many corollaries behind. There was the demand of Oriental trade. "We have to look not only to cotton, but to anything that will furnish us business going to the West, whether it is going to the Pacific Coast or to Alaska, or to Honolulu, or to the Orient or Manila—anywhere; we must try everything. During the season of open water, during the season of navigation, we can make rates from Buffalo and the lower lake ports by way of Lake Superior on our own lines, but that does not reach to the South, and only takes the manufacturing districts south of the lakes during the season of navigation. A line reaching St. Louis and all the trunk lines of the South and the trunk lines of the East, between St. Louis and Chicago, puts us in a vastly different position; and that is the reason why it was of such importance for us to control the situation. We could not control it without controlling the access to the main centres. We could not control it unless we could give a market for the production of the line—products raised along our road—whether it was out of the mine, from the farm, or out of the forest. If the man who produced it could not sell it, he would stop producing. And that was the problem we had to meet, and with the Burlington we find ourselves able to meet it."

There was the matter of fuel demand and supply. "The Great Northern Railway Company and the Northern Pacific Railway Company have an interest in this country and in people living here. Our winters are cold, it would be difficult for them to live here without fuel, and it is a very serious matter for the railways. We don't know now that we will be able to run our trains to the 1st of February, with the lack of supply of coal, without bringing coal from Illinois, and we don't know but we will have to give up a portion of our supply of steam coal to keep people from freezing before spring. It is due to the inability of the railroads between Lake Erie and the mines in West Virginia, Pennsylvania, and Ohio to move the coal. They are unable to move the coal up to Lake Erie ports, and we are unable to get a supply. At this time we have not been able to get one half of our purchases for the year, and navigation will close some time next month. That is the importance of the control for us of access to the coal mines of Illinois, which are the nearest coal mines to this country, and the importance of that will be apparent more and more as time goes on."

Here as always, his public utterances, when checked by his personal correspondence with friends and others who were interested with him financially, ring true. The above quotations are extracts from his testimony. In April, 1901, with the deal just closed, he wrote to Lord Mount Stephen: "The best traffic of the Great Northern and Northern Pacific is the cotton and provisions west and the lumber and timber eastbound. The San Francisco lines run through the cot-

ton country from New Orleans through Texas and
Arkansas. The great provision centres are Kansas
City, St. Joseph, Omaha, Chicago, and St. Louis, none
of which are reached directly by the Great Northern
or Northern Pacific. Both companies have to divide
the through rate with some other line to reach those
important points. Now as to lumber from the coast,
we have to divide our rate with lines south to reach
Chicago, Wisconsin, Illinois, St. Louis, Iowa, Nebraska,
Kansas, etc. The Burlington lets us into all these districts and commercial centres, over better lines and
with better terminals than any other road." He never
changed his opinion of the value of this studied development of his system. Years later, in making a summary
of it, he wrote: "The last and most important step was
the Burlington purchase, in connection with the Northern Pacific, which places our lines on a permanent basis
as an independent railway system, which includes
within itself all the necessary conditions of production
and distribution which will for all time give the property great internal strength, covering a wide distribution of traffic resources with access to all the best markets, so that we can never again be dependent on one,
two, or even three crops for our revenue. Nor will a
failure of wheat or corn be so serious a matter as
formerly."

Last, but perhaps not least, there was another good
reason for wishing to take the Burlington into camp.

The Union Pacific people had already been nibbling at this tempting bait. They had visions of a control which would give them undisputed sway south of the Northern Pacific line and through the Middle West. They also wanted to build a fence across the southern and eastern line of their northern rivals. They aspired to domination of all the country west of the Mississippi, save a northern strip reduced to such helplessness that it, too, would finally be absorbed. Mr. Harriman and Mr. Schiff took up the purchase of the Burlington with Mr. Perkins and Mr. Harris, who represented it. Mr. Perkins had what amounted practically to an option on the property. Mr. Harriman made an offer, but it was too low to be taken into serious consideration. Then, believing that he could make terms satisfactory to himself later, he went back to New York. During the fall of 1900 or early in 1901, Union Pacific interests had purchased eight or nine million dollars' worth of Burlington stock in the open market. Not enough of it could be obtained in this way for a control, and the enterprise was stopped by Mr. Hill's negotiations. His ear was quick to catch the warning signal. The Burlington in Union Pacific hands would be even more dangerous as an enemy than it would be profitable in his own hands as an ally.

As usual where he was in command, no time was wasted. When negotiations were opened with the directors of the Burlington, about the middle of March, 1901, no attempt was made by Mr. Hill or Mr. Morgan or anybody connected with either of the purchasing railroads to approach individuals or brokers or to obtain any of the stock in open market. Neither man would have dreamed of it for a moment. Each of them repudiated vigorously the idea of any transaction for so much as a single share on private or firm account. This was a deal to be concluded exclusively by and for the railroad companies concerned. The stockholders of the Burlington were widely scattered. A large number who had inherited their holdings did not care to sell at any price. The directors of the road believed that if they could obtain the figure they asked for the stock they would be making a good bargain for its owners, and the event proved them right. Their executive committee entered into this negotiation. The price of $200 a share was agreed upon. It could not fail to satisfy the old holders of the securities, who saw their property valued at a figure above their most sanguine hope. What the other parties interested thought was stated by Mr. Morgan; and reflects light, not only on a transaction that caused surprise at the time, but upon the character of Mr. Hill, as understood by his business associates. Mr. Morgan said: "It was the only price at which it could be bought and we had great difficulty in getting it at that; and, in the next place, I felt, and Mr. Hill must have felt also—because he does not think of making transactions he does not think are profitable—

that it was worth a great deal more than that for the purpose for which we wanted it, and it would pay a large profit. He thought it would pay both the Northern Pacific and Great Northern a profit on that price." He explained carefully and emphatically that by this he meant not only a profit for the purpose for which it was wanted, but a profit in operation on its own account. Any one who will take the trouble to look up the traffic and revenue records of the Burlington system, comparing those prior to the date of sale with those under its later management, will learn that his opinion was correct.

So speedily had the great transaction been carried through that the sale was agreed upon, subject to the approval of both parties, in March, 1901. Both the courts and the public accepted the facts to be as stated briefly by Mr. Hill's counsel in the Northern Securities case: "The evidence is, therefore, uncontradicted and conclusive that the Great Northern and Northern Pacific Companies each purchased an equal number of shares of Burlington stock as the best means and for the sole purpose of reaching the best markets for the products of the territories along the lines, and of securing connections which would furnish the largest amount of traffic for their respective roads, increase the trade and interchange of commodities between the regions traversed by the Burlington lines and their connections and the regions traversed or reached by the Great Northern and Northern Pacific lines, and by their connecting lines of shipping on the Pacific Ocean, and as the best, if not the only, means of furnishing an indispensable supply of fuel for their own use and for the inhabitants of the country traversed by their lines."

At the directors' meeting of the Great Northern Railway Company of April 20, 1901, a preamble and resolutions covering this important deal were adopted. These stated the opinion of the board to be that it was desirable and for the best interests of the company that it should obtain, either separately "or in harmony and connection with the Northern Pacific Railway Company," an interest in the Chicago, Burlington, & Quincy Railroad Company. After asserting that it could not be obtained except by such joint purchase and the issue of 4 per cent. joint bonds at the rate of $200 par value for each $100 par value to be acquired, and that the Northern Pacific had agreed to the proposal, the president was authorized to enter into this agreement for the purchase of the whole or not less than two thirds of the shares of capital stock of the Chicago, Burlington, & Quincy Railroad Company. The two systems actually acquired 96.79 per cent. of the total authorized issue. The report of the 'president for June 30, 1901, covers all these transactions officially as follows: "The Great Northern Railway Company and the Northern Pacific Railway Company have jointly purchased 1,075,772 shares of the capital stock of the Chicago, Burlington & Quincy Railroad Company, and in payment for the same have issued their Joint Collateral Trust Bonds and scrip to the amount of $215,154,000. Further bonds of the same series, up to a total of $222,400,000, may be issued for acquiring the residue of the stock." "The Burlington system includes 7,992.60 miles of standard gauge railroad (on which are 423.15 miles of second track, making 8,415.75 miles of standard gauge single track) and 178.77 miles of narrow gauge railroad. It is located in the states of Illinois, Iowa, Missouri, Nebraska, Kansas, Colorado, Wyoming, South Dakota, and Montana, a territory of great extent; rich in all resources except timber; already well populated and developed and containing many large cities." "The Burlington is favourably located, with ample terminals in the important traffic centres of this territory, including Chicago, St. Louis, Peoria, Kansas City, St. Joseph, Omaha, Denver, St. Paul, Minneapolis, Burlington, and Des Moines. The territory served by the Burlington produces most of the machinery and implements used on the farms, in the forests, mines, and mills of the tier of states reached by the Great Northern and Northern Pacific. It also produces a large part of the iron and steel products exported to Asia via the Pacific Ocean. Chicago, Kansas City, St. Joseph, and Omaha, are the largest provision centres in the country. At St. Louis it connects with the chief cotton-carrying lines of the South and Southwest. On the other hand, the Burlington territory takes for fattening the live stock raised on the northern and western farms and ranches. It consumes lumber in all shapes on a large scale."

Writing personally to Lord Mount Stephen, Mr. Hill said: "It is true we pay a great price for the property. This could not be avoided. Seventy-five million dollars or $80,000,000 of the Chicago, Burlington & Quincy is held by small holders, many of whom got it by inheritance. The average holding of the stock by the company's books is 68 shares, in the hands of nearly 15,000 stockholders. . . . Our plan is based on securing not less than two thirds of the 'Q' shares which enables us to form a new company which will lease the property to the present company, the rental being the interest on the bonds paid for the purchase; the stock of the new company to be divided between the Great Northern and the Northern Pacific equally, $50,000,000 to each. The new bonds to be payable at our option any time after five years."

If the price, measured by the 175 to 180 at which the stock had previously sold in the market, was high, there were two compensations. First, the property could not have been bought for any less; indeed, the new owners might congratulate themselves on being able to get it at all. Second, it was actually cheap when measured by mileage cost and earning power.

On these points Mr. Hill said: "The matter was the subject of negotiation on several occasions. The books or transcripts of the accounts were produced, showing its earnings—the income—I remember its income as shown was $10,400,000, including the sinking fund, and that was more than 10 per cent. on the outstanding stock at that time, or about 10 per cent. The Burlington road had a very heavy sinking fund; for many years the miles of main track—something more than 8,000—had a bonded debt, less the sinking fund, of about $15,800 a mile, and stock was about $13,000 a mile. Take the Burlington stock at 200 and add to it the bonded debt per mile of the road and it would give the average cost of the Burlington about $42,000 a mile, which was about what it cost us; that is $10,000 or $12,000 a mile less than any of these granger roads are selling at on the market. In other words, the Burlington was the cheapest property altogether, and reached the points we desired to reach, and it would cost us less money per mile than it would to have acquired any other."

A few weeks later he sent to the same associate of his thought as well as of his work, a lengthy exposition of the broad lines of American railroad development. The Burlington purchase appears there in its true place; not as an act of aggrandizement, but as one of the pieces in a big mosaic which was being put together according to a predestined pattern by forces so great, so far above any permanent individual contradiction or interference, that he looked upon himself as their servitor: "The recent combinations of railway lines in this country, following what has occurred in England, are rapidly bringing the properties into groups, generally on the basis of territorial control. About all the lines south of Washington are under the control of the Southern Railway. The Pennsylvania controls the Norfolk & Western, Chesapeake & Ohio, Baltimore & Ohio, and in fact all the lines between the Southern Railway lines and the Erie, as far west as St. Louis. The New York Central controls the Michigan Central and Canada Southern, a large mileage in Michigan, the Lake Shore, Nickel Plate, Big Four, and practically all the lines between the Pennsylvania Company's lines and the Great Lakes except the Erie, and I have no doubt they or the Pennsylvania Company will control the Erie in a very short time. The Union Pacific now controls the Southern and Central Pacific, the Colorado, Denver & Gulf, the Chicago & Alton, and other lines in that territory. They also tried hard to control the Chicago, Burlington & Quincy but failed. The Chicago & Northwestern Railway is controlled by the New York Central people. This concentration of lines has already resulted in arrangements between the lines east of Chicago which practically farm out or divide the western traffic in both directions so as to take the lion's share of the rates for the lines east of Chicago. The old companies like the Alton, the Rock Island and, to a degree, the Chicago, Burlington & Quincy, and the St. Paul are forced to accept divisions of rates and conditions which have practically made them no longer independent. For these years past the trunk lines east of Buffalo demanded from us that we should hand over to them the rate-making power of our Northern Steamship Company's boats on the lakes. So far we have been able to prevent this for the reason that our lines originate so large a grain and flour traffic that we have been able to hold open both the Lackawanna and the Lehigh. However, even these lines are, during the past year, passing under the control of interests allied with the trunk lines. The time had arrived when we should make our own territorial combination."

It need only be added that the purchase in every way justified the calculations of the men who advocated it. In the same letter Mr. Hill outlined vigorously the new strategic position: "With the Great Northern, Northern Pacific, and Chicago, Burlington & Quincy under one grand control, we have placed ourselves in a position of strength as to traffic, terminal cities and terminal facilities, and territorial control, which is now the strongest in the West and will daily grow stronger. We have secured another advantage by being in the best position to receive the western movement of population, which is beginning to assume proportions never before reached in the settlement of this country. Now, where have we lost anything? I must say that I am not able to see any such loss. We may have a year or two of hard work, but the end attained will be well worth the effort, and the result will be that we will have a compact property, well in hand, with a constantly increasing future from natural and constant causes."

The Burlington remained a powerful system. Neither its shareholders nor its public had any reason to regret the transfer of control. Its business increased, especially to the south and southwest. Nowhere was it injured. Mr. Hill put into effect upon it the methods proved so successful wherever he had applied them. He sought and found economies in operation that made its reports a cause of pride to him. His directing mind and hand were behind its accomplishment. He saw, scrutinized, analyzed, corrected. Not only as an explanation of the new progress of the Burlington, but as a light thrown upon his grasp of practical method and the way he enforced it everywhere, the following letter to an official, having almost the precision of a military order, is given here: "In looking over the performance sheet I can readily see how you would increase your engine power very materially without much expense and no outlay by increasing the train load. To illustrate: The figures show between Savannah and St. Paul four freights a day each way with an average of 400 tons each. A good engine on that division can easily haul 2,000 tons in a train, or more than the four trains are hauling, and if they haul but 800 tons, which is only 40 per cent. of the capacity of the engines, the number of engines used would be cut in two. The same thing applies to cars, although in a somewhat less extent. I have frequently said that this is not a matter that can be regulated in a day, at the same time there is so very much room for improvement in the matter of train loading and saving in train miles that there is nothing connected with the entire operation of the Burlington road which calls for as close attention and that will give as good results. Every engine on the road in service beyond what is necessary to do the work adds directly to the expense." Five years after the road came under the new control, the normal average train load had risen from 200 to 376 tons per train. The Burlington was then handling, with a smaller number of trains, a traffic more than half as large again as it was in 1901. This is a practical demonstration of what Mr. Hill's system of railroad operation could accomplish.

The reasons that he had given before the event were found valid afterward. He said that the buying of the Burlington had increased commerce between the states and with foreign nations more rapidly than he had known business of such magnitude to grow in his forty years' experience. The total tonnage of the Great Northern increased about 30 per cent. The foreign business increased more than 100 per cent. The Northern Pacific reaped a similar benefit. He summed up in the following words the broad general effects of a policy which had been fitted to national and international requirements. This is what constitutes its greatness and his, as compared with internal reorganizations which look no farther than the progress of the system to which they are applied: "It has created traffic. Now, how much of that traffic would have been created or would have existed, it is very difficult for me or anybody else to say. But we know that the traffic has increased since the acquisition of the Burlington to an enormous extent, and we know further that we are able, not to compete alone with railways, for that is a small matter in this business, but to compete in the matter of rates with the ships going from New Orleans or from Galveston, or the railways carrying it anywhere, or in connection with any other system of transportation. Now, we are able to make a rate that will take that business."

Finally, the matter is brought down to the ultimate test, its consequences for the public as a whole. While the pieces were being shifted in the big game and the players were winning, how did the people fare? The answer is unequivocal. Along with increased business and profits went decreased rates. Mr. Hill said, at the same time that he made the statements quoted above: "We have been able to reduce rates from 10 to 15 per cent. in a year on the local business between the Pacific Coast and the Twin Cities and Lake Superior. The

Northern Pacific rates have also been reduced, and their revenue has been such as to enable them to make this reduction, without any reduction of their dividends." No act, no policy in the history of American railroading was more completely vindicated. None was less the offshoot of impulse, personal ambition, or the will to wealth and power. None was more simply the embodiment of a thought so true and living that it compelled events themselves to realize and to justify it. It was a natural and almost necessary evolution from Mr. Hill's whole career as a master of transportation. So was completed the first part of the trilogy.

CHAPTER   TWENTY-EIGHT

A BATTLE OF GIANTS

THE prologue to the second portion of the trilogy had
been prepared before the action of the first was
completed. Late in 1900 or early in 1901, the
Union Pacific interests had, as has been said, bought
some eight or nine million dollars of the stock of the
Burlington. The same idea was in more than one mind.
The struggle for control of mighty machines of transportation and the business of an empire did not originate in a day. Its tap root was not local ambition or
personal pique. Whatever attitude one may take toward the several actors in the drama, he would misjudge
them absurdly if he measured them by any such pica-
yune standard. Giants in power, they were also above
the common stature in judgment, strategy, anticipation
of events and their logic, clear understanding of ways
and means. One who turns back to the chapters on
the reorganization of the Northern Pacific and on early
railroad developments and struggles in the Pacific
Northwest will find there germs of trouble. The situation was not unlike that in the Balkans in the summer of
1914. Spheres of influence, not yet determined, over-
lapped their claims. Debatable ground was coveted on

both sides. Between North and South, west of the Mississippi River, there was, in the railroad world, another irrepressible conflict. Should this immense portion of the continent be virtually controlled by one system, with a France and a Belgium remaining here and there so long as they did not assert an independence too , great, or should there be different groups of railroads, and consenting community of interests between powerful equals? That, at bottom, was the question to be decided. The two contradictory principles were personified in Mr. Harriman and Mr. Hill. The purchase of the Burlington fired the first gun; because it established, if confirmed and uninterfered with, a permanent advantage.

There is abundance of data here, because the facts were subsequently threshed out over and over again in the courts. The Northern Securities Company trod upon the heels of the struggle for control of the Northern Pacific, which itself was an immediate consequence of the annexation of the Burlington by that road and the Great Northern. It led a litigious life. In one suit after another, carried on bitterly by state and national authorities, it was hunted from court to court and all its antecedent affiliations were brought to light. Among these, both the Burlington purchase and the struggle for the Northern Pacific played leading parts. The most trifling detail was examined and read into the record. All the principal actors, Mr. Hill, Mr. Morgan, Mr.

Harriman, Mr. Schiff, and their understudies in the telling situations were on the witness stand. The ablest counsel in the country saw to it that nothing material should be omitted or remain unexplained. Motives were probed, and suspicions light as air examined as Holy Writ is searched.

Mr. Hill was a central figure. He was surrounded and supported by those to whom a lifetime of fidelity had made him not only a leader but a friend. About the rock of his purpose and his magnificent steadfastness to his word, the waves of the frenzied storm of May, 1901, raged in vain. It is far from the most important, but it is one of the most dramatic, episodes of his career. The opposing interest to Mr. Hill and Mr. Morgan, who represented the Great Northern and the Northern Pacific, was the group that may for convenience be designated as the Union Pacific interest. Sometimes the properties named, the holders of stocks, the acting agents, were other corporations or individuals: the Oregon Short Line, the Southern Pacific, one or other of the big financial houses in New York that were backing this combination. But always, if the action is to be free and the understanding simple, they may be summed up in the name of one man and the insistence of one idea. The man was Mr. E. H. Harriman, whose rise and power were shown with sufficient fullness for the purpose of this work in the chapters already referred to. The idea was that neither the

136

group of railroad interests dominant in the South nor that in the North must permit its power to be impaired, its expansion limited, by a too great preponderance of the other in intermediate territory. For years the forces on both sides had been mobilizing. Now they came into contact.

It has been mentioned that Union Pacific interests had, late in 1900 or very early in 1901, bought in the market a relatively small stock interest in the Burlington. Finding this route a "no thoroughfare," they had sold it again. Mr. Hill was not ignorant of the significance of this. Neither was Mr. Morgan, to whom, as more particularly responsible for the financial future of Northern Pacific, it was of even greater interest. For the Burlington system and the Burlington territory alone intervened as neutral ground between the Northern Pacific and the Union Pacific. The Milwaukee & St. Paul had not yet built its Puget Sound extension. It and the Northwestern were in the field, but did not hold it strategically. Yet Mr. Morgan did not grasp fully the significance or the danger of the occasion. One has but to consider what would have happened if it had proved feasible to carry out his plan for the purchase of the St. Paul, to which Mr. Hill had at first reluctantly yielded. Undoubtedly Union Pacific interests would then have bought the Burlington. They would have had, at that time and for the ends aimed at, the stronger ally. The dangers to which the northern transcontinentals and their territory were exposed would have been lessened, but by no means removed. The situation would have remained serious, and the struggle must have continued almost indefinitely.

Early in March the Union Pacific interests, using the term as defined above, because sometimes one and sometimes another of the men included were acting, sometimes they represented themselves as individuals and sometimes acted for one or all of the interests concerned, made a request for a share in the Burlington property. They proposed to put up part of the cash and receive representation and influence. But the buyers refused. They had seen their peril. They realized the value of their holding. Not only were they practically in possession of a useful and remunerative property, but they had interposed a buffer between their territory and that of their most aggressive rival. They saw no reason to exchange a certain victory for a doubt-ful truce. The incident was closed. These things had not been done in a corner. The Union Pacific people knew what was in the wind, for Mr. Hill had advised them of it himself. He wrote to one of those interested with him in the negotiations, May 16, 1901: "So as to remove any ground for the charge that we were working secretly to acquire the Chicago, Burlington & Quincy, I said to [one of the representatives of the Union Pacific interests] in January that if he at any time heard that we were conferring with the 'Q' board of directors looking to the joint acquisition of that property, I wanted to be the first one to tell him that we intended to take up the matter seriously. In April, after Mr. Morgan had gone abroad and the Burlington matter was taking definite shape, I again told him that matters were progressing toward a close. He said he should have bought Burlington in the market and saved the advance." Mr. Hill replied that the other side had tried that method themselves, and "found themselves up against a stone wall," consisting of the great body of small shareholders, "who would not even give him one director, and who resented his attempt to buy into their company." "I told him our plan was an open and fair attempt to agree with the 'Q' board, as the only means of gaining control of that property."

The Union Pacific interests felt that they could no more submit quietly to this latest development than the Great Northern and the Northern Pacific would have felt that they could acquiesce in Union Pacific ownership of the Burlington. Every argument adduced by Mr. Hill in his statement in favour of the control that he had secured was an argument in Mr. Harriman's mind why it could not be allowed to stand. Every possibility of alleged encroachment to the north revealed new attractions of the prize that had been snatched from him. In that system paralleling his own, in that territory not to be demarcated from his own, from Chicago west to Denver and Cheyenne, he

139

saw potentialities of endless trouble. When the Union Pacific people demanded a participation in the purchase, the answer was that it was against the law, because the Union Pacific and the Burlington were undeniably parallel and competing systems in an important territory. Also, the directors of the Burlington were unwilling to sell where the Union Pacific would be a party. Shortly after buying the Burlington, a road leading to important coal mines in Illinois was added. The Union Pacific people asked that it be turned over to the Alton, and that the Burlington should buy its supply of coal from the Alton road. "The railroad coal used on the eastern end of the two northern lines," said Mr. Hill in a letter at this time, "amounts to something over a million and a half tons a year, or over five thousand tons a day, and the coal for domestic and other use to about fifteen hundred or two thousand tons a day more. You will see at once how unreasonable it would be for the Burlington and the northern roads to depend upon some other line and some other mines for a permanent supply of coal without which the roads could not be operated nor could the people live in our northern country during the winters." Probably some or all of these demands were intended to lay a foundation for the policy that was now to be adopted; to give a colour of reason for the hostilities that were soon to be begun secretly and in full force.

If Mr. Harriman could not get the less, he must take

the greater. He would buy the mare to get the filly. He formed a project whose daring commands admiration from friend and foe; whose execution was so swift, so unsparing, so successful, that but for a single oversight his stroke would have gone home. Had he won to his goal, the future of the Great Northern would have been limited and uncertain indeed. The Union Pacific interests had determined on nothing less than the capture of the Northern Pacific itself, by purchasing a majority of its stock. The boldness of the plan, so different now in magnitude from the old days when Mr. Villard had realized it—$78,000,000 to put up instead of $8,000,000—allied it to a work of genius. From those two grim old lions who guarded the way, the quarry was to be snatched before they sensed the presence of an enemy. The implications of the project were tremendous. Suppose the Union Pacific interests gained control of Northern Pacific. At once the Great Northern would have had to make terms with its new owners, or bear the brunt of incessant hostile attack along two thousand miles of battle front. It would have been shut into the narrow strip between its line and the Canadian border. As the Union Pacific would succeed also to a half interest in the Burlington, the situation there would be a permanent deadlock. All the system of relations and the scheme of traffic worked out so carefully by Mr. Hill would have been either suspended or destroyed. There could be but one issue from a position so intolerable. He would have had to make the best terms he could. And the terms dictated by an interest that would then have reached from New Orleans and Galveston to Winnipeg, and from San Francisco and Portland and Tacoma to Chicago and St. Paul and Duluth, were not likely to be tolerable. The victor could have made them almost what he pleased.

With a clear vision of this, making the great venture worth while, win or lose, the Union Pacific interests started their campaign for buying control of Northern Pacific. After all, it was not such a hopeless bit of crusading as it seemed at first glance. The latter company had outstanding $80,000,000 of common and $75,000,000 of preferred stock. Holders of both shared in the control and direction of the property. It was not the custom for the managers and directors of a railroad system to own an absolute majority of its stock. From 30 to 40 per cent. was usually deemed ample to secure or protect control. Mr. Hill personally never needed anything like that amount. The loyalty of his stockholders made it unnecessary. He said, speaking of this very occasion: "I may say that I think I controlled the policy of the Great Northern Railway Company and its predecessor as fully as the policy of any railway ever was controlled in this country, and I never owned more than 10 or 12 per cent. I never owned a majority of the stock, but I always had a following of good, loyal stockholders, and the men who were most active,

142

covering about 33 or 35 millions out of 125 millions, practically formed the company, and they desired that their other shareholders, whoever they were, new or old, might participate in anything that they were doing, if they thought it would be any advantage to them as shareholders." There was little possibility of uniting the scattered stockholders, representing the balance of power in any large corporation, into a coherent opposition which could overthrow those in control. At worst, no such operation in Northern Pacific was likely to be carried through without sending bubbles to the surface in time to give ample warning.

So the interests represented by Mr. Hill and Mr. Morgan did not have a majority of its stock. It had not occurred to them that they would need it. There was no dissatisfaction in their camp. They did not do business that way. A frontal attack was something they did not expect. For once in their lives they were caught napping. They had not overlooked the possibility, they had discounted it. Examining it coldly, they had dismissed it as a chimera. Mr. Hill said: "As I remember it, one of our directors raised a question that inasmuch as the purchase of the Burlington stock and the creation of a bond to pay for it involved the joint and several liability of the entire amount of the purchase, it was a matter of consequence to the Great Northern to know that the Northern Pacific would not pass into the hands of people who might be interested in other directions, in developing in other directions or other sections of the country; and I remember I answered that, with what myself and friends held at that time and what Morgan & Company held, we would have somewhere in the neighbourhood of 35 or 40 millions of the stock out of a total of 155 millions, which was larger than is usually held in any of the large companies. I did not think at the time that it was at all likely that anybody would undertake to buy in the market the control of 155 millions of stock." In March, 1901, Mr. Hill said that he had no knowledge of any Union Pacific parties holding stock in the Northern Pacific. Early in May they advised him that they had secured a substantial control. And they had reason to believe it. So lightning-like was the assault.

Mr. Hill was under no illusion as to what the success of the Union Pacific in this foray would mean. It was the counterstroke to the Burlington purchase. Every consideration which made the latter advisable made the former ruinous. This was not a question of prestige, it was a matter of life or death. At the time, and again in later years, he described it as such. "The value of the property would be destroyed. Its growth would be restricted. It would be controlled in the interests of another property or body for the reason that it would be restricted or might be restricted so as not to interfere with the growth of the other property. We were making great efforts, and very successful

144

efforts, at that time, to settle up all this northern section between the Great Lakes and Puget Sound, and
bringing in an enormous number of people, many of
these people coming from the line of the Union Pacific
in Kansas and the Southwest, bringing them up here.
And I remember one reason why they wanted to get a
joint interest in the Burlington; they said we were
getting too strong for them, we were going down into
their country and taking people from there. That was
one of the reasons they gave." Still more explicitly
he explained the inevitable consequences. "If that
stock had not been redeemed, and the Union Pacific
controlled the Northern Pacific, and half the Burlington, they would very soon control the Great Northern.
Because if the Union Pacific controlled the Northern
Pacific and controlled the Burlington to the extent
that the Northern Pacific half-interest would control
it, we would be deprived of any access that we
could control for a moment longer than the good will of
another company; and we could not go on building up a
business on any such condition. And let me add, further, if I may, that it would have almost destroyed the
value of the Great Northern property or its shares for
its shareholders. I would have recommended them to
sell their line at once on the best terms they could get.
It was not a question of competition. It was a question of physical inability to reach the market. We
would be shut out from the markets." Mr. Morgan,

145

of course, who had handled the reorganization of the Northern Pacific, and had both pride in his work and interest in the outcome, was not handing it over to a rival if he could help it.

The secret had been well kept. During the month of April the Union Pacific interests were quietly gathering in all the Northern Pacific stock they could reach. Many holders who were friendly to those in control were taken unaware and, to their lasting regret, parted with their shares without any idea of the purpose for which possession of them was to be used. One stockholder to the extent of three and a half millions had already sold when he received a telegram from Mr. Hill asking him not to. He said afterward that he would rather have burned his stock if he had known what it meant. This buying continued through the first week in May; and by that time the Union Pacific people had secured $41,000,000 of preferred and $37,000,000 of common. The total, $78,000,000, was a clear majority of the $155,000,000 outstanding capital stock of the Northern Pacific. They believed that they had a sure control and rested on their oars.

After the Burlington purchase had been concluded, Mr. Morgan, whose health was poor, went abroad. His first news was that the control of Northern Pacific was in danger, if it had not already been lost. Mr. Hill and his friends, who were advised at last, by the steady rise in price of the stock and by whispers of something going on, such as inevitably circulate in the most covert transactions, had now sized up the situation. It was very late in the day and much ground had been lost. On the second day of May, only one week before the storm burst, Morgan & Company had, in the ordinary course of business, unsuspectingly sold more than a million dollars of Northern Pacific. On the same date the treasurer of one of the proprietary companies of the Northern Pacific sold 13,000 shares of the common stock. Mr. Hill had reached New York only the day before. He lost no time. The steady rise in price to from $110 to $120 was to him like a steady fall of the barometer. Soon, also, glittering possibilities were dangled before him. He was assured that control of the Northern Pacific had already passed into other hands and would be held there firmly. But his position and his power, he was told, would be made greater than ever before. It was a kingly crown in the railroad world that was offered to him. This was his reply: "I simply said that it was not necessary to bribe me to do the fair and respectable thing toward so close a neighbour as the Union Pacific; and on the other hand I could not be bribed to do wrong in any way. I at once told Mr. Baker and Mr. Perkins, they wired Morgan, you know the result." The cat was out of the bag. Mr. Morgan was advised by cable, and he and his friends and Mr. Hill took counsel. On May 7, Mr. Hill and his friends on whom he could depend held

147

only from $18,000,000 to $20,000,000 of common, and the Morgan Company from $7,000,000 to $8,000,000. At a disadvantage here, they had the all-important certainty in their minds that upon the common stock alone rested the ultimate control of the property. The $37,000,000 held by the Union Pacific was less than a majority of $80,000,000; but the margin was fearfully narrow.

Everybody knew what it would mean to go into the market and buy the amount necessary to convert the Hill-Morgan holdings into a majority. Prices would soar; speculative purchases and sales would confuse and impede the transaction; and the almost irresistible temptation would be offered to those really friendly, but not absolutely identical in interest, to sell out at the big figures that were offered. It was a time when millions, literally, were to be made, not by treachery, but merely by a lesion in friendship. But it was a time when men counted for as much as millions. Absolute confidence existed between the two men most concerned. Exactly as the four associates made all their arrangements to buy St. Paul & Pacific, and pledged their "fortunes and their sacred honour" without a word in writing, so Mr. Hill and Mr. Morgan agreed to stand by each other, let come what might. It was man's word against the world. Mr. Morgan described the position, his quick vision in a time of doubt and danger and his instant decision, in this

148

laconic fashion: "We had reorganized the Northern Pacific. We had placed all the securities of the Northern Pacific, and I knew, as I had always supposed, that there were people—friends of ours and other people— who held practically enough Northern Pacific—we always supposed we had with us people upon whom we could depend to protect our moral control of the property—and consequently when that news came to me I hadn't any doubt about the fact of the matter and at the same time this news came so strong, whoever had acquired it, I felt something must have happened. Somebody must have sold. I knew where certain stocks were, and I figured it up. I feel bound in all honour when I reorganize a property and am morally responsible for its management to protect it, and I generally do protect it; so I made up my mind that it would be desirable to buy 150,000 shares of stock, which we proceeded to do, and with that I knew we had a majority of common stock, and I knew that actually gave us the control and they couldn't take the minority and have it sacrificed to the Union Pacific interests."

That "which we proceeded to do," covering in five words an undertaking so great and apparently impossible, is delightful. What the Morgan firm had to do was to go into the market, where the waves were already telling of rapids and cataracts ahead, and buy about $15,000,000 of Northern Pacific stock. Before doing so they asked Mr. Hill if he and his friends would hold their stock and not sell out. His reply was character-istic: "I said myself and friends would stand without hitching." And they did. For himself it was easy. Money could not make him break faith. To be able to answer in the same positive and confident way for the band of friends who had retained large interests in the projects with which they knew he was connected by ownership or by his personal activity, was something to be prouder of than possession of a dozen railroads. He appealed to their loyalty. The way in which those friends stood by him through this crucial time is one of the highest tributes that could be paid to any man. When the $15,000,000 of stock was bought and the sky cleared, the Union Pacific people were found with a majority of the total stock of the Northern Pacific. The Hill and Morgan interests had more than $42,500,000 of the common stock, a majority of about $3,000,000.

Dealings of this magnitude and meaning could not occur without shaking the financial world to the centre. The so-called panic of May 9, 1901, was the conse-quence. It was not a panic in the ordinary sense. Lurid tales have been told of the scenes of that great day, and the exciting efforts and excited words of the principals in the struggle. These are fairy stories. When Northern Pacific soared to the unheard-of price of $1,000 a share, brokers were not buying it for Mr. Hill or Mr. Morgan or Mr. Harriman or Kuhn, Loeb & Company. None of these men did business on those

150

terms. Before the crisis they had done what they could, and each side believed itself sure of victory. But the fact that the market was bare of Northern Pacific, while buyers were still eager to get it, sent prices rocketing. Many shareholders in the West and South sold their stock but could not deliver it immediately. Speculators who sold short saw the price jump point after point, and could not furnish the stock to stop their losses. But it was not what is ordinarily called a "corner." Nobody was trying to force prices up that he might sell at a profit. "How could we sell at any price?" said Mr. Hill; "we were investors. We were not speculators. I never bought or sold a share of stock for gambling purposes in my life. And I don't want to earn money wrung from people by a corner." This was not the kind of panic that originates in depression or want of confidence. Therefore, although it was the talk of two continents at the time, it produced no lasting consequences.

It could have done so if it had ended in a war to the death of the financial powers engaged. But nobody wanted that to happen. The facts and the immediate results were summed up thus by Mr. Hill: "There was a very strained financial condition; people were failing and the trouble was very great. Something had occurred that never had happened in New York before—an attempt to buy a control of $155,000,000 of stock on the market—and the high price caused people to sell stock they did not own. The bankers and financial men of every description were deeply interested, not only in New York, but in London, and in financial centres on the continent, and the result was, I think, maybe two or three meetings. I know certainly there was one between the bankers at that time. The Union Pacific people claimed that they had the control by the ownership of a majority of the stock of the Northern Pacific Railroad; that wasn't conceded by Messrs. Bacon and I think Mr. Steele—Mr. Robert Bacon and Mr. Steele—because they knew they held, as long as myself and friends held our stock, a majority of the common stock which would control the property. They made an agreement that as far as the election of the directors was concerned they would leave it to Mr. Morgan to name the directors, and that was done." Somebody on the other side had suggested previously that all interests might be pooled, with one general direction of the combined properties; but Mr. Hill would not hear of it. "I simply said that such a combination was illegal, and even if it was legal was one that sooner or later would turn the courts of all the states against us, and for that reason it could not stand and should not be considered."

The great advantage of Mr. Hill in this struggle was that, having participated in the reorganization of the Northern Pacific, he knew the conditions under which its stock had been issued and by which it might be retired. The Morgan firm, of course, had them by heart. The all-important one was that the preferred shares could be retired on any first of January prior to 1917. The Union Pacific interests could scarcely have been ignorant of this, but neither could they have appreciated what might be done under it, or they would have bought more common and less preferred. The election of the Board of Directors of the Northern Pacific was fixed for October. When the smoke cleared away, after May 9, the Union Pacific interests had stock enough to choose the next Board of Directors, since both classes of stock were entitled to vote at this election. With their friends in a majority, they could, if they were present and voted at the October meeting, name their own directors and so prevent the retirement of the preferred stock. On the other hand, the existing directory was, of course, friendly to and representative of those in possession. It had power to postpone the annual meeting from October till after January 1, 1902. Thus extending its own period of life, it could have retired that stock before its holders ever had a chance to vote. The defenders of the property had won a clear and undoubted victory.

Nothing was to be gained for either side by fighting. Both might have continued to tear up Wall Street and injure large property interests, including their own. They could have engaged in endless litigation, which would have cost a lot of money without materially altering anything. They might have maintained their divided ownership of Northern Pacific and kept up a jolly tug-of-war until the rope broke. The end of that would be two pieces of rope, and two parties covered with bruises from some severe falls. After all their animosities, and with all that they had done or left undone, again it has to be remembered that on both sides these were big men. They were big not only by the measure of achievement, but also because they were not actuated by a blind, vindictive desire just to crush and kill. They were big enough to see that the interests in their charge ought not to be made coppers in a game of pitch and toss. They had already accepted, not merely as a theory but as a conviction, the necessity of community of interest to a certain extent. Recent events had broadened and instructed their view. Things being as they were, they were ready for some agreement.

They did not wait to scrap it out in October, but agreed to place the Northern Pacific interests practically without reserve in Mr. Morgan's hands. The following bulletin was published June 1, 1901: "It is officially announced that an understanding has been reached between the Northern Pacific and the Union Pacific interests under which the composition of the Northern Pacific Board will be left in the hands of J. P. Morgan. Certain names have already been suggested, not now to be made public, which will especially be recognized as representative of common interests. It is asserted that complete and perfect harmony will result under the plan adopted between all interests involved." Shortly after May 9 a conference was held at Mr. Harriman's office, where all parties agreed that the Board of Directors to be elected at the annual meeting in October should be named by Mr. Morgan, and this agreement was carried out. Mr. Harriman was placed on the board of directors of the reorganized Burlington. Union Pacific interests received a representation on the new Northern Pacific board of directors. Mr. Hill explained it thus: "I don't know but they feared we would swallow them or something, and they professed great fear that the Burlington was going to build through to California and to southern California and what is known as the W. A. Clark road, building from Los Angeles into Utah. I remember being asked by some of them if our company or the Northern Pacific or the Burlington were connected with it or expected to be. I told them no; we were developing an entirely different section of the country, and we were not anxious to extend into southern California or San Francisco, and I think that largely led to those people being put into the Burlington board that they might be witnesses; that there was nobody going to dig pitfalls, etc., for them in that country."

November 13 a resolution was passed, giving notice of the retirement of Northern Pacific preferred stock. This was executed on the first day of January, 1902, by the delivery of the stock to the Morgan firm for payment in cash at its par value. Before that date the whole face of affairs had changed. The idea of a holding company, latent in Mr. Hill's mind for a long time though for a more limited purpose, had been transformed into fact. The Northern Securities, expanded into a corporation which should hold the securities of these great properties and make them immune from future attack, promised to allay or remove antagonisms. Its chief stockholders would be a sort of General Staff for the transcontinental systems and their allies. For this last and greatest action of the trilogy the stage was already set and the actors ready with their rôles.

CHAPTER   TWENTY–NINE
THE NORTHERN SECURITIES

AS THE *dénouement* approaches, the action quickens. The adoption, November 13, 1901, of a resolution directing the retirement of its preferred stock wrote "finis" after the struggle for control of the Northern Pacific. On the same date the Northern Securities Company was incorporated. This was more than coincidence. Although the strenuous denial that the new concern was a product of compromise between the interests so lately locked in deadly struggle must be accepted in good faith, although it is beyond question that the general idea of a holding company had been conceived by Mr. Hill years before and was but waiting a favourable opportunity to take material shape, it is hardly to be questioned that this process was hastened and the practical form in which the idea was now embodied was more or less modified by the stirring events to which this embodiment was a sequel. Succession in time did not prove a relation of cause and effect. It did indicate a kind of family tie. No work of human logic, no devotion to the dramatic unities, could have arranged with better art the procession of events that led to this concluding action of the

157

trilogy. The very principles by which the Great Northern had been constructed and operated made it certain, as has been shown repeatedly, that ultimately the law of survival would dictate some form of "benevolent neutrality" between it and the Northern Pacific. The scheme for trans-Pacific development, as part of a commercial expansion greater than had been seen since Venice was in her prime, required the addition of the Burlington. The jealousy of rivals and their plan to meet this new condition broke into a flame that swept through Wall Street and threatened commercial and financial solvency in many capitals of the world. It was desirable to change the truce that followed into a lasting peace. Was it not possible to build a strong fortress where, in peace or war, those who had seen the work of their hands grow great might establish it against all assaults and for all time to come? The question was as natural as the proposal to substitute a steel bridge for a ferry that any freshet might sweep away.

These events were not needed to suggest the thought to the mind of Mr. Hill. He may have had his peer in some of the great financial strategists and some of the organizers of railroad consolidation of his day. But he had no equal as a prophet of the future. From the watchtower where his mind sat always gazing into space that to other eyes was only thick darkness, it had seen the possibility of new battlefields and other risks to come, since men die and the world changes; had fash-

158

ioned tentatively a defence against time for the interests that were bone of his bone and flesh of his flesh in life's achievement. Five or six years before, his thought began to prepare for this moment. His task was verging toward completion. His life was passing to a stage where he did not wish always to carry the spear and wear the buckler. Like every man who has wrought a great work with diverse elements, and inspired scattered units with a single mind and purpose, he wished to make its future secure. He meant to consolidate his forces and his fortifications. After the impulse to create, comes surely the impulse to maintain and to protect. It had been working powerfully upon Mr. Hill. But now he might not act alone. His genius for organization must be applied not merely to the problems of a single system, under his complete command, but to groups of systems, and to men whose aims might be other than his own.

Turning back to the "argument" of the play, Mr. Hill's statement at the close of Chapter Twenty-five, the reasons which first suggested to him a holding company for the main interests with which he was identified will be found plainly and emphatically set out. Those that he gave to the public were those that he had given to his friends in private for years. Some time between 1893 and 1895 it became manifest to him that such a concern would be the logical complement of changes in the corporate world in which he had been active or influential. Exactly when the plan first took the shape of a future certainty it is not now possible to say. Time was aging the small group of men who were the core of that splendid following that answered to his splendid leadership. To bind together their holdings in some form of corporate unity that should defy decay and death within, and danger without, was his final thought. Over it he still pondered when the events of 1901 forced his hand and safety called for action. The seed had dropped into his mind early and was germinating there. The forcing heat of this eventful year gave to the plant a growth and fruitage quite different from his first intent.

Confidence in the security of any railroad had received a rude shock. The men whose property had so narrowly escaped what they regarded as destruction were not minded ever again to run a similar risk. They did not wish themselves or their successors to have to make another fight like that of the struggle for control of Northern Pacific. Both sides had had a warning. Each would always have to stand on guard. But who could answer for the future, when large holdings should be broken up by the changes incident to human life? Some of these men were more than eighty years old. All of them wanted "peace in their time." Mr. Hill had talked of his idea of a holding company to Mr. Morgan and Mr. Kennedy. Mr. Morgan said later that it was a thing of Mr. Hill's planning. Mr. Hill said so himself.

His original thought had been to erect such a concern for his own system and its subsidiaries. The consolidation of these which took place in 1907 was almost in sight. Long before the Northern Securities was formed, this less inclusive proposition had occupied a good deal of his thought. Now circumstances hastened the maturity of the project and compelled an enlargement of its scope. It appeared to all those interested in recent controversies that the only permanent safeguard of the independent existence of these great properties and of a successful, because harmonious, conduct of their business was a sort of tribunal of ownership, where all would have representation and power; where their differences might be arbitrated and their common welfare assured.

The kind of thing contemplated had been done often, to all intents and purposes, indirectly. Many railroad corporations held the stocks of other railroads as part of their assets. But in these cases the purpose was not avowed, and the holding corporation called itself something else. Industrial combinations had grown great as aggregations of smaller units, or had divided themselves, amoeba-like, in order that their subsidiaries might be free to accomplish what they themselves could not or dared not undertake. The devil had been whipped around the stump so merrily both before and after the Sherman Anti-Trust Act of 1890, that it was almost refreshing to see somebody propose to act in the open and move in a straight line. Nevertheless, so to depart from precedent would draw down upon the bold operation all the anathemas that had been stored up against these others who were believed to be skillful evaders of the law. The Northern Securities attracted to itself all the thunderbolts with which the sky of a time stormy for large corporations, and especially for the railroads of the country, was surcharged.

Mr. Morgan said that this form of holding company presented itself to him as practical and desirable only after the ninth of May, 1901. "My idea was, I can't live forever, and J. P. Morgan & Company may be dissolved." This fell into step with the anxiety that had been pressing upon Mr. Hill for some years about the future of the Great Northern. So all these more or less nebulous ideas drew together and coalesced in one solid purpose. A future possibility became a present necessity. With these men, to perceive that something ought to be done was to go ahead and do it. The definite plan, as announced to the stockholders, was matured about the first of November, 1901. Before that, of course, the exact form that it should take had been the subject of exhaustive investigation and minute legal scrutiny of advantages and dangers. It was intended as a purely defensive measure. Was it the carrying out of some compromise agreed upon in May? In answer to the direct question what connection there was between the formation of the Northern Securities and the agreement to have Mr. Morgan name the new Northern Pacific board, Mr. Hill said: "There was absolutely no connection whatever. The time at which it was agreed by the banks to allow Mr. Morgan to nominate the directors was in May. The Northern Securities Company was actually formed in November. It had been discussed without any reference to Mr. Harriman's holding, or anybody else's holding for several years, and they had no more to do with each other than you have to do with either of them."

These are the authentic outlines of Northern Securities' genealogical history. Its life story has been open, from beginning to end, to the most pitiless light that an uninterrupted series of legal prosecutions could throw upon it. The student of this unique effort in corporation-building has the advantage, not only of the court testimony of all those who played important parts, but also of a careful and authoritative digest of the whole. In a bulletin of its Economical and Political Science Series, the University of Wisconsin published, in 1906, "A History of the Northern Securities Case." It is the work of Dr. B. H. Meyer, then a professor of political economy in the institution and a member of the State Railroad Commission, later one of the Federal Interstate Commerce Commissioners. Dr. Meyer's monograph is clear in its analysis and complete and reliable in its inquiry into facts. It has been consulted freely in compiling the statements of law and of fact that follow. The inferences and conclusions reached in this chapter rest upon the voluminous evidence in the case, and the corroborative testimony of confidential letters whose sincerity is not open to question.

When it was determined, soon after the agreement of May 31, 1901, that settled the controversy over Northern Pacific, to form such a company, some of the ablest lawyers in the country were employed on the preliminaries. From the beginning, the main features of it were agreed upon without serious difference of opinion. The plan, Mr. Hill said, was practically determined by Mr. Kennedy, Mr. George Baker, Mr. James, Mr. Thorne, Mr. Clough, Mr. Perkins, and himself. Mr. Hill gave in his own words the explanation of the general lines followed: "We were particularly anxious to put a majority of that stock where it could not be raided again as it had been. We wanted to put it in a corporation that was not a railroad company—a company that would hold it as an investment, and the larger the company the more difficult it would be to secure a majority of it. Then, again, a reason why we preferred an investment company: railroad charters, I think I may say almost entirely, are drawn or granted on terms that do not permit railroad companies to buy the shares or own the shares of investment companies. Railway companies, under certain conditions, can buy the shares of other railways, as a means of consolidation, or they might buy the shares of a road that they would otherwise build. We were advised that we would be safer with the shares held by an investment company, the stock of which could only be held by individuals or by corporations that were not railway companies, and to that extent we would be more free from such raids by interests that were anxious to destroy or restrict the growth of this country—such raids as had been made by the Union Pacific interests, so-called."

For the sake of clearness, let it be repeated that the original idea of making a holding company had no reference to the Northern Pacific at all. It was entertained by Mr. Hill before the reorganization of that system. Now, the whole position and all the elements of the problem were changed. In view of the relations established with the Northern Pacific and their joint interest in the Burlington, such a holding concern for the Great Northern alone would have been absurd. All the closely allied interests must join. They desired to. In the consultations held, Mr. Perkins represented the Morgan interests. Mr. Morgan not only cleared the air of gossip about internal machinations, but paid to Mr. Hill the highest tribute he could give. "I would have given him all my Great Northern stock. He could have done what he liked with that, because I had confidence in him and he has confidence in me. It is not a coterie or anything of that kind." Compare Mr. Hill's public statement with his private correspondence, a test convincing for

165

historic accuracy. Here is an extract from a letter written in May, 1901. It is a document preparatory not to aggression, but to defence: "The cost of administering the affairs of the holding company would be practically nil, as it would only draw dividends on the shares held by it and divide the money so received by check to its own shareholders. You will see how strong the holding company would be. It would control the Great Northern and Northern Pacific, and those two roads would control by ownership the Chicago, Burlington & Quincy. The holding company could also, if at any time it seemed best, hold the shares of coal or other companies which, while of value in themselves and of value to the railway company for the traffic they would afford, the charters of the railway companies are not broad enough to enable them to hold with safety. I think the completion of the plan of which the above is a fair outline would greatly enhance and insure the value of every share we hold in the railway companies. For myself I feel that the future would be secure, and we would have a certainty in the situation and the control of these properties safe. Unless we do something of this kind, we will always be subject to attacks like the recent one to secure control of one or other of our properties."

The charter was taken out in New Jersey, whose laws were supposed to be especially friendly to this kind of undertaking. It differed from that of most other large corporations formed in this epoch particularly in the fact that its powers were severely limited. The custom was to provide against every contingency by authorizing each of the new corporations now being spawned so rapidly to conduct practically any business in which it might conceivably wish to engage. The charter of the Northern Securities confined its activity "to the acquisition of valuable paper held by domestic and foreign corporations, exercising the rights of property over the same, aiding corporations whose paper is thus held, and acquiring and holding the necessary real and personal property." Its authorized capital stock was $400,000,000. At first a much smaller capitalization was contemplated. But neither Mr. Hill nor Mr. Morgan was willing that any one should ever be able to accuse him of sharing in a profitable venture from which others were excluded. Mr. Hill had a lifelong reputation for working for his stockholders all the time. If there were any conflict of interests, his rather than theirs must suffer. But if only those were admitted whose age and long connection with the company had inspired the project, and if it were a financial success, people would not be lacking to stigmatize it as the plan of a chosen few on the inside to make money for themselves. He said: "I had the feeling that we would give each shareholder the opportunity to come in at the price we put our own in, if he desired. If he preferred to stay out, that was his privilege." Mr. Morgan

167

took the same position. Adherence to that principle necessitated a capital stock at least as large as that of the Great Northern and the Northern Pacific combined. The authorized share capital of the two was at this time $280,000,000. Of course, an exchange at above par would raise this limit. Other interests also would want to be admitted from time to time. About 76 per cent. of Great Northern stock was exchanged for the new security at the rate of $180 for each $100 turned in. Mr. Hill had suggested this basis, which was approved by all. About 96 per cent. of Northern Pacific came in on the basis of $115 for $100. The Union Pacific people were admitted also, for a lasting harmony was desired, and surrendered to the Northern Securities the holdings of Northern Pacific which they had acquired in the fight for possession, receiving in exchange about $82,500,000 of its stock. The first Board of Directors consisted of fifteen men. Six represented Northern Pacific interests, four Great Northern, three Union Pacific, and two were what might be called "at large." The presidency was unanimously conferred upon Mr. Hill.

The original project to unite the Great Northern with the Northern Pacific by a more intimate tie had roused bitter public opposition and been defeated in the courts. It was determined to carry this new scheme, which was represented as a repetition of attempted railroad amalgamation in a larger and more daring way, before the same Cæsar. In part the heated protest was sincere. The public had in the past suffered grievances at the hands of some of the carriers of the country. It was angry and suspicious. Political parties had found in railroad regulation an issue as unfailing as the tariff, and in denunciation of railroads a charm that seldom failed to rouse the passions on which their own success might depend. A public educated for a generation by this kind of argument was not in a mood to examine facts impartially or to draw judicial conclusions. On the other hand, the form taken by the attack disclosed clear traces of a political motive. January 7, 1902, the State of Minnesota attacked the company in the Supreme Court of the United States. Denied permission to file a bill of complaint, it brought suit in the state court. In the meantime, the Federal Interstate Commerce Commission had, at a meeting on December 20, 1901, adopted a resolution calling for an investigation by it into "consolidations and combinations of carriers," including "the community of interest" plan; and, February 19, 1902, the Attorney-General of the United States announced that, complying with a previous request of President Roosevelt, he had given his opinion that the "merger," as the Northern Securities was called, violated the provisions of the Sherman Act of 1890. Thereupon, March 10, suit was brought in the United States Circuit Court at St. Paul against the Northern Securities, Great Northern, and Northern Pacific. Happily it does not come within the field of this work to tread all the dreary mazes of the legal labyrinth into which these proceedings led the way. A sketch will suffice.

First, however, let the whole transaction, with its legal aspect to those who had studied it and felt sure of their ground and their right, be set down in Mr. Hill's own words. The following is from a personal letter to Mr. James, written in March, 1902, less than three weeks after suit was begun: "We are fully prepared for anything we have to meet, and in this case the question is simply, was there a conspiracy between the shareholders of the Northern Pacific and the Great Northern shareholders to form the Securities Company for the purpose of restraining or restricting interstate commerce? You and our other Great Northern friends know that the Securities Company was not a conspiracy, and that it has been under consideration for years. When it was formed, or rather decided that it would be formed, there was no meeting or conspiracy. The question had been under consideration for a long time, and it only embraced the holdings of fifteen men out of eighteen hundred. It was first considered as a close corporation, with not more than fifteen shareholders, owning about one fourth of the shares of the Great Northern and about one fifth of the Northern Pacific. In order that it might not be said that a few of the larger shareholders who had practically managed the company had undertaken to form a corporation in the company's business in which every other shareholder might not participate, it was decided to allow all Great Northern shareholders the privilege of doing with their respective holdings what those who formed the company had done. The company was formed by the holders of one fourth of the shares, and the option was left to all others to decide for themselves individually whether they would join in the new company or not. When the company was formed it controlled but one fourth; and the individual action of each shareholder, deciding for himself, without any conference or advice, to sell his shares to the Security Company is very far from a conspiracy to restrain trade. All of our counsel feel that our case will be easily won, and that in the end we will have the advantage of having our charter rights confirmed by the Supreme Court. In fact, our action will show that we prevented the Union Pacific interests from holding the Northern Pacific, and through it and the joint control of the Burlington restraining and practically destroying the trade of the Northwest and of the whole country, as it concerns the Oriental trade. We have taken this year about three fourths of the entire Asiatic cotton exports via Puget Sound. Our business on all these railways is very large. It really seems hard, when we look back on what we have done, and know that we have led all Western companies in opening the country and carrying at the lowest rates, that we should be

171

compelled to fight for our lives against the political adventurers who have never done anything but pose and draw a salary."

These two cases resulted in two different decisions by circuit courts, before the Supreme Court of the United States was reached. The first, which was rendered by a tribunal made up of four circuit judges, found that "the Securities Company accomplishes the object which Congress has declared illegal perhaps more effectually than other forms of combination generally known in 1890 when the Anti-Trust Law was passed." It said that, although the motives which inspired the combination might have been "wholly laudable and unselfish," although it was "the initial and the necessary step in the accomplishment of great designs," the only question before the court was whether or not it constituted a combination having power to "suppress competition between two or more competing and parallel lines of railroad engaged in interstate commerce." This question the judges answered in the affirmative. The Northern Securities was enjoined from voting stock, acquiring additional stock, paying dividends or exercising corporate control. The return of stock held by it to persons holding Northern Securities shares in exchange for shares deposited was permitted. In the state case, the United States Circuit Court found that the formation of the Northern Securities did not involve any act or contract in restraint of trade. The real

172

distinction between the two was that, while the one court decided that the purchase of a majority of shares in the two companies by a single interest was illegal, the other held that the mere possession of power does not warrant an assumption that such power will be used criminally. This distinction represents the vital point in the case, and presents the issue on which its determination would finally rest.

Both these cases now went up to the Supreme Court, where the opposing parties were represented by some of the ablest lawyers in the United States. It would be tedious to follow in detail the conduct of the case whose importance here is in its relation to the life and work of Mr. Hill. The opinion of the trial court of four justices was sustained by a decision given March 14, 1904, by the casting vote of a single justice. Four members of the highest court were of the opinion that the formation of the Northern Securities Company had not transgressed the limits of the law. Four others declared that it had. The ninth judge tipped the scale against it. It was ordered to dissolve. Besides the decision of the majority, there were one concurring and two dissenting opinions put on file by individual judges, to express shades of difference between their views and those of their associates. Seldom has a great case been involved in more legal subtleties, or determined with more doubt by our great tribunal. The dissenting opinion of the four minority judges denied that the Anti-Trust Act applied to the

particular case in question. It showed that such consolidations had been made prior to the passage of the
Anti-Trust Law, and held that the power to deal with
them lay with the states. It concurred with the position taken by Judge Lochren in the state case, that the
power to commit a wrong does not imply that the wrong
will be committed; and that until some law has been
violated, such power may not be prohibited. In the
state case, the Supreme Court held that it had no
jurisdiction and remanded the case to the state court.

Two years and a third had passed between the organization of the company and the final decision. During
this time the former had, of course, kept on its way, in
the firm presumption of legality. This was a time of
continual anxiety for Mr. Hill. From the day when
he first conceived the plan of a holding company to that
on which he took steps for its dissolution, he never
wavered in his fixed belief that it was organized well
within the sanction of the law. That he had warrant
for this faith is seen both in the unpunished existence
of similar combinations in the East and in the fact that
four Supreme Court Justices out of nine agreed with
him. He studied the question from every angle, he
pored over every bit of evidence, he searched for more,
he brought every legal principle and every fact involved
under the scrutiny of his powerful and analytic mind.
Lacking special professional training, he was nevertheless one of the busiest and most helpful members of

the Northern Securities' legal staff. Had he believed at the bottom of his heart that this project was actually illegal, even technically, he would never have approved it. He was not one of those who seek their ends by deliberately overriding the law. For that he had supreme respect wherever it was definitely stated and applied. "We must all bow to the law of the land" was his unvarying comment on any dictum that ran counter to his plans. Through all this time he was as sure that the Northern Securities was within the law's protection as he was that he had a right to build a station or put in a water tank somewhere on the railroad right of way.

Until the court's decision was made public, he entertained no doubt that it would be favourable. It was a bitter surprise and disillusionment. That it was adverse struck him no more severely as a checkmate to one of his plans than as a denial of what were to his mind unchangeable principles. He never believed, at this time or later, that the Sherman Anti-Trust Act was intended to apply to railroad corporations. He never accepted the rule that the power to act unjustly is equivalent to the commission of an unjust act. A great many people agreed with him. Bar and bench were divided. Years have passed since then, and public opinion has experienced some enlightenment and some change. It is at least a doubtful question whether, if the same issue were presented to-day in the same way, a majority of the Supreme Court would reach the same conclusion. It is an open question whether, on a popular vote, a majority of the people of the Northwest would declare against the Northern Securities now. The practical accomplishment by other means of what it set out to do, without injustice to the people or escape from the strict control of law, has proved that much of what was then hated and feared was only a nightmare terror.

This decision, of course, created an immense stir and much excitement in the stock market. It required a readjustment from which came more litigation. Eight days after it was rendered, Mr. Hill sent out a circular announcing the approaching dissolution of the Northern Securities Company and the distribution of its assets. This circular noted that, since the formation of the company, the railways included had extended and improved their facilities, while the rates paid by the public had been materially reduced. It once more declared that the buying of Northern Pacific and Great Northern shares was done "in the full belief that such purchases were in no wise obnoxious to any law of the United States." Since, however, the court thought otherwise, the company would proceed to comply fully and promptly with its decree. Therefore, 99 per cent. of its capital stock outstanding was called in and cancelled.

Immediately a question arose precipitating a legal struggle on lines similar to the fight for stock control of the Northern Pacific which followed the Burlington purchase. What should the holders of Northern

Securities shares receive in exchange for them? Would they get back exactly the same number of shares in the same corporations that they originally deposited, or only their portion of a ratable distribution of all the assets? Mr. Hill and his friends proposed the latter. For each share of Northern Securities surrendered, there was to be delivered to the holder $39.27 stock of the Northern Pacific and $30.17 of the Great Northern. To ratify this plan a special stockholders' meeting was held April 21, 1904. At this meeting about 75 per cent. of the stock was voted for the plan. The Harriman interests had already protested against the proposed scheme of distribution. They had from the beginning held more than $82,000,000 of the stock. This they had received in exchange for the Northern Pacific shares turned in by them in 1901. As they had attempted, in May of that year, to control the Northern Pacific by purchase, so they now attempted to reach the same end by overthrowing the plan of pro rata distribution, and compelling the return to them, share for share, of the stock of that company which they had originally put in. Let Mr. Hill disclose his absolute confidence in the strength of his position, even as affairs now stood, through an extract from his ample and intensely earnest correspondence of this time. Its insight into opposition strategy, its bold confidence, its phrasing, are all inimitable. Time has proved its concluding sentence to be not a wrathful defiance, but a prophecy

177

of the reasoned and the foreseen. "During the time when railway combinations were being made throughout the country, we got together the strongest and most promising in the country, and they found themselves in the same place as was the Chicago & Alton, Rock Island, Michigan Central, and other so-called conservative companies, who lost their chances to their more enterprising neighbours and were compelled to sell out. The St. Paul and Northwestern were both customers for the purchase of the Saint Paul & Pacific from the Dutchmen, but they lacked movement. These two lines with the Burlington were all right for a time, or until the transcontinental lines began to dominate the situation, and when we bought the Burlington they were like 'Ginx's Baby,' nobody's child. And they will remain so until they build a line to the coast, which I hope they will do, and also that they build it to Puget Sound. The addition of the business of two such lines to Puget Sound would greatly help that seaport and would enlarge the whole business, and in the end would do us much more good than harm."

April 2, 1904, the Harriman interests had taken legal measures to enjoin the carrying out of the plan announced. Again let Mr. Hill tell some of the preliminaries, in a letter to a trusted friend, where he can give full vent to his honest indignation: "Before closing let me again refer to their statement that they only wanted protection for the Union Pacific. Mr. Harriman was the first director of the Northern Securities Company to whom I went after the decision of the Supreme Court to consult as to how we should dissolve the company, and he immediately said the only thing we could do was a pro rata distribution. This he repeated on several occasions for four or five days, and at the end of that time came to my rooms to tell me that he was afraid he could not carry it out, and the next day he wrote me a personal letter to the same effect, after he had assured me that we would have their full co-operation; and, in the meantime, having had his own counsel present with the Northern Securities counsel in consultation as to the legal steps to be taken, and his counsel agreed fully and said that it was the only legal and moral course that could be pursued under the circumstances. Within ten days from that time they brought the present suit, giving as the reason: 'We knew, of course, that Mr. Hill wanted the control of the Northern Pacific, and it would be a great property in his hands, but we wanted to get control of it if we could and we are going to make the effort, because to make the effort would only cost us the lawsuit.' In which case the Great Northern would be hemmed in along the northern boundary without any outlet anywhere except on terms to be made for it, and our property would follow the course of the Alton and other roads like it which were lacking in foresight to protect themselves against what might occur in future."

179

The Circuit Court unanimously denied the application to intervene. Then came more litigation, whose purpose was the same and whose devious course and voluminous record need not be considered here. An injunction against the distribution plan adopted was granted, and through the usual tortuous legal channels this secondary and final question about the partition of the estate of the Northern Securities reached the Supreme Court. This interminable carnival of lawsuits was an almost intolerable burden to a man who had tried to do what he believed right and for the best interests of all. Sincerity rings out in this extract from a letter written to a friend in the summer of 1904: "The present lawsuit is brought, as the parties admit here, not because of any wrong done them, but because they think they have everything to gain and nothing to lose, 'as Mr. Hill will protect their stock as well as that of everybody else, as long as he is in charge.' This, however, is cold comfort. If they desire to continue holding their stock we can have no objection and will treat theirs as well as we do our own, but we cannot allow them to impair or destroy our property. You have but little idea of the difficulties I have had to deal with and get along with during the last two years. You know that I never would be connected with a property that was run for the benefit of those in the saddle and not for that of the shareholders."

The whole controversy was summed up by Mr. Hill

in a letter to a high public official, late in 1904. It has that quality of condensed and luminous statement which the reader will have learned by this time to expect: "The affirmance by the Supreme Court of the decree of the lower court restraining the Northern Securities Company from voting and receiving dividends on the railway stocks of the Great Northern and Northern Pacific Railway companies rendered the stocks unproductive and made it necessary that the Securities Company in the interest of its stockholders should reduce its capital stock and distribute the surplus as corporate assets. Proceedings were taken in conformity with the laws of New Jersey which resulted in the adoption of a resolution for the reduction of the capital stock and distribution of surplus corporate assets with the approval of the stockholders of the Securities Company. The Securities Company proceeded upon the ground that each share of its stock had an equal value and that it had acquired title to the railway stocks and had a right to distribute them as corporate assets.

"The Oregon Short Line Company, a part of the Union Pacific system, was the beneficial owner of the Northern Securities stock which stood in the name of Harriman and Pierce. Harriman and Pierce contend that the decree in the government suit adjudged that the Northern Securities Company has repudiated the contract and abandoned the trust, that the law, therefore, implies a promise on the part of the Securities

181

Company to return the railway company stocks it holds to those from whom it received them or their assigns.

"You will note that Harriman and Pierce contend that the Northern Securities Company has no stockholders as such, that its certificates of stock are mere evidence of a right which the present holders have in the identical property on account of which its stock was issued, and that the present holders can trace their interest to identical stocks now held by the Securities Company."

All the courts, Circuit, Circuit Court of Appeals, and Supreme Court, held for Mr. Hill. The decision of the last mentioned, unanimously rendered March 6, 1905, in which the plan of the Northern Securities Company for distributing the stock held by it was sustained in every important particular, put a quietus on the trouble makers. It was now free to execute its plan for dissolution, and did so. That Mr. Hill, after the pressure of these years of contest in the courts, neither felt an enduring animosity nor permitted rancour to distort his views or change his attitude toward others is shown in a striking way by a personal letter written two months after the court had spoken its last word. Coming from a man of stern temper and thwarted purpose, who had all along believed and still believed himself right in principle, and who had been opposed at every turn, it is a really notable utterance: "I have told all the Union Pacific people that we should let the past be cast aside, and take every proposition between the two or three systems without any prejudice and consider all interests fairly and honestly, and have peace by each company, regarding at all times the rights of all the others. Where there is a disposition to agree on fair terms there should be no difficulty in securing harmony; and this can only be done where there is no right or disposition to encroach upon or invade each other."

The dissolution of the Northern Securities marked one of Mr. Hill's few great disappointments. It cannot properly be said to mark a failure. The plan as it was outlined in his mind, away back in 1893 to 1895, was a limited holding company for Great Northern stockholders only. Time and circumstance, rather than individual judgment or desire, had compelled its expansion to the form taken by the Northern Securities. The forces which struck at this, both state and federal, were inspired, in part at least, by a political motive. The decision pictures the court in doubt. The vote of five to four was almost equivalent to "not proven." The after event amounted to a vindication. For, just as the reorganization of the Northern Pacific, planned in 1895 and prohibited by the court, was accomplished in another fashion, to the same end but in conformity with the law, so the main business and economic purposes of the Northern Securities have since been realized. About the only thing actually accomplished by the court's decision was to prevent eight or ten old men from

183

placing their investments where these would be secure after their death. "If this is failure," Mr. Hill might have said, "make the most of it."

The finale upon which the curtain falls in the last act of the trilogy is, like most of life, neither pure comedy nor pure tragedy. Legally, perhaps, the course of events had been a good deal like John Gilpin's ride. But of both events and actors it is far from true that "where they had got up, they did again get down." Contrast January, 1901, with April, 1905. Complete confidence, assuring intelligent co-operation between the Great Northern and the Northern Pacific, had been assured for the future by the same sort of bond that unites the veterans of a war in which they fought side by side. The control of the Burlington was vested in them jointly beyond the power of any foe to disturb. Exactly as the rule of law which forbade, ten years before, the ownership and guarantee of Northern Pacific securities by the Great Northern corporation, had drawn into a more sympathetic understanding the parties interested, and assured their harmonious action, so the disappearance of the Northern Securities as a holding company delimited interests on the one side and cemented them on the other. Little use hereafter of an attack upon these last, or of seductive offers and suggestions. They had passed through an ordeal where they had learned the need of confidence and had seen it supremely justified. Their new knowledge of the

184

ground and the issues was as superior to the old as is the soldier's acquaintance with the battles and sieges he has passed to an account of them in a newspaper. Mr. Hill said that during this time he rejected a proposition to become the head of a holding company including substantially all the railroad interests west of the Mississippi. The unity of purpose and the indissolubility of allied individual interests which the Northern Securities was framed to effect and represent were forged into one bar by the blows, welded into one homogeneous mass by the fierce currents of these electric years. The man who says or thinks that the Northern Securities Company was a fiasco, that its brief life accomplished nothing, reads facts only with the raised letters of the blind. A stray meteor in the stormy skies of its time, it had part in the moulding and rearranged the orbit of constantly changing worlds.

By the time the audience that witnessed the trilogy had dispersed, one of the motives that had inspired and directed its performance had grown weak and pale. The flaming vision of an Oriental trade, and of a revolution in world commerce hitherto undreamed of, at its brightest in 1901 and 1902, had faded by 1905 to a gentle glow. The light of Asia died down, under new regulations and orders of the federal power, into the pale promise of a day whose dawning was not yet to be. But the agencies prepared to serve a mighty concept were not left, like the ma·

185

chinery abandoned along the old Panama Canal, sad monuments of an enterprise born out of due season. They served their purpose and their time. They were the tools by which Mr. Hill continued to build, and to fashion the work of his life into the completed whole that he left behind him. The Northwest of to-day, the railroad system of this country, would be something other than they are, less complete and less fitted for new times and new men, but for the events narrated here and the new understanding and outlook through which they entered into their inheritance.

On Mr. Hill the influence of these years was profound. They did not embitter him. From them sprouted no bud of vengeance to come. His philosophy, indeed, was one that looked before and after. But, emphatically, it did not sigh for what is not. He continually created and reconstructed. The letters contained in this chapter paint the intellectual man and the moral man in him. They have little need of commentary. At the beginning, in the thick of the *mêlée*, after the smoke had cleared away, he maintained his mental attitude; he kept the poise of his thought. The element of personal fidelity, his to others, others' to him, was the most precious jewel that shone among the ashes of this crucible. Always it had been to him a token of the best. Now it was the crown of life. Fair dealing, loyalty to any pledged word, had been articles of his faith. He found them worthy to become the cult of

186

the business world. His purposes were carried out by agencies different only in form from those he had imagined. From this moment the country, the world, knew him better. That comprehension was, perhaps, the best gift of these disturbed times. After the whirlwind of accusation and the cleansing thunderbolts launched in quick succession, his form stood outlined against the sky with more distinctness and more nobility than ever before. In the years that followed from this time to his death, the projects of Mr. Hill were considered by the people, his words were listened to, his cautions and his recommendations were heard everywhere with constantly growing respect, esteem, confidence, and something that it is not too partial to name affection.

CHAPTER   THIRTY
SOME INTERLUDES

IN HIS talks to farmers and his numerous articles on the improvement of agriculture, Mr. Hill repeatedly emphasized the diversification of crops. He applied the principle rigorously to his own life. No single-crop idea for him. Such a contest as that over the Northern Securities, which lasted from the first days of 1902 until the adoption of the plan of stock distribution April 21, 1905, following the final decision by the Supreme Court, was surely enough to occupy to the fullest extent the energies of the man in command. He gave to it, as has been seen, tireless study and a dauntless enthusiasm which could not have been exceeded, which could not have been equalled, had the matters in jeopardy been wholly personal. What room was there in these years, so crowded with the strategy of desperate campaigns of life or death, for any lesser interest or any other concentration of thought or deed? Mr. Hill found so much that the remainder of the story of this time will be almost as full of action, and in some respect as replete with vivid and startling interest, as during the development of the trilogy whose audience had now departed and whose lights were fled.
188

The largest and most unprecedented act whose fulfilment runs through these years, beginning indeed as far back as 1899, must be reserved for separate treatment. This was the disposition of his interest in rich ore lands acquired in northern Minnesota. In the light that it throws upon the character of Mr. Hill, upon his conception of his duty to the stockholders of his system, and upon his proud refusal ever to permit personal interest to prevail over his idea of perfect integrity, it is as striking and as characteristic as any event related or yet to be set down in these pages. But it did not stand alone. While the future relations of the Great Northern to its associate systems, to the Northwest and to the commerce of this country at home and abroad, were being determined in the courts, defended by its president, who was also the president of the Northern Securities, the company itself was not permitted to stand still. The same work of expansion that had been going on for more than twenty years must proceed without interruption or slackening of pace. New country to be opened and settled, new lines to be built and old ones extended for that purpose, new instruments to be provided for new ends, and the financing of the whole with that conservative forethought which Mr. Hill always brought to the performance of this part of his task—all laid urgent hands upon him. Trains could not cease to run, not a wheel of the complicated mechanism of

189

which he was builder, master mechanic, and engineer could skip one revolution while the big creation called the Northern Securities, in which interest seemed relatively so distant and so vague, was on trial for its life.

It will be remembered that preparations for invasion of the Orient went briskly forward. The two huge ships for Pacific trade, the *Minnesota* and the *Dakota*, were built. The intricate network of traffic arrangements designed to fill their mighty holds was perfected. The danger of being held up between Chicago and New York by the eastern trunk lines for a disproportionate part of the through rate had disappeared. Mr. Hill had shown, when he put his ships upon the Great Lakes and when he built, in 1897, the circular steel tank elevator of his own design at Buffalo, with a capacity of 3,000,000 bushels, and broke the elevator pool there, that he was not to be trifled with. Nobody was going hereafter to invite recklessly a blow from that puissant hand. Armed as he now was with power over so great a traffic west of the Mississippi and to the Pacific coast, he had more to concede than to demand. He could act henceforth as the dispenser of benefits, toward whom none of the lines that ran to the Atlantic seaboard would dare to take an attitude either arbitrary or unjust. So the six ships of the Northern Steamship Company and the elevator property at Buffalo were sold to and taken over by the eastern trunk lines. His friendly interest in the affairs of the Erie and the Baltimore & Ohio completed the strengthening of his defences.

The stir of ordinary human life, intent upon its sustenance and its increase, was continually changing the fields of the Northwest from vacant land to fertile farm and happy home. An encouraging breath fed and brightened its steady flame. Immigration was sought everywhere; especially among progressive farmers, looking for a chance to better themselves in a new country. Cheap and rich land attracted population. The machinery to promote immigration was extended and improved. The report of the year 1902 said: "The large movement in the Northwest during the last few years, which still continues without abatement, has resulted in the settlement of a vast area of vacant lands adjacent to the Company's line. During this period more than 5,000,000 acres of Government land in the northern part of the country have been taken under the Homestead Act. It has also been satisfactory to note that many of the large farms in the state are being cut up into smaller ones." Up to this time what was called "bonanza farming" had caused curious and often gloomy inquiry among students of agricultural economics. Thousands of acres of farm land in single tracts were taken up or purchased by men with capital, who made use of the latest machinery, were able to buy, sell, and ship on the wholesale system, and realized large profits. It was feared in many quarters that this

191

competition might crowd the small farmer to the wall. Economic alarmists predicted the speedy concentration of all small farms in the country into a relatively small number of large holdings whose owners, veritable "patroons of the manor," would lord it over the multitude of hard-pressed farmers, reduced by the system to the status of tenants, and sinking gradually almost to the level of serfs. There were some of these "bonanza farms" in the Northwest. The report of the railway company just quoted declared that their subdivision into small farms, then actually taking place, was "satisfactory."

The head of a railway might have been expected to believe it most profitable to deal in agriculture as elsewhere, with a few large concerns rather than with many smaller ones. Mr. Hill did not think so. He saw always the prosperity of the transportation interest and the prosperity and safety of the country itself resting upon the independent successful industry of the individual farmer as its cornerstone. This conviction shaped his policies. Nowhere in the country, during these years, was the settlement of new land carried forward with more vigour and intelligence than in the territory subject to his care. The general public looked upon it now with better knowledge and a new interest. In 1889 and 1890 a tier of new states in which the Great Northern operated, from North Dakota to Washington, had come into the

192

Union. The mental attitude of people toward a territory was curiously different from that toward a state.
Industrially speaking, the two had, of course, if identical in other respects, equal advantages to offer. But
settlement and capital looked with less favour on the sections sometimes weakly, often unwisely, always selfishly
governed from Washington, than on those where local self-
government guarded the local interest with a watchful
eye. Again, these communities that had been widely
advertised by statehood recently conferred attracted and
held people by merits of their own. The immigration
into the Western and Pacific states during 1901 and 1902
was greater than that of any previous year. It was the
fruit of a policy consistently pursued from the first day
when Mr. Hill exercised real power over the old St.
Paul & Pacific. Naturally the business of the company
felt the new stimulus. The gross earnings of the Great
Northern for 1902 were $36,000,000, as compared
with a little more than $28,000,000 the year before.
The operating expenses increased less than $2,000,000.
This was a proof, at the same time, of growing volume
and density of traffic and of the continued application
of that rule of Mr. Hill's which required the increase
in expenses to be always a little less than the increase
in earnings, or the decrease in expenses to be a little
more. Nobody ever made a more thorough-going application to the financial side of railroading of the motto,
"Safety first."

Financing, also, as related to capitalization must now proceed on a larger scale. It is amazing to what a narrow basis it had been held down. Cities explain the gross inflation of their bonded debts by pointing to increase in population. Such a rule would have swollen the capitalization of the Great Northern beyond recognition. In the report of 1904 it is stated that "no additional permanent capital has been obtainéd by the Company since the issuance of $25,000,000 capital stock under authority of resolutions adopted by the Board of Directors February 27, 1901." In the meantime, all sorts of expenses had to be met out of current revenue. "The total amount paid out substantially within three years for securities, additional mileage and equipment, and additions to the property of proprietary companies was $48,499,894, or $23,499,894 in excess of the proceeds of the last stock issue. In addition to that, in the same three years the improvements made to leased Manitoba property have cost $5,114,130." So, in October, 1905, the capital stock was increased to $150,000,000. The money thus obtained was used to liquidate indebtedness already incurred, and to pay for or acquire stocks and bonds of subsidiary companies. The Great Northern was now financially among the big concerns of the country. Its capitalization per mile, and its ratio to the total value of the property, remained, as it always did, surprisingly low. Here was a margin of value which might have been, and in so many instances elsewhere

194

was, converted into stock by those in control, and assigned to themselves and their associates in one way or
another. Mr. Hill was proud of the low capitalization
as measured by either actual cost or present value.
To his mind it was, like low cost of operation, a title to
distinction. Very rarely, in the history of a new country, has financing on so large a scale as that which he
planned and conducted for more than thirty years been
directed by a rule so stern. Another issue of 600,000
shares for similar purposes in 1906 increased the total
capital stock to $210,000,000. In this way funds were
provided for the consolidation of the system already
determined upon by the purchase of all its subsidiary
companies.

This carries the history of the capitalization of the
road down to Mr. Hill's formal retirement from the
presidency. Only the bare skeleton of it could find
place in chapters so crowded by vital and fecund events
as these must be. It deserves to become the subject of a
connected story, apart from the other activities of his life.
The exigencies of a work like the present break it into
parts which, though not unrelated, have been distributed
necessarily through many chapters. A life so rich, so full,
so varied as that of Mr. Hill defies continuity along any
one line. It expands not so much on straight lines, or
even on lines branching and divergent, as by the giving off
of parts which, like the fragments of a stellar system,
assume, though always in harmony with the whole, a

195

form, a motion, and an inner energy which are all their own. The financial story of the Great Northern, separated from all the other interests interwoven with it, pays tribute in its entirety to his character. For, after the principle had been adopted, and the method adjusted to the principle, the money must be forthcoming. It was never lacking. It was never even difficult to obtain. It yielded gladly to the counsels of that supreme confidence in his integrity, as well as his ability, of which the natural and true course of this story has given so many and so convincing proofs. There remained still one concluding and triumphal act by which Mr. Hill provided, so far as human ingenuity and forethought could, for the financing of his company for many years to come. In the proper time and place the blanket bond authorization, making the Great Northern like a town that has been fortified and provisioned against all possible need within or attack from without, for half a century, will be touched upon. This was one of his great primal thoughts, and became a model to be followed by nearly all the leading railroad corporations of the time.

Not only the bitter struggle for supremacy between railroad corporations recounted in preceding chapters, but the leading tendencies and much of the discussion of the time found their nervous centre in a conflict of opinion over the legality and the desirability of industrial combination and consolidation. Mr. Hill, whose mind had always an economic trend, naturally debated this question with himself. The general course of development in the country pointed common inquiry in the same direction. The issues raised by the lawsuits in which his own interests were involved were suggestive of the same problem in theory if not in fact. For at least ten years before 1890, industry of every form in the United States openly obeyed more and more some unseen centripetal force. That force even appeared to be world wide. Everywhere small business concerns were uniting into large ones, or throwing up their hands in surrender to combinations already formed. It was the era of what were popularly but erroneously called "trusts." Apprehension was general, vivid, and not altogether without warrant. The public saw control of many of the necessaries of life passing into the hands of large corporations. It believed that the main purpose of these was to secure excessive returns on capital through the extortionate prices that these monopolies could and would impose. Almost every day grew up before its eyes some company which issued stock enough to buy all the principal establishments scattered over different parts of the country and engaged in the same line of manufacture or trade. Upon these skilful promoters had already obtained options. Often there was little relation between the actual value of plant and product and the par value of the stock given in exchange. The first object was to secure control. After that, the union of these separate concerns under one management enabled those at the head of it to buy cheap and sell dear. They could make their inflated capitalization pay a good return, at the cost of the consumer.

The public not only had a grievance, but it was honestly alarmed. A future half opened before it in which the many could exist only by the payment of whatever tribute the few should see fit to exact. In response to this condition and this fear, Congress passed the so-called Sherman Anti-Trust Act in 1890. A dozen years later it was to play an unexpected part in the life story of the Northern Securities. Its actual purpose was to check the process just described, by declaring such combinations illegal because "in restraint of trade." Thoughtful people had little faith in the efficacy of this law. Restraint of trade, according to common law, had always been illegal. The new statute lacked definiteness. Many years more were to pass before, in the effort to break up under it some of the consolidated interests, notably the Standard Oil Company, its feebleness was to be demonstrated and its few real teeth were to be drawn. There was, from the first, both doubt of its value and suspicion that it would not be rigorously enforced. Practically it made no change in the situation. Companies continued to combine and to swallow others. Many small concerns were bribed or forced out of existence. Ten times as many, which were unintelligently or inefficiently han-

198

dled, found here a welcome excuse for their misfortunes. As in nearly all times of change and of crisis, the country felt blindly that something was radically wrong, without having any clear conception of the nature of either the disease or its cure.

The phenomena were too interesting not to attract the thought of Mr. Hill. Although no present or contemplated plan of his own came, in his opinion or intention, within the purview of the statute, it touched nevertheless so closely all large undertakings and all national growth as to call for study by those feeling any responsibility for the future of their fellow men. As a railroad manager, as a practical student of economics and as a citizen, Mr. Hill thought deeply about this apparent conflict between a universal tendency of the time and the public interest. He was full of righteous wrath, both because the poor and thrifty would feel the pressure of a higher cost of living and because their savings were being coaxed into a thousand pretentious and promising corporate adventures from which they would never return. Here, as everywhere, he went straight to the heart of the matter. He set out on one side, to be accepted without question, the underlying laws of human association. It was of no more use to attempt to defeat or deflect these than the law of gravitation. On the other side, with that clarity and incisive grasp which distinguished all his thinking, he set out what could and ought to be done. In an address delivered before the Illinois

199

Manufacturers' Association at Chicago, in June, 1902, he condensed into a few paragraphs the essential fact of all that the country had been mulling over for many years:

"There is one plain evil connected with the creation of certain great corporations that has not been corrected, although it is easily reached. The valid objection to many concerns, especially some of those known as 'industrials,' is that they appear to have been created in the first place not so much for the purpose of manufacturing any particular commodity as for selling sheaves of printed securities which represent nothing more than the good will and prospective profits of the promoters. Nearly all the large concerns engaged in manufacture or trade that have come to grief owe their downfall to excessive capitalization. This is a real menace not only to their successful existence but to the public, which pays prices based to some extent on the desire to make profits on more than the money invested.

"If it is the will of the general Government to prevent the growth of such corporations, it has always seemed to me that a simple remedy was within its reach. Under the constitutional provision allowing Congress to regulate commerce between the states, any company desiring to transact business outside of the state in which it is incorporated should be held to a uniform provision of Federal law; namely, that all should satisfy a commission that their capital stock was actually paid up in cash or in property taken at a fair valuation, just as the capital of a national bank must be certified to be paid up by the controller of the currency.

"It is only fair to a dealer in Minnesota or California or Oregon that, if a company claims to have ten, twenty, or fifty millions of capital, and wishes to do business in that state, he should know that its solvency and the honesty of its alleged capitalization have been passed upon by a Federal commission. With such a simple provision of law, the temptation to make companies for the purpose of selling prospective profits would be at an end; and, at the same time, no legitimate business would suffer. Nor could any number of individuals desirous of engaging in business as a corporation suffer any hardship by being obliged to prove that their capital was as advertised; that they were not beginning to deal with the public under false pretenses.

"I am convinced that this is the simplest, most effective and necessary regulation to be applied to modern business methods. It begins at the beginning. It not only attacks the practice by which millions of the people's money have been coaxed into bad investments, but it also bears directly upon the main evil attributed to the existence of big corporations. With it they would lose most of their incentive to any such wrongdoing as may be within their power. With it there would be little inducement to claim exorbitant profits

201

by raising prices, because the fact could no longer be concealed by spreading the net return over a fictitious capitalization.

"And of course it follows equally that where capital has been fully paid in, no interference should be allowed, because no injustice would be likely to be done."

This has the simplicity of a scientific statement and a mathematical demonstration. The size of a corporation is not a danger. It cuts no figure whatever. He added: "Consolidation of wealth does not mean the hoarding of money in a bag that its single possessor may delve up to his armpits in it. It means rather the effective organization of effort, the intelligent use of money which represents exerted mental or physical energy. No man grows wealthy along broad and legitimate lines without turning the resources of nature into remunerative channels of usefulness for the talents of other men. We are, as yet, only on the threshold of the new era in the business world, and no one can say positively that the present order of things is and will be for the best. That is still to be proved, and it can be proved only by time. All that we can say is that, as far as we have gone, the results are certainly favourable. Against the alleged injury that is intangible can easily be put the benefit that can be shown by figures—benefit to the workingman, benefit to the consumer, benefit to the capitalist. Wages are higher, prices are lower, investments are safer, more productive, and more certain of return." The weak point is the unrestricted power of capitalization. The so-called "trusts" were all capitalizing the future. The securities they issued could only make good, and many of them did make good, by the growth of the country. Meantime, the whole of that growth, so far as it affected them, was absorbed by them in advance. Both before and after this growth occurred, the public must pay a tribute of interest or profits upon it, as represented by industrial stocks and bonds. Here, and in the infinite possibilities of fraud by conscienceless promoters, who had no sincere purpose beyond the collection and appropriation of stock subscriptions, lay the danger and the wrong. The people furnished the principal and then paid interest upon it indefinitely. Here, and not in any hypothetical "restraint of trade" or crushing out of competition, the lasting evil would be found. Mr. Hill pointed out an easy and proper remedy. Compel every corporation issuing a paper security to show that actual value in cash or in property had been put up before allowing the securities to be issued. Where capital had already been inflated and stocks watered, compel the holders either to make good the difference between the total capitalization and the money and property actually turned in, by paying assessments, or else cancel the excess of securities over that total. It represents only greed and ambition to power.

His analysis of the situation was never contradicted

or set aside; but authorities, state and national, lacked the wisdom to understand or the sincerity to adopt or the courage to enforce his idea. Several states have, indeed, exercised the power to control the issue of railroad securities. This is of little consequence; because the state has already exercised, in some cases savagely, the power both to increase the expenses of railroads by all kinds of impositions and to reduce their rates. Whatever corrective the public might need can thus be supplied on either end of the scale. Industrial combinations, whose exactions come so much more closely home because they control things of prime necessity, remained, as shown by prosecutions under the Act of 1890, relatively immune. The public desire to subdue them to the helpful service of mankind settled down into a kind of hopeless inaction. It remains true, as any one can see who studies the paragraphs quoted from Mr. Hill's address, containing a doctrine that he held without the change of a word or a letter to the end of his life, that his method of dealing with the dangers of industrial combination, his plan of utilizing its enormous force for good while shearing away the locks in which resides its evil force, is impregnable in theory and would be effective in practice. This is one of his earliest, as it is one of his most valuable, contributions to the economic study of the times in which he worked and thought. It awaits acceptance by some wiser and sadder generation.

This chapter may well conclude with a notable act of disinterested service rendered by Mr. Hill to the business interests and to the whole people of Montana. One of the events of 1903, it also belongs to the chronicle of these fateful years. The reason for selecting it from so many others of its kind is rather its great moment to a whole community than its merit as a type. Mr. Hill was always responding to some such call as this, though most of them were less imperative. No disturbance of the ordinary and orderly course of prosperous, busy life left him cold. Where that was interrupted or menaced, to help restore it was a work of humanity. He was the head of a Red Cross service among business organizations and communities. Thousands of instances where his intervention rebuilt an interest or prevented its destruction gave vent to the helpful impulse that always stirred him in answer to any call for actual reconstructive work. Most of them were known only to the parties concerned. He shunned publicity. But sometimes they were on so great a scale that the bushel was too small to hide the candle. Then it was possible to know something of his disinterested service. Some instances have been given. One more, and this among the greatest, prevented an apparently certain demoralization of all the business interests of Montana. For the circumstantial account the writer is indebted to Mr. John D. Ryan, who was personally cognizant of them and furnished the details of the following story.

Montana, great in area, agricultural possibilities, scenic values, resources of wonderful range and abundance, was at this time most noted for her mineral wealth. Her rich copper deposits had built up a mining industry of great proportions and added hundreds of millions of dollars to the wealth of the world. Among the corporations and the men who owned them the struggle for control became bitter. The Amalgamated Copper Company was one. The remarkable and remembered personality of Augustus Heinze stood for implacable opposition. Everybody familiar with the events of that time remembers him and the battle royal that took place. Five years of litigation and political strife ended in a sort of deadlock which, in November, 1903, threatened to prostrate the state. One John Mac-Ginnis, a lieutenant of Heinze, was a minority stockholder of the Boston & Montana Mining Company, about ninety-nine hundredths of which was owned by the Amalgamated Company. To cripple the company he brought suit for an injunction and receivership. District Judge Clancy granted an injunction prohibiting any direction of the Boston & Montana's affairs by its directors or officers, on the allegation that these were under the control of the Amalgamated Copper Company, which held the stock. Most of the producing properties of the great Butte camp were involved. A receivership would have followed the injunction speedily had not the Amalgamated Company suspended its operations. The properties which it controlled at that time employed about 10,000 men in the Butte camp and about 15,000 in the whole of Montana. Winter was approaching. The forced idleness of so many men and the consequent paralysis of industry in all the mining and industrial centres of the state created a dangerous situation. It promised to set back the progress of Montana for many years. So bitter was the feeling between the contending parties that no one could see any likelihood of an end to the feud.

Seeing that ruin was impending, the business interests of the different towns took the matter up, as they do in large cities confronted by a general strike. Acting on a suggestion made by the Great Falls Chamber of Commerce, indorsed by similar business organizations throughout the state, a board of arbitration was selected and asked to meet in Butte and endeavour to bring about either some modification of the court's decree or some action by the litigants which would reopen the mines and put the men at work again. The arbitrators chosen were Mr. Hill, United States Senator Paris Gibson, and Mr. W. A. Clark. Mr. Hill immediately left St. Paul in answer to this distant summons. Arrived at Butte, the arbitrators held a session that lasted forty-eight hours almost continuously. At the end of that time, being unable to reconcile the conflicting interests of the hostile parties, the conference dissolved with the statement that nothing had been accomplished. Mr. Hill was not accustomed to endure patiently the collapse of anything to which he had set his determined hand. He was bent on saving the people of Montana from the suffering and loss ahead of them. His fierce wrath would not brook the obstacle raised by private interest or political animosities. When the arbitrators adjourned he got into action. The remainder of the story can be told best in Mr. Ryan's own words:

"Mr. Hill individually, after learning that the Amalgamated officials were willing to resume operations on condition that the Governor of the state (Joseph K. Toole) should call a special session of the legislature to consider the enactment of what is known as a change of venue law, which would permit cases to be taken from a prejudiced court or a prejudiced judge or a prejudiced district, to one where fair play could be had, discussed the matter with the Governor on his special train between Butte and Helena, where the Governor, who had been present during the conference, was returning. His broad vision and sound judgment undoubtedly impressed the Governor. Although there had been much discussion and every other legitimate pressure brought to bear without result on the Governor by those who wanted to see the litigation between the big mining corporations of Butte tried before unbiased and unprejudiced judges, and under circumstances and conditions where both sides could have equal opportunity, within two or three days after the return of the Governor to Helena, and after Mr. Hill had returned to St. Paul, the Governor called a special session of the legislature to consider the enactment of such a law, and instructions were issued by the Amalgamated officials to re-open the mines and all of the works of the company, and operations were again under full headway immediately. It has always been remembered of Mr. Hill with gratitude by the people of Montana that in the time of their adversity he dropped everything and came to help them as best he could."

CHAPTER THIRTY-ONE

A ROYAL GIFT

ONCE more the hand upon the dial of the crowded and kaleidoscopic years that end the old century and begin the new must turn backward.   In 1899 the rounding out of his railroad system in northern Minnesota brought Mr. Hill into direct contact with the new mineral industry of the state.   From that connection, at first unsought but clearly necessary and helpful to his railroad interest, emerged, in 1906, a fine and unselfish conception, and a princely act.   No wonder that he always had the utter confidence and loyalty of those connected with him by the ties of business relationship and fidelity.   Right royally was it now remembered. Mr. Hill matched his chivalry against theirs.   The unconditioned gift of property worth actually, at one time, in the market, about $135,000,000, property which has, since that time, distributed a total of $11,250,000 to the holders of its certificates, without any other consideration than a personal unwillingness to profit by any transaction growing primarily out of the development of the railroad, and a desire that all who had put money into it should share, dollar for dollar, with himself in the benefits, was something unprecedented in

210

business experience. The original investment from which these mighty values grew was made by him as a private individual. By no obligation of law, of morals, of friendship, or of equity, except in the fine and high sense in which he understood these words, was he required to divert any portion of this wealth from his personal fortune. An act so impressive in itself and so significant in the motives that directed it well deserves a place of distinction in his biography. The seven years covered by it included, in addition to planning and supervision of the unceasing extension of the Great Northern's lines and traffic, the purchase of the Burlington, the struggle for control of the Northern Pacific, the formation and militant life of the Northern Securities, the preparations for building the Spokane, Portland & Seattle Railroad, and the study and labour devoted to the promotion of national conservation and the improvement of farm properties and farming methods throughout the Northwest—all of which have been or will be described in other chapters. Superhuman strength of body and of mind would seem called for to accomplish triumphantly tasks so many and so great. Yet to these one more, by no means the least interesting or impressive, was added. The history of Mr. Hill's acquisition of large ore properties in northern Minnesota, and his disposal of them, reads like a work of the romantic imagination. To friend and enemy alike it carried conviction of his inner quality.

The secret of iron ore deposits in northern Wisconsin and Minnesota, the latter soon to be known as the richest in the world, had been well kept by nature through the ages. It was exactly the middle of the nineteenth century, the year 1850, when the first trial shipment of Lake Superior iron ore was made from the Marquette Range, and the first discovery of iron ore in Minnesota was reported. Of the three productive iron ranges in Minnesota, the Vermilion, the Mesabi, and the Cuyuna, all of them of great richness and extent, this story is mainly concerned with the second. The first disclosure of importance in Minnesota had been made on the Vermilion Range in 1865. The tale of the development of this section is an interesting and almost thrilling record of personal struggle, failure, and success. While it was known in general in the latter part of the last century that there were iron deposits of promise elsewhere, exploration and development of the Mesabi Range were slow. The greater part of the preliminary work on it was done between 1890 and 1900. Even at this time there was no general knowledge of the extent and value of these ore beds. Of course, they were more talked about and more hopes were built upon them in Minnesota than elsewhere. Like the prophet in his own country, it is also true that in Minnesota they were regarded, by all except a few, with doubt and distrust. From the ore-bearing tracts of this land of forest, swamp, and barren rock, exposed for untold years to the action of the weather, other elements had been leached away; leaving concentrated iron deposits of unexampled richness. The geological formation is such that these masses of hematite ore are of wide area and, on this range, do not exceed 500 feet in depth. Capable of being worked as open mines with the steam shovel, and yielding an ore with a very high percentage of the best quality of iron, they have since taken the leading place in the iron industry of the world. A bulletin of the University of Minnesota on iron mining in that state, by Mr. Charles E. van Barneveld, says: "Actual productions from the Lake region may be said to date from 1855. During the first nineteen years of its life the Mesabi Range produced 224,905,184 tons, roughly 45 per cent. of the total Lake Superior production, and, in 1910, the Mesabi is credited with 29,201,700 tons, almost 70 per cent. of the Lake Superior tonnage for the year, producing the raw material for approximately 40 per cent. of the American and 17 per cent. of the world's pig iron output."

Mr. Hill had eyes and ears always open for the discovery of new sources of mineral wealth. His exhaustive study of the coal supply has been mentioned more than once. He had given less time and thought to iron, because it was supposed to be absent in any considerable or paying quantity from the territory in which he operated. He was, however, familiar with the general facts of the world's iron ore districts, consumption and demand. After his interest had been captured, he carried his studies into this field. A few years later he could describe the location and possibilities of all the known iron ore deposits of the world. He knew what variety and amount was furnished by Sweden, by Spain, by every country of South America where iron existed. He could say where each would find its best market, and how much of that market it could supply. He would give you in casual conversation the dimensions of actual mountains of rich ore in remote parts of Brazil, concerning which he had sent for and obtained accurate information. He investigated this subject as systematically as he had the trade possibilities of the Orient; and, later, the uses to which peat was put in Germany, with a view to the development of the immense deposits of it in Minnesota. But up to the time reached here he had taken only such interest in Minnesota iron ore lands as arose from their present or prospective contribution to railroad tonnage. These properties were largely in territory that his lines could reach or expected to control. It was clear that for many years the ore would have to go east, and would choose the cheap route of the Great Lakes. Its transit over a railroad would cover only relatively small distances, but its volume and weight and the ease of handling it by modern appliances make this profitable business. These considerations did

214

not, however, as yet, command his attention, because the whole industry in Minnesota was in its infancy. He became an owner of ore lands, in the first instance, not by forethought or studied intention, but in an almost accidental way.

The general scheme of extending the Great Northern's lines, after the construction of the Eastern Railway Company of Minnesota into Duluth, included a railroad from Duluth northwest, to connect with the existing lines at or about Crookston, Minnesota, thus affording a rail outlet for grain shipments from the West to the head of Lake Superior. As an initial step to this end Mr. Hill acquired the Duluth & Winnipeg Railway, a single track line between Duluth and Swan River, and organized the Duluth, Superior and Western Railway Company for the purpose of taking it over. The old Duluth & Winnipeg had a traffic arrangement with a logging road, running from Mississippi, Minnesota, through Swan River to a point near the present town of Hibbing; under the terms of which it hauled iron ore from the Mahoning mine, delivered at Swan River by the logging road, to the ore docks at Allouez Bay. This introduced a direct interest in iron ore production and carriage into the affairs of the Great Northern. A personal interest of a different and powerful nature had intervened before this to dispose Mr. Hill to consider and look into the whole question.

His eldest son, James N. Hill, and his second son,

Louis W. Hill, had both entered the railroad service in 1893, after leaving Yale University. Like every father whose life has been devoted to the handling of large affairs and the creation of great properties, Mr. Hill hoped that one or all of his three sons would take up and carry on, after him, what he had brought to such splendid consummation. He did not propose to constrain any of them. The third son, Walter, was still too young for railroad harness. To the others he gave their opportunity to learn the business under his thorough-going tutelage. They could then take it up as a life work, or turn to some other form of interest and occupation, as their aptitudes and their tastes, after a suitable experimental period, might decide. Both the boys were put through such a course of education as Mr. Hill, and every other father whose affection does not run away with his judgment, knew to be necessary. They began at the beginning. In the nine years of his connection with the road, J. N. Hill served in seven different offices or positions. L. W. Hill remained continuously in railroad work, and became president of the Great Northern in 1907. He began, like his brother, as a clerk in the comptroller's office, and appears, by the payrolls, to have been employed successively in eighteen different offices, one after the other. There was no doubt that the practical education of these young men would be complete. It included every kind of labour, from overalls up, where a man might get knowledge of railroading, beginning with the alphabet and ending with the encyclopedia. Both made good. After his novitiate, J. N. Hill decided that another line of activity was better suited to him. He had shown conspicuous ability, and was made vice-president of the Great Northern in 1902. But his choice led him elsewhere, and was justified by his subsequent success in the other interests to which he decided to devote himself. Louis W. Hill remained with the Great Northern. He received his father's ideas, was in all the later years his right hand in carrying them out, lifted burdens by acting on his own initiative, and became, by his loyalty and filial devotion, expressed in a thousand acts rather than in words, the business confidant and helper of all Mr. Hill's later life.

The connection of both these young men with the purchase of the ore properties that came into Mr. James J. Hill's possession is close. The Eastern Railway of Minnesota, giving entrance to Duluth, has been mentioned several times. J. N. Hill was vice-president of this company for more than two years, from 1897 to 1899. L. W. Hill was president of it from January, 1901, to April, 1902. Both of them had, of course, not only lived in Duluth but traversed the outlying country and become familiar with the ore interests of northern Minnesota and their possible future. Both believed that the road should build into the iron country and get its business. J. N. Hill advised it. Louis

217

W. Hill was especially enthusiastic in the faith. He studied the formation of the country, drove over it in winter, examined ore samples, and made acquaintance with the owners of some of the lands. He invested there on his own judgment and responsibility. He kept talking to his father about the great future of this section and these values. Still, up to 1899, Mr. Hill was only partially convinced. At that date the railroad interest and the ore land interest, by sheer force of circumstance, reached a point of junction. The time had come to shorten the through line of the Great Northern from Duluth to the wheat fields of the Red River Valley and the farther West. Access to the lake terminals from the south and southwest was ample. The route from the Northwest was still too roundabout. So the Duluth and Winnipeg was bought and the building of the link by Cass Lake was decided upon. In the path was what was known as the Wright and Davis property, including the logging road just mentioned and some lands. Part of these were known to contain iron ore, one mine having been opened and leased. The natural assumption was that there might be more of it in the vicinity. But nobody knew to a certainty. The future of the properties as ore producers was as indeterminate as any other "prospect" in a mineral-bearing country.

Mr. D. N. Philbin was general superintendent of the Duluth & Winnipeg when Mr. Hill bought it. He re-
218

mained with it. He had been for years an enthusiast about the iron interest in northern Minnesota. He had talked it over many times with both the young Hills. He now added his efforts to persuade Mr. Hill that here was something worth his while. The Wright and Davis property, originally timbered and much of it now apparently made valueless by the lumbermen, included about 25,000 acres of unexplored lands on the Mesabi Range. On it was the Mahoning mine that became famous later. The new cut-off for the Great Northern must be built anyway. The line of the old logging road might be made, almost had to be made, a part of it. The lands would go with it. Such a purchase, as a whole, involving an element if not speculative at least not altogether identified with railroading, was not the kind in which a railroad enterprise directed by Mr. Hill was wont to engage. From the beginning to the end of his career he insisted on keeping it free from every such entanglement. So he decided to make this a personal transaction, and bought and paid for the entire property himself. The purchase was completed and the papers passed May 1, 1899, for the entire Wright and Davis property. For this, including the Duluth, Mississippi River & Northern Railroad, and the lands, some of them cut over, some under stumpage contract, and some known or supposed to be mineral, he paid $4,050,000.

The funds were furnished by him personally. The property was now his own. He had a right to do as he pleased with it. He could have turned the portion of it necessary for the new line over to the Great Northern at an advance. Other men high in the railroad world and the financial world found no impropriety in making that kind of deal years before and years later. He could have kept the ore lands in his name and added all the values to be realized from them to his fortune. There was no more shadow on his right to do this than on his right to sell the milk of his cows. The point to be made is that at this moment everything was in his hands; not merely by accident of position or power, but by the same title that a man has who buys a city lot or a farm and pays for it with his own money. The Mahoning mine was at this time the only one shipping ore. Only one other deposit was known certainly to exist on the property. Explorations were going on and, of course, after these lands were bought, partly because they went with the railroad and partly because the existence of large quantities of iron ore there was suspected, they would be prospected and developed if results were favourable. Mr. Hill determined that this ore should be shipped over the Great Northern. This is the way he looked at the situation: "I did not want to carry on the ore business personally, for the reason that I had made it a rule that nobody working for the company, myself, or any one else, could have any business that called for the transaction of business with the company in anything along the railway where the company

220

was interested in the carriage. If the stockholders of the railroad company held the ores or if they were held in trust for them, the railway company would have a reasonable right to expect that the transportation of the ores on these lands would go over our line."

An analysis of this shows plainly the working in his mind of the laws of his code of business honour. The little railroad running in the direction where his line must go ought to be acquired for the Great Northern. The lands attached to it might be valuable as ore property. By this time he was ready to believe they were. The ore from the one mine opened and the others possibly to be opened ought to go to swell the traffic and earnings of the Great Northern. But the railroad must not be mixed up in a land deal. Nobody connected with the company ought, by holding these lands, to have powers and interests so largely distinct from those of the company itself. This tangle of conflicting principles could be straightened out in only one way. Mr. Hill must buy the whole property himself. He must render to the railroad the things of the railroad; namely, the logging line, right of way, and necessary property. He must turn this over at cost, so that no taint of personal profit could touch the transaction. He must, for the same reason, get rid of the ore lands; lest they should bring him wealth that he, as representing the company, could not accept when accompanied by this indirect and purely speculative admixture of personal advantage, flowing through the channel of his office. If large ore deposits should be uncovered, this valuable traffic must continue to be so controlled that it would go over the Great Northern. Set all these ideas in motion at once, and the resultant of their forces is the line that Mr. Hill took. It pointed him straight to his almost quixotic resolution.

The Lake Superior Company, Limited, was organized to carry it into effect. That could do what he did not feel at liberty to do. In it could be shut up the property and interests which were to be transferred later to the stockholders of the Great Northern Company direct. To turn over the ore lands to them before these had been proved valuable would have been like giving them a lottery ticket. The whole thing must be worked out as it was worked out, through years of boring, analyzing, surface stripping, and other incidentals of development, until the ore property became a thing of ascertained and independent value. This the Lake Superior Company could do. Then the whole—definite, enlarged, compacted, a going concern—could be transferred to the Great Northern stockholders. This is the way Mr. Hill talked about it before a legislative committee in February, 1907: "I got my share simply as a stockholder, and that is all the interest I have in it—the same as any other stockholder. The lands went to the Superior Company at exactly what they cost. I haven't made the value of a postage stamp, directly or indirectly, out of the transaction, in any way or manner. There is nothing private about it, nothing secret, nothing to conceal, and nothing to be ashamed of. I hope that I did right in the matter, and what I did will meet the approval of honest men. A great many people seem to be unable to realize that a man could hand over an immense property of that kind. Well, I did it. It hadn't the value when I did it that it has now, but I am glad it was put in that way, and if it had been twice as valuable I would have the same feeling."

The Lake Superior Company, Limited, was organized in 1899. This concern not only answered the need of the moment, but also dovetailed into other needs which had not yet specifically appeared. This Lake Superior Company became a holding company for various interests related to the railroad company. Some, like the ore mines and the great dock property at Allouez Bay, were matters already needing a caretaker. Others had to do with projects on different parts of the system where it was desirable that plans for contemplated construction should not stand openly in the name of the Great Northern, because this would rouse rivalry, raise the price of property, and promote innumerable lawsuits. Neither is it clear how these great ore interests could have been kept intact and subject to continuous development in the years that followed, if they had not been handled in exactly this way. The idea of a holding company for the railroad was at this time in mind.

In 1901 it materialized in the Northern Securities. Instead of being involved in the maze of litigation continued down to 1905, as they would have been if they had been mingled with Great Northern interests as a part of that company's holdings, and therefore forbidden to develop, the ore properties were kept in a separate and independent position until the Northern Securities case was out of the way, the atmosphere cleared, and an open route for the future secured. The Lake Superior Company could go on with its own business, handle mineral lands, invest its profits and act for the stockholders, without danger of interference while merger questions were threshed out in the courts. A lot of important odds and ends, coal mines, iron mines, elevators, and docks, not only in the Lake Superior region but at Buffalo, in the East, and in the West, were accommodated here until the time should be ripe for a general consolidation of the railroad company's interests. The Great Northern's report of June 30, 1900 said: "It is considered that these properties can be handled to better ends by a separate company. . . . The income from these properties or securities (belonging to the Lake Superior Company) will belong to the Great Northern shareholders." Mr. Hill said that, so far as the ore properties were concerned, which is the only matter to be dealt with here, "the Lake Superior Company was formed to hold them in trust, so that the profits, if any, from the mines, would

LORD STRATHCONA AND MOUNT ROYAL
A life-long friend and business associate of Mr. Hill

go to the stockholders, and the transportation would go
to the railway; and the stockholders, being interested
in the railway, would be a guaranty that the shipments
or iron ore from these lands would go over the Great
Northern Railway." The Lake Superior Company
held the properties and administered them down to the
time when, in 1906, a board of trustees to take charge
of them permanently was formed.

During these years the work of exploring old lands
and acquiring new went forward steadily. Louis W.
Hill was active in looking after its details. James J.
Hill was now convinced of the immense intrinsic importance of something which he had at first regarded as
little more than an accessory of straightening the Great
Northern's main line to the West. Money was spent
in examining and buying other promising tracts, in
drilling on those already owned and, in general, in
creating a large mining interest about the property
which in itself was apparently inconsiderable. Enormous development took place. The ore from the Lake
Superior region was sought for eagerly. The value of the
deposits grew, along with an ever-growing certainty of
their extent and richness. Not many years were needed
to make the Mesabi range famous. These properties
waiting in the hands of the Lake Superior Company were
sponsor for millions of wealth to be realized through long
future years not of hope, but of certainty. The Duluth,
Superior & Western Railroad and the old logging road

together made a complete line from Lake Superior to the Mesabi Range. Over the single track of this road 873,739 tons of ore were hauled in 1899, the year of the purchase. By 1906, when the definitive trust was organized, over 6,000,000 tons were carried on a railroad now grown into a double track line, maintained in the highest state of efficiency and repair. A few properties had been leased or sublet to provide traffic. At the time the trusteeship was created, the proprietary companies held approximately 65,000 acres of land. Everything expanded on a magnificent scale. Along with the Duluth & Winnipeg Railway had been acquired a small plant for handling ore at Allouez Bay. In 1903 the Allouez Bay Dock Company was incorporated, its stock being held by the Lake Superior Company. It was acquired in 1913 by the Great Northern. So immense was the development during a decade that in 1916 the Great Northern plant at this point consisted of four docks, one of them a concrete and steel structure with a total storage capacity of 335,430 tons, which afforded facilities for handling, in one navigation season, approximately 16,000,000 tons of iron ore. At least 300,000,000 tons of controlled ore were known to be available for future shipment. The railroad company received fifty-five cents a ton in freight revenue. Shipments reached highwater mark in 1912, when the iron ore traffic of the Great Northern was nearly 14,000,000 tons. For reasons to be stated, it fell below this figure later. But it recovered quickly. Its past has realized, its future will transcend the estimates of Mr. Hill.

In 1906 the importance of these ore properties was so great as to call for continuous systematic development on a large scale; and so well understood that producers of iron at the East were anxious to have access to them and, if it might be, to control their output. Both ends were served by an arrangement concluded by Mr. Hill with the United States Steel Corporation. Negotiations had been going on for a long time. Even at the end they moved slowly; so that while this important document bears date of January 2, 1906, it was not completely executed and delivered until September 16 of that year. It was based upon a sliding scale of prices, according to quantity of ore mined and varying with the lapse of years, with rather complicated details which need not be recited here. Both the royalty and the amount taken out were to increase until a fixed maximum was reached. The time had now come to carry out Mr. Hill's idea about the disposition of this immense and valuable interest. Litigation over the Northern Securities was ended. The affairs of the Great Northern were in settled shape. The lease just concluded was expected to last indefinitely. Everything was ready for the distribution of these splendid values and profits according to Mr. Hill's fixed determination. December 7, 1906, all of the ore properties, title to which was in several different

227

corporations, were placed in a trusteeship. The trust agreement was made between the Lake Superior Company and Mr. Hill's three sons, Louis W., James N., and Walter J. Hill, and Edward T. Nichols, as trustees. The outstanding capital stock of the Great Northern Company was then $150,000,000, or 1,500,000 shares. The entire beneficial interest of the trust, therefore, was made to consist of the same number. Share for share, these certificates were distributed as an outright gift to the stockholders of the Great Northern Railway Company of record at the close of business December 6, 1906.

The lease to the United States Steel Corporation was to run until all merchantable ore in the lands leased had been exhausted. It contained, however, a provision that, by giving two years' notice, the lessee had the right to cancel the lease on January 1, 1915. For various reasons, industrial and possibly political, this notice was given in October, 1911. During the time its lease was operated, the United States Steel Corporation took out, in all, 26,573,808 tons of iron ore and paid to the trustees a total of $45,174,225. After the cancellation of the lease, the trustees formed their own separate organization, and mined and marketed the ores, in addition to leasing properties direct to furnace and consuming interests from time to time on a royalty basis. With greatly increased demand for iron and steel and higher prices, the enterprise promised to yield

228

large and uninterrupted returns for an indefinite time in the future. That the change in system of operation did not affect the standing of the trust property as a business concern is shown by the fact that the cash distribution to the certificate holders remained at $750,000, paid at some time during every calendar year, down to and including 1916. At the end of the calendar year 1914, the trustees had paid out to the railroad company for freight on ore shipments nearly $15,000,000. Royalties paid were about as much more. There was a cash balance in the hands of the trustees of approximately $8,500,000. The total payments to Great Northern stockholders or those to whom they sold their certificates from the formation of the trust to June 27, 1916, were $11,250,000. This sum, added to freight payments, makes a total amount of between twenty-five and thirty million dollars, the magnificent yield to that date of the bounty of Mr. Hill, presented to the stockholders of his railroad system.

If, to the figures of cash already received, there be added the certain income from the hundreds of millions of tons of ore in the properties administered by the trust, always growing in value, always most available for consumption because of the cheap open mining system and the nearness to water transportation, the total ultimate money value of this royal gift will reach startling figures. It was a deliberate act. It is more enlightening and more conclusive than volumes upon the character of the man; because, from that character, it drew its motive and necessity. There was no reason in the world, in law or morals, why he should not have added these many millions, coming from a property purchased with his own money, to his own fortune. The truth is that he never thought of such a thing. Not to do so was for him both a matter of conscience and a point of pride. He recognized that inner compulsion which has ruled a few great men in those crises that express from human nature the essence of its greatness or its littleness. He "could do no other." It deeply delighted him to pass over this huge honorarium to the men who had been interested in his enterprise from the beginning, and who had stood by him so loyally through storms and among rocks and shoals that promised shipwreck. In the constellation of the Great Northern's success a new star of striking brilliance was to appear. Of his own part in what he did he thought little. Its magnificence consists partly in the simplicity of his own thought about it. There is impressive royalty of mind, something far higher than the just satisfaction of being a benefactor on a colossal scale, in the matter-of-course words in which he himself answered a leading question: "A great many people have asked me why I didn't keep the lands. I suppose I might have kept them—I don't know any reason why I shouldn't when I bought them —except that I prefer to have the shareholders have whatever there was in the transaction." His refusal of personal profit was like his reply to the lure of control of a continental railroad combination; to more than one temptation to some great betrayal or some minor meanness; to the multitude of suggestions made to him during his life that for some purpose, high or low, he should be "falsely true." Hè did not strike an attitude. He just said quietly, with that look of mingled surprise and scorn which no one who saw it failed to remember, "No, I couldn't do that."

CHAPTER THIRTY-TWO

A PIONEER OF CONSERVATION

ALTHOUGH Mr. Hill's mind seemed always busy with the details of his transportation system, with construction, operation, maintenance, financing and the thousand and one demands made on his attention by his life's work, it was continually engaged, in some deeper depth, with large economic problems. He pondered everything, and was fascinated by curious researches among the fundamental facts and laws that environ and shape the life and labour of man upon the earth. This serious and systematic study, enlarged by experience, enriched by the contributions of years, tested by observation and revealing to his ardent nature a present crisis, led him to certain practical conclusions which he found it both a duty and a pleasure to give to the public. He opened, in 1906, a campaign of popular education in the wickedness and dangers of waste, from which the whole conservation movement in this country, and its actual accomplishments in legislation and in custom, trace their origin. His expert knowledge of the farm, and of the value of live stock to agricultural progress, his interest in drainage in Minnesota, his familiarity with irrigation past and

232

present, had all contributed to lead him to the threshold of a broad generalization. He crossed it in the memorable address that he made at the Minnesota State Fair, September 3, 1906.

Up to this time the conservation of natural resources in the United States had been in theory ignored and in practice a thing of shreds and patches. Like the habits of industry and thrift, it could be commended as most excellent for somebody else to adopt. But its adepts were few. The big interest and the community were both making too great haste to be rich to bother themselves about any such ideality. "Until late in the nineteenth century," says President Van Hise in his sketch of the conservation movement, "the resources of this country were commonly regarded as inexhaustible." American literature on the subject scarcely extended beyond Professor Shaler's admirable little outline sketch, "Man and the Earth." There had been much experimenting with soils in other lands, little in our own. Forestry had made a little headway, but was not taken much more seriously than an attempt to find Robin Hood's barn. Irrigation, of course, of immemorial antiquity, was common in many parts of the West. Mr. Hill interested himself in that; and even before the date from which the essential portion of this chapter begins, he had, in 1905, read a paper before the National Irrigation Congress, at its meeting in Portland, Oregon. But reclamation work, such as this, is conservation only in the largest and loosest sense. The general principle of a prudent preservation and careful use of all natural resources, and its direct applications, captivated both his imagination and his strong sense of practical values. So he now engaged in a deliberate study to bring together and concentrate upon a focus the wandering beams of light from different portions of a vast but nebulous firmament of knowledge and of warning.

He investigated and verified world statistics of production and consumption. He massed his facts. Then he drew conclusions logically inescapable. When his message was ready, he selected the great agricultural anniversary of his state for the occasion, and the farmers of the Northwest for the audience. Before a throng of many thousands whose interest he held for hours, he delivered his impressive address on "The Nation's Future." Nine months had been devoted to the preparation of the material that was condensed into a little pamphlet of less than thirty pages. The theoretical starting point was essentially the same as that of Malthus and Ricardo. The purpose was to show an escape from the *impasse* into which their mathematical theorems, as applied to beings with life and will, led their followers, and from the black doom that they had hung above the world. Like Malthus, Mr. Hill set out from the law of population increasing in a geometrical ratio. Unlike him, he looked, for the salvation of

the future, not to established checks upon the multiplication of the human species, but to an equivalent
multiplication of its means of support. Like the older
economists, he admitted the law of diminishing return
as applied to land. But, instead of looking hopelessly
to the day when the people of the world must be satisfied
to eke out a wretched and dwindling existence upon soil
just at the level of cultivation, he predicted and would
prepare a world made rich everywhere in productive-
ness beyond the dream of past imagination. He opened
new vistas. He drew away a veil from murky skies
where the early theorists of the "dismal science" had
read signs and wonders and written prophecies according to their kind. He mingled with the word of reproof
and warning the word of promise and of cheer.

To the logical arrangement and expression of his
conception Mr. Hill gave more care and thought than
to any other public utterance of his life. Like all
great ideas, his is essentially simple. "The Nation's
Future," is a document weighted with real concern
for the economic welfare and the political safety of this
country. It worked out, necessarily, into a system
applicable to all the world, and may be summarized
briefly. Man's physical life is supported and his progress guaranteed by two kinds of material and indispensable resources. The first is food; the second, those
commodities that protect and aid the body in its work
and growth—clothing, shelter, implements of every kind.

When statistics of every country and every industry are examined, it appears that both classes of these necessaries or supports to human advance are being either actually exhausted and totally extinguished or levied upon for present consumption at a rate that will impoverish the future. The consequence, if the process continue, is as certain as that of drawing water perpetually from a reservoir without replenishing it. The inquiry made by Mr. Hill included the basic staples of all the main kinds of industry in the leading countries of the world. As to food, the investigation led into territories of fact that he had made peculiarly his own. He knew what had been done in Europe. He was familiar with the Rothamsted experimentation. For nearly twenty-five years he had been telling the individual farmer, and the farmers of the Northwest as a class, that they were neglecting opportunities and throwing away offered wealth. He had urged upon them deep ploughing, repeated cultivation of the soil, rotation of crops, fertilization and the raising of live stock. Thus only could they add to their wealth and prevent soil decline. All he needed now was to enlarge the dimensions of the picture and deepen its background. The problem of the individual farmer became the problem of the world. Since population will go on increasing, while the land area of the globe must remain substantially fixed, it will be necessary to increase and maintain the productive power of each acre at least as rapidly as population grows. On one side this meant new methods, and on the other the preservation and improvement of soil quality. The latter is conservation, pure and simple. As to the accessories of life, things of wood and iron, fuel supply, all the external agencies that destroy natural resources to minister to our needs and at the same time to enlarge them, conservation must also come into play. We cannot rely upon the assistance of future discoveries or applications of science. That would be to squander all we possess to-day in the vague hope that somebody some time is going to leave us a comfortable legacy. There is just so much coal and iron and other useful mineral wealth stored in the earth. Extracted and used, it is not reproduced. There are just so many billion feet of standing timber on the globe. This, it is true, may grow again; but it would not reach the useful stage for decades or centuries. Impending scarcity can be averted only by economy; and the future made secure only by a scientific system of forestry. Every resource useful to man depends upon him for preservation, in the same bond that he depends upon it for existence and development.

Under each item of this programme Mr. Hill gave facts and figures from the records of the world and its different industries. He dwelt most forcefully upon the conservation and improvement of the soil; because that, in the last resort, is man's one unfailing support.

237

He bent all the persuasive and convincing vigour of his mind to compel the people to see the urgency of a problem before it hung its sword above their heads. He pointed out the danger to intelligence, to morals, to democratic institutions, in neglecting the clear mandate of the future. He called upon the Government to establish model farms everywhere in the agricultural states, to "show exactly what can be done on a small tract of land by proper cultivation, modern fertilizing and due rotation of crops." More briefly and rapidly, but with no less evidential conclusiveness, he traced a plan of conservation for manufacturing, commerce, all the varied complexities of a modern industrial society. He tried to make the individual see himself as necessarily involved in the success or failure of all humanity as an economic unit. The eyes of the country must be opened. "Only thus may the struggle for existence, that has power either to curse or to bless, be brought to any other termination than the peace of death."

It would be difficult to exaggerate the effect produced by this statement. It came at a psychological moment. It emanated from a source of power. The occasion resembled that on which a scientist of world renown tells for the first time his discovery of a new metal, a new gas, a new law of physical or chemical action. But while the latter appeals in the first instance to an educated few, Mr. Hill's words were meant for and were taken up by the many. An emergency—

238

believed, whenever it was thought of at all, to be too distant to touch our present, like the effect of the gradual cooling of the earth—was shown to be already knocking at the door. His address was published in full by the *New York Herald.* It was taken up by newspapers from one end of the land to the other. Huge volumes of scrapbooks are filled with public comments upon it. He received letters about it from all over the world. Requests for leave to reproduce it came flooding in. It was republished nearly a score of times by individuals, institutions and societies in this and other countries. It was translated into several languages. Best of all, it did not end in a temporary sensation and a dying echo. Seldom have counsel and warning borne such immediate practical fruit. The time was ripe, the word fitted the time, and the conservation idea sank deep into the mind of the American people. It dates its real origin, as an accepted rule of conduct, from Mr. Hill's memorable address. So great was the interest and so general and continued the discussion which followed his statement of the nation's need that political powers took cognizance of it. It was one of those not-too-common cases where many leaders saw that to support and further a wise economic principle would win popularity. The truth was so plain and the facts had been so clearly and convincingly stated that public opinion stood up solidly behind them. Men might, some did, question whether the fate of the waster would come upon us in just the number of years that Mr. Hill thought it possible or probable. They did not question the law, or attempt to deny the ultimate fact. In all the states the topic was soon alive. It did not escape the notice of so keen a reader of the people's thought as President Roosevelt. While not unwilling to fall in with a popular tendency, his facile intelligence also appreciated the worth of the idea. Together they made an opportunity. The statesman in him joined hands with the politician. He called a conference of the Governors of the several states, to consider measures for the conservation of national resources.

This body was in session three days beginning May 13, 1908, at the White House in Washington. It was the official beginning of conservation as an organized movement covering the whole country. Mr. Hill was invited to address the meeting. He made an impression as profound upon these representatives of public opinion in the states as he did upon the farmers who had gathered to hear him at St. Paul, and upon the thinkers in every large centre of intelligence throughout the world where his first discourse had been read. This White House address began with a restatement of the thesis and a condensation of the argument of "The Nation's Future." He gave it a keener point for this occasion, however, by forecasting the effect of a decline of national resources upon the political future of the
240

United States. He said, "No people ever felt the want of work or the pinch of poverty for a long time without reaching out violent hands against their political institutions, believing that they might find in a change some relief from their distress." He quoted the letter of Lord Macaulay, predicting that our day of trial would come when increase of population should press hard upon a territory fully occupied, and enhanced in value beyond the reach of the poor. He took the broadest possible ground: "Since the unnecessary destruction of our land will bring new conditions of danger, its conservation, its improvement to the highest point of productivity appears to be a first command of any political economy worthy of the name. The first task, it seems to me, must be to force home the facts of the situation into the public consciousness; to make men realize their duty toward coming generations exactly as a father feels it a duty to see that his children do not suffer want." To this end he called for an extension of the work done by the Department of Agriculture and the agricultural colleges of the various states. He elevated the truth which this meeting had been called to consider from an economic theory to a "patriotic gospel." He had gone into this work himself in the true missionary spirit. That spirit inspired him as he spoke. The New York *Sun* gave this account of the effect he produced: "Before Mr. Hill had finished one-half of his address the bell sounded the warning which

241

meant 'three more minutes,' and Mr. Hill paused but the chairman made a gesture indicating that he should proceed. Three minutes later came two strokes of the bell, and Mr. Hill stopped again; but loud calls of 'Go on! Go on!' encouraged him to proceed and he was not interrupted again. After the reading of his paper Mr. Hill was personally congratulated by Secretary Cortelyou and Secretary Garfield and Secretary Wilson, who occupied seats on the platform, and the applause of the governors and delegates lasted nearly two minutes." This address complemented that made a year and a half before; and, with it, reached all the different levels of the public thought. From this time the conservation movement gathered impetus. Shortly afterward the President appointed the National Conservation Commission. It held its first meeting a month later. Scores of organizations, local as well as general, were formed to explain and enforce the practice of conservation of our resources. The principle, though far from triumphant over the lust for wealth and power, became an unquestioned law for national life and action.

Mr. Hill never looked back after having put his hand to the plough. Once in the grip of this great general idea, he applied it scientifically and followed wherever it led. Its virtue and the vastness of its scope were first fully revealed to him, perhaps, in its application to soil preservation and renewal. That was the main artery through which his interest in it throbbed. There will be occasion to speak of this at more length and from abundant materials in the description of his accomplishment in the restoration and improvement of agriculture. That subject, so immense in itself and filling a place in his life almost equal to that assigned to the problems of the carrier, demands and will receive an analysis of its own. It is sufficient here to follow, through his words and acts, other developments and ramifications of the conservation idea. It was constantly fermenting in his mind, and from it flowed through many years the heady wine of new and helpful thought. Naturally, after his initial service as inspirer of the conservation movement on a national scale, his advice and assistance were in great demand. This, as an organized mission, made but slight appeal to him. Few such organizations did. Like all men of supremely high mentality, he pinned his faith to the life and reproductive power of the idea. That was fluid, penetrating and creative. Once embodied in an organism, it lost something of freedom and of worth. So, although he seldom refused the stimulus of his presence and his speech to the associations now so numerous and so active in spreading the conservation gospel, he went on developing and applying it in fields and ways distinctly his own. In 1910, he addressed both the National and the Minnesota Conservation Congresses. He spoke to the Minnesota Association again two years later; but the body and purpose of his thought were now bent mainly in two directions. One led to the first object of his intention and care, conservation on the farm; the other struck out a new path. This was the fit and necessary relation of conservation to capital and credit. In it were foreshadowed the office and right rule of the banking and general financial interest which was to occupy so large a place in the closing cycle of his life.

It is difficult to untangle the closely twisted filaments in a mentality such as this, or to analyze as independent entities the activities so closely and harmoniously blended. A chronological life of Mr. Hill, treating each year or group of years as a whole, would be a collection of fragments instead of a building architecturally complete. The most faithful attempt to explore, without divergence, tracts of it which appear uniform or at least closely related, runs up, unless the analysis goes deep enough and spreads wide enough, against the difficulty of tracing the organic connection between apparently unrelated things. His natural antipathy to waste and his solicitude for prosperity on the farm, both of them traits that were derived from his earliest years and were rooted in the primary character of the man himself, led him to the principle of conservation. Throwing contemptuously aside the petty detail and the bobbins of red tape by which that principle was presently swathed, through the hectic industry of men of great sincerity but limited vision, he followed it into another territory, that of finance, which also it had been a part of his life work to occupy and to know. Conservation he had accepted as a general rule for wise human action. It applies to the forest, to the mine, to the field, to manufacture, to all the obvious forms of human effort. Where it is neglected or denied, life forces are impaired. Has it not elsewhere an incidence equally apt and possibly as necessary?

To carry it into the financial realm, and develop the theory of conservation of capital and credit, was but to make a metaphysic of his own work in financing a railroad system. Less captivating than the idea of conservation of natural wealth, this was less instantly and cordially received. Eventually, perhaps, its consequences may be even wider and more lasting. Men who see a tree cut down understand that many years must pass before another can fill its place. If they see a bucket of coal shot up from the bowels of the earth, they know that nature will almost certainly never restore a similar mass of matter to the space left vacant. They are slower to see and to believe that the same law prevails in the less tangible world of capital and the intangible world of credit. To illuminate this truth now became Mr. Hill's particular care. In one of the addresses of 1910 he made an exhaustive study of the public abuse of capital and credit. Comparatively few federal statistics on this subject were then available. The reports of the treasurers and auditors of all the states were called for, examined and collated. Thirty of these that were found consistent and intelligible were tabulated It appeared that state expenditure in the nine years ending with 1909 had increased more than 201 per cent.; while the wealth of the whole United States between 1890 and 1904, a period half as long again, had increased but 65 per cent. This was a destruction of capital to which the conservation rule ought to be applied. If it were not, Mr. Hill pointed out plainly the inevitable result: "You cannot cheat the first four rules of arithmetic. As you cannot eat your cake and have it too, so you cannot spend your money for one thing and also use it for another." In this stupendous growth of public expense for non-productive purposes he saw the greatest check upon progress, and one of the heaviest and most impoverishing burdens upon labour. Here was room and need for conservation.

The same was true, on an even larger scale, of credit. Money for expenditures such as those reflected in a considerable part of these totals must be obtained by borrowing. No people could endure the taxation that cash payments would require. Besides, the country had been assured by Daniel Webster that "Credit has done more a thousand times to enrich nations than all the mines of the world." Communities not only believe this, they take it crudely at its face. They do not turn the coin over and look at the other side. The converse proposition, the misuse of credit, gives rise to the most terrible calamities of modern times. Mr. Hill, in 1913, urged the conservation of credit with almost angry emphasis. He pointed out that in the five preceding years between eight and nine billion dollars' worth of paper had been put out by corporations. Again and again he reiterated the law that excessive spending, based on unlimited borrowing, must sap the foundation of the social structure, just as it rots the fibre of the man himself. "Grant credit unwisely and you open Pandora's box." Let the lumbermen fell all your forests, and soon you cannot build a roof above your head. Shut up all your forests in reservations or bar access to them by the hedge of useless regulations, and tomorrow again you will be houseless. Somewhere between the two lie comfort and sanity and progress. Use all your cash capital to buy automobiles, or to sustain a horde of useless officeholders, or to underwrite vast schemes of paternalism based on that sort of humanitarianism whose motto is "Let the other fellow pay for it," and the community goes bankrupt. Use credit in like manner, and the result is veiled. When the actual dollar goes, you can see the empty place that it leaves behind. But debt is a winged thing. It reproduces itself in secret chambers until your imagined prosperity falls to pieces because the moth and the worm have eaten it.

Once more an intelligent and prudent people is driven back upon conservation. Use capital and credit; but use them wisely, scientifically. A public or a corporate treasury should be guarded more carefully than a waterfall. The latter will furnish power to the end of time. Even if control of it should be given away in folly, wisdom may one day recover it. The former is a lake fed, indeed, by constant secret springs, but of limited volume and flow. Start the steam pump at a thousand gallons a minute, and after a while you have nothing there but mud and crawling forms of lower life. Worse than that, the burning sun upon the hidden fount will dry up the living source once thought inexhaustible. In place of perpetual power and refreshment you have made drought and death visible; in order that, for a little space, adjacent land might be drenched with a destructive torrent, where a few inches of water would have ministered to it in perpetuity. This was Mr. Hill's conception of the need and the uses of conservation in the broad field of finance. If it was less popular than his work on similar lines elsewhere, that was only because it was a more advanced and unwelcome form of effort and instruction. He could see no difference between an acre of ground left barren because its occupant had exhausted every atom of fertility in the soil and the same acre lying waste because its whole product could no more than pay interest and taxes. His grip upon the general principle never relaxed. He meant that men should work hard, live thriftily, save money, and put it at work again productively. He meant it be-

248

cause he believed that nature meant it. He was terribly in earnest, because he knew that she could and would enforce her decree.

It has seemed proper to follow out here one line of Mr. Hill's thought and purpose, although the applications of it cover many fields and stretch through many years. From the address at the Minnesota State Fair in 1906, to his address on "The Use and Abuse of Credit," in 1913, there is a natural evolution of mental and moral ideas. In the first he said that we must conserve our national resources that "our children's fortunes may be made secure." In the second he said: "Nothing casts a darker shadow toward our future than the misuse of credit. . . . It is perhaps, the meanest form of stealing ever invented; because it adds to the criminality of breach of trust the baseness of embezzling the future resources of our own children." The railroad, the farm, the bank have come together. They acknowledge one guiding hand. Through them all, one unceasing mandate runs. If Mr. Hill wrought a mighty work in diverse ways, it is because he disdained the superficial; and sought in nature and in man the few simple, immutable laws that must eternally prevail. So grasped, comprehended and applied, the idea of conservation becomes no less than an intellectual and moral apprehension and use of the mysterious ways of Providence.

CHAPTER THIRTY-THREE

SETTING HIS HOUSE IN ORDER

THE attempt of Union Pacific interests to compel the return to them of the same stock that they had turned over to the Northern Securities was more than a straw to show the direction of the wind.   It meant, if successful, an immediate renewal or a permanent possibility of hostilities. Control of the Northern Pacific would always have been in danger. The defeat of this attempt and the distribution of Northern Securities assets, by order of the court, as Mr. Hill had planned, closed that chapter. But the relation of the Northern transcontinentals to that large portion of Pacific Coast business finding its natural outlet through Portland was sure to be unsatisfactory.   Indeed, it was little more natural or final than at the close of the period described in the chapter on early railroad development in the Pacific Northwest. The Northern Securities properties having been "unscrambled," to use a term afterward coined by Mr. Morgan, the hoped-for community of understanding and action on general lines between the Harriman interests and the Hill-Morgan interests could not materialize. That policy had suffered a compound fracture by the cool rejection of a plan of compliance with the court's

250

order which had at first been approved and accepted. The bitter prosecution through all the courts of the attempt to retain a dangerously large holding in Northern Pacific, and the blocking of plans believed by the northern lines to be essential to their future, made close coöperation over large areas and the joint use of any considerable length of trackage by the two interests undesirable even if it were not impracticable. Confidence in the permanance and fair execution of such an arrangement would always be weak. The Union Pacific was actively at work to procure independent entrance and terminals in the Puget Sound region. There was going to be more or less open war in Washington and Oregon. It behooved a good general to plan and make preparations for an impregnable defence and an independent control of the bases of his own position.

Mr. Hill had never, from the first, left out of his scheme some provision for traffic rights into and out of the City of Portland. It will be remembered that long before his line reached tide-water at Everett he had arranged for such accommodation. The business of which Portland was the collecting and distributing centre could not be overlooked or sacrificed. That city divided with Seattle the commercial honours of the North Pacific Coast. The government engineers had opened for it a deep channel from the Willamette to the sea. From the wheat fields of southern Washington and northern Oregon there was a water-level grade down the banks of the Columbia. It was a great advantage not to be obliged to pull heavy trains over the summit of the Cascade Mountains. The Northern Pacific line through to Tacoma and thence southward to Portland was too indirect. The business of a large and fertile area was naturally tributary to Portland. So long as the traffic over the northern lines might have a choice of exits to the sea, all would be well. In the present disposition of affairs and people, indefinitely continued use of the tracks down the Columbia of the old Oregon Railway & Navigation Company, controlled by the Union Pacific, could not be counted on upon reasonable terms. Mr. Hill saw clearly not only the immediate act, but the general principle that each competitive group should be independent. His mind was as open when this seemed to operate against him as when it marched with his interest. In a letter to President Harris, of the Burlington, in May, 1905, he said: "If I were at the head of the Northwestern or the St. Paul, I would never be satisfied with a connection over some other line that was a natural competitor from the common point eastward. The Northwestern and St. Paul, with over fourteen thousand miles of railway, would if they built to Puget Sound, be a great acquisition to the business of the sound and would go far toward putting it on a foundation, viewed from the commerce of the world, ahead of San Francisco. This would, in my judgment, help our lines much more than any possible injury it could do; in other words, if we cannot hold our own in competitive trade we must make room for whoever does it better than we do." This was a wonderfully courageous and farsighted view. It was not "brag" to discourage an enemy; but a confidential expression, to a friend and business associate, of his inmost belief. Most railroad managers would have lain awake nights, imagining the damage that such competition might do and scheming how to head it off. Mr. Hill saw business enough for everybody; and believed that, whatever might happen to the hindmost, the foremost could take care of himself. The building, later on, of the Puget Sound extension of the Chicago, Milwaukee & St. Paul, creating a profitable traffic for itself coincident with a rapid and uninterrupted growth of business on the older lines, proved the justice of his view.

In the southwest he saw the same conditions turned end about. There must be an outlet independent of the Union Pacific from Pasco, to the mouth of the Columbia, and a short line through from Spokane. This was vital to the future of Great Northern and Northern Pacific interests in that section. If it hurt anybody, that, according to his conviction just stated, would be the sufferer's own fault. With an open field and no favours, things must always come out about right. This determination took effect in the building of the Spokane, Portland & Seattle line. In August,

1905, the Portland & Seattle Railway Company was organized to build from Spokane to Seattle, from Spokane to Portland and from Seattle to Portland. Its powers covered also the construction, purchase and operation of boats on the Columbia River. The capital stock was placed originally at $5,000,000. Directly or indirectly, the stock of the company from first to last was controlled or owned by the Great Northern and the Northern Pacific, acting jointly. The north bank road, occupying that shore of the Columbia, was to make them both independent of any other system in the triangle included within the lines joining these three cities and in their tributary country. It could, at need, be used as a base of operations, offensive or defensive, should future developments in Oregon call for action. The Northern Pacific and the Great Northern had but one opinion in this matter. In July, 1905, Mr. Hill had made the following explanation in a personal letter: "Tuesday last the Northern Pacific Executive Committee appointed Messrs. Robert Bacon and James N. Hill as a committee to confer with our company, taking steps to build a line from Pasco along the north shore of the Columbia River to Portland. As this line would furnish access to Portland for both the Northern Pacific and the Great Northern, it has been determined to build the line through an independent company, the bonds of which will be guaranteed by the Northern Pacific and Great Northern and the stock equally divided between the two companies. The Great Northern can turn its business over to the Northern Pacific at Spokane, or they can build from a convenient point west of Spokane down to a connection with the Northern Pacific at or near Ritzville. The main object of having the line owned equally and jointly from Pasco to Portland is to preserve for each company independent rights through that territory, and, while taking possession of the north shore of the Columbia River, avoiding the necessity of any duplication of mileage hereafter."

With the ownership of the Spokane, Portland & Seattle vested in the two powerful and prosperous northern transcontinentals, money and credit were already amply provided. Construction began in 1905, the road was built in the most substantial manner, and the last spike was driven March 11, 1908. Always generously appreciative of the work of others, especially when they, too, had been pioneers, Mr. Hill said, in his address at the celebration, in Portland, of the opening of the North Bank Railroad, "I think you ought not to forget the memory of Henry Villard." The two parent companies now had a line 556 miles long, holding the north bank of the Columbia, and the permanent financing followed. In April of this year the capital stock was increased to $25,000,000. To complete the history of this cap stone to the railroad edifice in the Pacific Northwest, it will be necessary to

255

go forward three years more. In 1911 the capital became $62,500,000, and the two owners entered into a detailed arrangement for the use and security of their joint property. The main points of this covenant were that they would purchase bonds of the Spokane, Portland & Seattle in equal quantity; that they would maintain with it a fair interchange of traffic; and that neither of them would sell its holdings of that company's stock until the mortgage had been satisfied. This extension and completion of facilities answered every expectation. It gave to the northern transcontinentals freedom of action, as well as freedom of access over their own lines to the entire North Pacific Coast. It put them in a strategic position of such strength that any attempt to invade their territory from the south, with a view to breaking down their business, could be met at once by effective retaliation.

It is clear that this rounding out of systems from the Columbia River on the south to the international boundary on the north, and extending to Vancouver, British Columbia, was both necessary geographically, and compulsory from the traffic point of view. It settled questions that had been in doubt and controversy for nearly or quite twenty years. It opened the front door and locked the back door of an important part of the Great Northern's territory. The public at the time took a more sensational view. There was always present to the reportorial eye, "in a fine frenzy rolling," a picture which the next reel of film would project upon the screen, of Mr. Hill and Mr. Harriman, as represented by the Union Pacific on one side and the Great Northern on the other, locked in a death struggle. Nothing of the kind was contemplated by either of them. Nothing of the kind could happen. Both were good strategists, both were out after business, and each intended to have his defences in good order. Current gossip talked of a through line to be built by Mr. Hill to San Francisco, and an equally vigorous attack in the north by the Union Pacific. What was in the mind of Mr. Hill and what was not are both stated plainly enough in a letter that he wrote in May, 1911, to a member of the Morgan firm:

"The Union Pacific started to build to Puget Sound, and, in order to avoid the reduction in revenue, etc., the Northern Pacific proposed a trackage arrangement, on a basis of about $5,000 a mile, to which the Union Pacific objected unless the Great Northern would join in the arrangement and, in that way, reduce the rental. The Great Northern had, years ago, run a survey on lower grade that would cost an amount which, at 4 per cent. per annum, would be but very little, if anything, more than it pays as rental for the joint line. In order to recover business lost to the Union Pacific from Puget Sound, we took steps to secure a part of the Oregon business, which had practically all been controlled by the Union Pacific. The Great Northern secured these

257

properties in the first instance and, in order to avoid any friction, turned over to the Spokane, Portland & Seattle a half interest at cost. Both the Northern Pacific and Great Northern have made what, for the length of the line, is, at least, an unusually heavy investment, in the Spokane, Portland and Seattle, which investment can only be made remunerative by securing for it a heavy tonnage, which its own line does not now and may never enjoy without extensions receiving tonnage which can be brought to its rails. This can only be done by securing a part of the traffic of Oregon and California. To build a railroad to San Francisco would cost, with terminals, not less than sixty million dollars. The Great Northern would not, under any present or probable future conditions, be a party to such an undertaking. The Tillamook line, with streamers to San Francisco, will secure the greater part of whatever advantage the long rail line would give, and can be in operation within two years at a cost of three and a half millions additional. With such a line into San Francisco, the Union Pacific would never have gone to Puget Sound, and, in the future, they would be slow to provoke any strife in common territory."

With the purchase, in 1907, of the Astoria & Columbia River Railroad, which included valuable Astoria waterfront, and with the completion and putting into commission of two modern steamships to ply between this terminus and San Francisco, the provision for the needs of his system in this direction were complete. The Great Northern Pacific Steamship Company was organized in 1914, and two steamers, each bearing the name of one of the two controlling systems, were put into commission the following spring. By their aid the northern systems carried through business to and from San Francisco. They became independent of the southern lines. On that advanced post Mr. Hill was well content to rest; and, after some encounters in debatable land in Oregon, which showed their mettle, all parties were satisfied to remain, for the time at least, in their occupied positions. So far as the Pacific Northwest is concerned, the plans of Mr. Hill were carried out with that completeness and success that distinguished his enterprises everywhere.

Before turning to the consolidation of the many allied companies into one, completing the quest on which he had entered nearly forty years before, mention must be made of some important services and some difficult problems which, as always, were woven during these years into the continuous fabric of his life. It is little worth while to build a house if you cannot furnish or heat it, or carry on the necessary household routine. He had, with a master mind and a master hand, created a mighty transportation machine. But a machine, in order to do work, must be supplied with motive energy sufficient to its task; and it must not be burdened with a labour exceeding its capacity to perform.

The mechanism of the Great Northern was in itself test proof. But the Great Northern was, after all, an organic part of the railroad system of the whole country. It could not escape the common lot. The entire railroad interest of the United States had begun to stagger under repeated bleedings. Neither political leaders nor the people who follow them usually foresee the complete and logical connection between what they propose and its necessary, especially its indirect, consequences. A wrong grins evilly at them, and they aim a smashing blow at its head. They do not stop to consider whether something behind it may not, when properly safeguarded, be indispensable to them. Almost always the recoil is painful. Sometimes it is disastrous.

The fortunes of what is commonly called the "railroad problem" had passed through this sequence. It began with abuses or arbitrary acts by railroads in the early days of steam transportation. These persisted and bred like rabbits. This led to correction by regulation. Regulation implied and established, through laws and courts, the power to fix rates, impose increased taxes and order at will changes in operation. The taxes paid by the Great Northern were $195,001 in 1882, and twenty-five years later were $2,050,923. Wherever the power to tax is beyond control by the tax payer, it will be abused. Add to it the power to make rates and compel expenditures, and the railroads were delivered unprotected into the hands of their enemies. The return on capital put into them lost in volume and in security. What was once a preferred investment, because its possibility of future profits balanced its risks, dropped into disfavour. Men with money could do better elsewhere. Then followed, in natural succession, crippling of resources, refusal to make large new investments, and inability of the railroads as a whole to add to facilities or even to maintain service in proportion to the growth of traffic. Like creeping paralysis, this disease had come upon the country unaware. Individual railroad managers realized their own predicament, but it gave them no disposition to go out and hunt for the troubles of others. The public saw trains running as usual, and went joyously on throwing the harpoon. It had considered little or not at all the situation of the country as a whole, and with what sort of future a continuance of past policies would bring not only the railroads but the people face to face. Here Mr. Hill stepped in to hold the mirror up to facts. His mind, unusual in so many ways, was especially remarkable in this— that its analytic and its synthetic powers were equally keen and vigorous. He had grasped the principle of conservation by study of an enormous mass of almost unconsidered details. By the same process he now envisaged the railroad problem as the country's danger.

As usual, he summed up the situation in one pithy sentence: "You can't bore an inch hole with a half-inch auger." He had been collecting facts, putting them together, tracing their connections, watching the needle of the trade compass. The facts were accessible enough. Helpless armies of them had been enrolled labouriously and scattered through voluminous records of the Interstate Commerce Commission, without anybody's taking the trouble to find out what they meant. Mr. Hill mobilized them and put them on sentry duty. He foresaw a crisis; not for the Great Northern, but for the entire railroad interests of the country, and through that for every man in it down to the poorest day labourer. The political authorities of his own state having long been especially active in railroad baiting, and one bill after another for reduction of rates being pressed at this time, he addressed formally, January 14, 1907, a letter to Governor Johnson, of Minnesota. In print it covers less than eight small pages. But it crystallized thought. It showed, from official federal reports, that in the ten years from 1895 to 1905 the total single track mileage of the country had increased but 21 per cent., locomotives 35 per cent., passenger cars 23 per cent., and freight cars 45 per cent. In the same time the passenger mileage had increased 95 per cent. and the freight ton mileage 118 per cent. These figures talk. They need no comment at all. It was no longer a question of making money, but of transacting the business of the country. "The disparity," said Mr. Hill, "between the growth of traffic and the additions to the railroad mileage and the extension of terminals shown by a new mileage of less than 1½ per cent. a year since 1904, to take care of a traffic increase averaging 11 per cent. a year for ten years past, presents and explains the real problem." He estimated that an immediate addition of not less than 5 per cent. a year for five years ought to be made to the railroad trackage of the country. If this were not done, part of the business offered would suffer vexatious delays, and part could not be carried at all.

This new work would cost five and a half billions of dollars; a yearly average of one billion one hundred million dollars. More tracks, more terminals, more equipment called for more money. More money could be obtained only if it were permitted to earn the profits usually accruing from other forms of investment. Failing this, transportation must slacken and development gradually cease, because the railroads would be physically unable to perform the services required of them. This thought had been maturing in his mind long before he gave it clear-cut, formal expression. In an address before the Merchants' Club of Chicago, November 10, 1906, he had given an emphatic warning. He said then: "There has not been a question since the Civil War of as much consequence as this." The letter to Governor Johnson became the real starting point of that campaign of publicity and that appeal to the business interests and the sense of fairness of the people which all the railroads afterward carried on so generally and effectively. It produced no instantaneous change. Appeals to reason seldom do. It did set people to thinking. It recalled and restated the forgotten identity of interest among all the people of every community. The public could maim or ruin the railroads if it wanted to. But on that line it could win only Pyrrhic victories. Prosperity and growth must accept the precept "live and let live." Almost all discussion of the railroad question in the next ten years either adopted the thought set out in this compact and convincing statement by Mr. Hill, or came back to it at last as to a just arbiter.

As part of any complete system of transportation, and in particular as a relief to overtaxed railway lines and terminals, he took a lively interest in the utilization of waterways. The natural division of traffic, followed in Europe, assigning bulky and cheap commodities, where speed is not important, to the river, lake or canal, was self-evident to him. He believed it both waste and discrimination to spend lavishly on so-called improvements intended as a sop to local greed and a penalty on legitimate enterprise. Deep waterways, favouring the economies that lessen transportation cost permanently, he advocated strongly. The commerce of the Great Lakes proved his point. He made several addresses at different congresses in favour of scientific waterway improvement. "The traffic of the country," he said, "needs, whenever normal conditions prevail, all the assistance that waterways can give." His recommendation was not to discontinue improvements or reduce the sums spent upon them; but to redeem the work from the curse of the "pork barrel," and carry it out along scientific lines. His own recommendations in "Highways of Progress" sum up the whole duty of the Government toward waterway improvement:

"A permanent commission, authorized to expend appropriations in its discretion upon national waterways in the order of their importance.

"A comprehensive plan, including the classification of rivers and canal routes according to relative value, and also including such reservoir and slackwater work as may be required to carry each project to success. This plan in its essentials to be adopted by the commission at the outset and adhered to without interference by Congress or any department.

"Insistence upon the development of trunk lines first, and upon a depth that will make these real carriers of commerce, able to aid the railroads in their task by transporting bulky freight economically and with reasonable expedition.

"A liberal standing appropriation annually for the commission's work until its plan shall have been carried out over the whole country; and a refusal to pledge the nation's credit for a single dollar of this, which is properly *our* work."

In 1907 a financial storm like that of 1903 broke upon the country. Its consequences were the same and it threw similar burdens upon his shoulders. As always in time of money stringency and general distress, pale faces distorted by fear turned first to him. Now that the bolt had fallen, the public came to him to learn what had struck it from the blue. He used this occasion justifiably to read a lecture to those who had maligned his motives and rejected his advice. He spoke his mind freely and, most were willing to admit fairly, in the following interview which appeared in the *New York Herald*: "The whole trouble is that capital has become frightened. There is nothing so timid as money. Look at about one-half the legislation pending in every state. It is all on taxation in different guises. When a man has been successful and accummulated property, there is a disposition to get much, if not most, away from him under forms of law. Investors do not dare to put out their money under such conditions. There is nothing wrong with this country, except what the Indian would call 'ghost dancing.' It is not the wealthiest men that will suffer in consequence of present and threatened disturbances. It is those of moderate means who have been dependent upon their small investments, added perhaps to moderate salaries, to support themselves and families. What is wanted is a spirit of fair play on both sides. When men with money see what all this hostile legislation promises to result in they say, 'I won't put up my money in such securities.' Capital, is, therefore, driven to its hole." This certainty that most of the troubles of the time were the fault of the people did not harden his heart or blunt his concern for the many who must suffer. One of the worst effects of the panic was its interference with the western crop movement. Up to this time and, indeed, until, at a later day, Mr. Hill had created the financial independence of the Northwest as he had created its railroad independence, the farmers of that section were largely at the mercy of the banking interests of the East. The products of the farm could not move from the land to the primary market, to the central markets, to the seaboard, across the ocean, and reach the ultimate consumer without a liberal provision for the journey. Money must be furnished to pay for the services of the army of people employed in the different functions of this great economic office. Local cash and credit were unequal to the demand. Millions were drawn from the East for this purpose. If the supply were cut off, the crop movement would stop. A panic in Wall Street might leave the product of a year's labour and privation to rot upon the soil, while distant thousands were starving because it could not reach them. Mr. Hill had always kept as close watch of the crop movement as of the railroad. He had helped many times, and again he put his powerful shoulder to the wheel.

In financial circles everywhere he was now an authority whose voice could not be disregarded. When the panic came, he wired to New York that money must be advanced to move crops. He wrote with satisfaction to one of his eastern representatives: "We have succeeded in getting the banks of the Twin Cities and Duluth to put up two millions against our ten millions of credit, which we agreed to furnish for ninety days at 7 per cent., to be used in moving the crop on the lines of the Northern Pacific and Great Northern roads. This is already making itself felt in the volume of our traffic, and I feel sure that it will keep our wheels rolling so that we will not greatly suffer by the general depression." During the first week of the stringency, when fright froze local sources of supply, he personally advanced some millions of dollars to keep the crops moving at a time when delay would have been disastrous. It is no exaggeration to say that he carried for a time the weight of Northwestern business interests upon his own shoulders, and saved from utter wreck not only many an industry, but millions of people. The danger and need of the farmers and labouring men roused him like a trumpet call. This was not his first service of the kind, but he determined it should be the last. Before the wheel of disaster could bring around another of those periods of depression that appear to recur in irregular and unpredictable cycles, he had constructed in St. Paul with his own hands, and

268

made strong with a portion of his own fortune, a financial institution which—aided, of course, by the rise and expansion of others inspired by his example—was able to protect the people of the Northwest.

The time was near to which Mr. Hill had looked forward with anticipations of mingled pleasure and regret through many of these later years. In 1907, twenty-five years would have elapsed since he assumed the office of president of the St. Paul, Minneapolis & Manitoba Railroad Company. A quarter of a century packed with such visions and such splendid achievements might well satisfy the most exacting ambition. He had always purposed to relax the bonds of duty and labour, however happily they held him captive, when the fitting time should come. It was practicable to do so now, because he could turn over the headship of this vast product of his brain and hands to the son whom he had trained for fourteen years to take his place. He could step down and not step out. He could be sure that his policies would be adhered to and his purpose fulfilled with a fidelity and determination that accepted the warrant of both duty and affection. He could always be consulted in an emergency. His partial retirement would be the first move in preparing the Great Northern to live on and work on after him, in the ways he had taught it. Of that time and that necessity he often thought and not infrequently spoke. He had not the slightest intention of withdrawing from active life. He had solaced himself in the burden and heat of the day by many a look forward to years of reading, recreation, travel and spontaneous delight in wandering along some of the many avenues where the human spirit loves to go untrammelled. The time had never come, because he could not will it so. He was the captive of his own unconquerable being. In him the man of action was supreme. But he did believe in setting his house in order. This thought escaped in more than one forecast of the future, made about this time, when he was talking to friends in St. Paul and to the veterans of the road. He reminded them that he could not be with them always; told them that there were hands skilled and safe to which he could commit his work; and added that he proposed to leave it a finished and perfected thing. Its growth has been traced step by step. From East to West, at either buttress, and all along the great span between, his railroad system stood strong and secure. A last hammer blow would weld its still separated portions into one homogeneous whole.

The Great Northern property consisted of many distinct corporations. The most important of these had been agencies indispensable in performing economically, swiftly and silently the work that must of necessity be accomplished piecemeal. That work was done. To promote future growth, to faciliate the final financing of a unified railroad interest through half a century to come, which was to be Mr. Hill's completing touch, the consolidation of interest already existing in fact must be made formal. The year 1907 saw all these proprietary companies purchased, assimilated and brought under the organization and the name of the Great Northern. It had originally bought the stock of some, guaranteed the bonds of others, advanced cash to still others and taken stock and bonds as collateral. Dependence and support must now be changed into identity. So the brood of the Great Northern was brought back under its wings. The children of the empire that had been built came to acknowledge one name and one citizenship, as they had long known but one household and one allegiance. At the annual meeting of June 30, 1907, Mr. Hill resigned the office of president, to which his son, L. W. Hill was elected, and himself became Chairman of the Board of Directors. He had finished in essentials, in everything but the working out of some still incomplete details, the work which he conceived in his young manhood. He had been its master spirit since the Dutch bondholders, in 1878, assigned to the associates control of the St. Paul & Pacific; virtually its sole ruler for the twenty-five years of his presidency. The record was now made up. A comparison of the principal items of the official annual report of 1882 with that of 1907* gives a bird's eye view of the efforts of a quarter of a century translated into

* See Appendix IX.

figures. It is the most unfavourable that could be made, because 1907 was the worst standard by which to measure progress. Large rate reductions had just been ordered, there had been a hard winter with heavy snowfall to impede traffic and swell expenses, and the country was in the grip of financial alarm and depression. For example, the percentage of gross earnings required for operating was temporarily raised to 59.05. The year before, under normal conditions, it was but 50.42. It had been 50.08 in 1882. Notwithstanding this inequality in the accompanying conditions, the two reports, set side by side, show an interesting uniformity and picture a surpassing deed. Everything had been multiplied by six, seven, eight, nine, ten. Tremendous increase for only twenty-five years. More impressive yet, because they reflect the influence of this growth upon the country, are some later figures of the federal census. The seven states in which the Great Northern operated most largely constitute what Mr. Hill first called "the zone of plenty." In the ten years ending in 1900 they increased their population 50 per cent., as compared with 20.9 per cent. for the United States. In the same period the average value of their farm land rose 188 per cent., and the total value of farm land and buildings 220 per cent.

In this development, stretching back to the days when Minnesota had only a few thousand people and those of the farther West were not worth enumerating at all, one may say soberly that history will conclude the Great Northern Railroad to have been the main contributing factor, and the creator of the Great Northern its inspiring genius. The world passed judgment upon it in wonder, admiration, and tribute of unstinted praise. In all that was written or spoken in appreciation of Mr. Hill and recognition of his services, there is a note of growing intensity and sincerity through the years.

CHAPTER THIRTY-FOUR

THE END OF THE GREAT ADVENTURE

MR. HILL had laid down unostentatiously a title and office which were almost part of himself. He had prepared everything for this step. He meant that there should be for him no wavering or return. But he neither desired nor intended to lessen his interest or to withdraw his counsel from the conduct of the property. The change from the Presidency to the Chairmanship of the Board of Directors meant that he himself need no longer make a daily study of the mass of detail inseparable from the conduct of an enormous system such as this had grown to be. He would always watch the weather gauge and, should grave difficulty and doubt arise, his, while he lived, would be the deciding thought. But he would be relieved of the routine of officialdom. He could give himself more unstintedly to other things. He intended that from this time should date an even larger and fuller response to the public questions that he loved to study and the public needs that he desired to serve. Nothing turned him from that purpose. There were, however, matters little and big that still chained him at times to his old desk as a railroad man. Such of them as fell within the period from

1907 to 1912 will be included in this chapter. Material development would no longer, to any great extent, take the form of spying out new lands and conquering alien territory. The pioneer period was over. Some collisions with other interests in central Oregon were partly the fading echo of an old controversy, partly the building of defences against attack, and partly an occupation of desirable and profitable country. The purchase of the Colorado & Southern, late in 1908, gave to the Great Northern a large additional mileage, with access to tidewater on the Gulf of Mexico. Through passenger service from Chicago to the Pacific Coast over the Great Northern began in May, 1909. Through trains on the Spokane, Portland & Seattle had been run to Portland the year previous. Physically speaking, there was little to be done for the Great Northern except to extend and improve track, equipment, and operation in proportion to the growth of the country. This had now become a task onerous enough to tax ability of the first order.

Through these years also litigation wound its troubling way. Some of it was an aftermath of the Northern Securities agitation; some, the device of leaders who saw political advantage in perpetuating strife, and of followers who either sincerely believed that they were unfairly treated or desired to use to their advantage the power that state control of railroads put into their hands. Few persons outside the Minnesota storm centre realized how trying were the continual and sometimes vicious attacks by local authority. The multitudinous details of legislative and court procedure need not be related here. A bare sketch of what happened will give some notion of the annoyance, and the interference with or burdens upon business, of the various legislative changes in freight rates at this time. No longer before than 1902 the railroad company had reduced rates on all classes of merchandise between stations in Minnesota, North Dakota, and South Dakota an average of 15 per cent. Rates on grain and grain products from the same states to eastern terminals were reduced 10 per cent. Rates on grain and its products, potatoes, onions, and hay from stations in the State of Washington to Puget Sound were reduced 10 per cent. All these concessions were voluntary. Referring to them, Mr. Hill's report for that year said: "It is the policy of the company to reduce freight rates as rapidly as the volume of traffic and earnings will justify." That had been the unbroken theory and practice of his management of the Great Northern. It now found itself brought under the scourge of compulsory sacrifice. The Railroad and Warehouse Commission of Minnesota had made an order, December 14, 1906, reducing rates on the carriage, within Minnesota, of a large number of commodities. A preliminary restraining order against the enforcement of these rates was obtained. While this order was in force the legislature, in April, 1907, passed two acts greatly reducing freight and passenger rates. Coupled with the reduction was a system of fines and penalties exhibiting the most savage hostility that had yet been shown to the interests of the railroads and, one might almost say, to their very existence. Certain stockholders of the Great Northern brought suit in the United States Circuit Court to obtain an order restraining the company from putting the new commodity rates into effect. This was obtained; but the other rates went into operation, while the questions at issue passed through the usual legal stages up to the Supreme Court of the United States. For the sake of clearness, even at the cost of a slight repetition, a summary of these suits, in which the position of the company and the results finally reached in all of them are briefly and clearly stated, is presented here from the official records of the Great Northern Company:

In these suits the main propositions asserted on behalf of the company were, *first*, that it was entitled to earn a fair return on the value of all property devoted to railroad use; *second*, that the cost of reproduction was the minimum value of its property for rate purposes; *third*, that the value of its property, thus ascertained, was largely in excess of its outstanding stock and bonds; *fourth*, that the Minnesota rates were a necessary interference with the company's interstate rates and, therefore, were unlawful; *fifth*, that the Minnesota rates, when applied to intrastate business alone, did not produce a reasonable return on the value of the company's property situated in Minnesota and apportioned to Minnesota business and, therefore, were unlawful. Upon the completion of the testimony, the Master-in-Chancery filed his report, finding in favour of the company upon each of these several propositions. His report established the value of all the company's property at

277

$457,121,469, the value of its property in Minnesota at $138,425,291, and held that the Company was entitled to a return of 7 per cent. per annum upon these valuations.

On June 9, 1913, the Supreme Court of the United States decided the so-called "Minnesota Rate Cases." The state of Minnesota had fixed a maximum passenger rate of two cents per mile between local stations, effective May 1, 1907. This was complied with. It prescribed a schedule of maximum freight rates on grain, coal, lumber, live stock, and other commodities, effective June 1, 1907. Charging confiscation and an interference with interstate commerce, certain stockholders of the company, in a suit in the Circuit Court of the United States, obtained a temporary injunction against all these state-made rates. In April, 1911, the Circuit Court, in a decision on the merits, made this injunction permanent. Accordingly, on July 1, 1911, the former higher rates were restored. The decision of the Supreme Court, reversing the Circuit Court, holds that the complainants failed to prove the state-made rates confiscatory or a direct interference with interstate commerce. Therefore, they were put into effect as of July 21, 1913, and the Company must refund the difference between amounts actually collected and amounts which would have been collected under the state-made rates. Refunds cover the period from July 1, 1911, to July 21, 1913, in all cases mentioned excepting commodity rates. These never were put into effect, and, as to them, refunds date from June 1, 1907.

A controversy such as this was no slight matter to Mr. Hill. As he had identified the interests of the railroad with his own when it was a question of profits to be distributed, so had he in the days of the Northern Securities and so did he now, when it was a question of losses and, as he firmly believed, injustice to be borne, consider the two as one. He studied the law and the facts, went over arguments as if his all were at stake, and resented every infringement of the company's rights as he would an assault upon his own. No one who did not see and hear him during the years when these battles were fought out could realize how intense was their personal effect upon him; not merely as one intrusted with the management of a railroad, not at all as an investor—for he had all that he wanted—but as a trustee for his stockholders, as a claimant for justice, as a citizen and as a man. He felt keenly an attitude inspired to some extent by political virulence. For a time at least he was partially alienated in sympathy from the community where he had lived so long and served so well. In 1906 he had purchased the residence, No. 8 East 65th Street, in New York City. Business drew him there oftener and for longer periods than formerly, and the arrangement served both comfort and convenience. For some time, in fact, he had serious thought of settling in New York permanently. That some of his children resided there was a powerful magnet. Old ties, however, were too strong. These and the pull of home affection, always so controlling with him, held him to the scene of his first triumphs and to the friends of early days whose ranks were thinning now so rapidly. After all that might be said or done, Minnesota and St. Paul had a place in his heart from which things that he resented for a time as ingratitude or injustice could not oust them. After the settlement of these cases, agitation died down. Every legislative session, of course, bore its crop of anti-railroad projects. But the plight of the railroads of the country could not be denied. The facts that Mr. Hill had stated in 1906 and 1907 had now become threatening forces. Excessive regulation and the flat conflict between state and federal authority, issuing in the absurdity that the latter could order a rate between points in adjoining states less or greater than the sum of the two local rates prescribed by the authorities of those states, had their effect. The local problem was absorbed in the national problem. Mr. Hill had long foreseen that federal regulation finally must reign supreme. This belief, his conviction that government ownership would be the beginning of "the end of this country as a free and democratic government," and his repeated demand for justice and fair play are the essential elements of his public utterances and his almost impassioned faith as a master of transportation during these years of strife.

He came now to his concluding act in the financing of the Great Northern. A wonderfully able and clairvoyant fiscal manager he had been from the day of the first bond issue to cover the cost of the St. Paul & Pacific. The same quality that guarded the cradle of the infant served to sustain and assure the future of its lusty manhood. As he had provided for the physical perfection of his system, as he had built up the completest and most skilled railroad organization in the country, as he had trained his son to stand at the head of it, so, with that same long look ahead, he arranged that its treasury should not suffer want for half a century to come. He conceived the plan of a first refunding mortgage for the Great Northern, under which a total issue of $600,000,000 of bonds would be authorized. In May, 1911, he made the following statement about it: "The size of the mortgage is explained by the fact that the outstanding obligations of the Company which are to be refunded amount approximately to $330,000,000. Included, however, in the figures last named is the direct and contingent obligation of the Company on Burlington joint 4's maturing in 1921 and aggregating $222,420,000. Covering a future of 50 years, approximately $270,000,000 in bonds, therefore, will be available for general corporate purposes, double tracking, and additional mileage. Since its beginning thirty-two years ago the Great Northern has expended between $350,000,000 and $400,000,000 out of capital and earnings. The provision made for the future, in consideration of the rapidly growing territory which Great Northern lines serve, would seem intelligently conservative. In no other part of the country has nature more generously bestowed those three great sources of all national wealth—the farm, the forest, and the mine—and nowhere else is there more room for such development as follows the occupation of a new country by an intelligent population."

The official ratification by the company of this issue of bonds, which were to bear interest at not to exceed 5 per cent., gives the following schedule and explanation: $45,000,000 to be issued at once; $30,000,000 as called for, both for corporate purposes; $332,162,000 reserved for retiring and refunding old bonds outstanding; $100,000,000 for general purposes, but not more than $3,000,000 for each calendar year beginning January 1, 1911; $92,838,000 for purchase of bonds or capital stock, or voting trust certificates of other companies, when these constitute a majority of the whole or when a majority of the whole has been pledged. All these issues, except that for refunding, were to be employed in the building of other lines or the acquisition of other properties, as from time to time might appear necessary or desirable. Mr. Hill explained the advantage of this massing of credit, which has since been adopted by many other systems, in these words: "It creates a financial clearing house through which its several outstanding securities may be converted into one of standard form and value; and it forms in addition a reservoir of authorized credit so carefully guarded by the conditions of the mortgage that it cannot be abused or dissipated, yet so ample that it will supply all needs for probably fifty years to come. No private estate in this country is more carefully provided against the future than is the property of the Great Northern Railway Company." The policy of using part of the surplus funds of the company to improve the property had been continued. The report of 1913 mentioned the fact that "there has been invested in the company's property more than $76,000,000 which might have been distributed to the stockholders, of which the public receives the benefit without making any compensation, and on which the company, therefore, receives no return." An increase in capital stock of $21,000,000 in 1912 and another of $19,000,000 in 1914 raised the total capital of the company to $250,000,000. Thus was written under Mr. Hill's guidance the final chapter in the financial history of the company that he organized so modestly in the year 1879.

His overflowing energy, stimulated and drawn upon by his keen concern in everything that touched the general welfare, spread to many subjects. It found congenial occupation in a series of remarkable addresses. For years he had been in demand at conventions and other gatherings where topics of general public interest were to be discussed. His clear thought, his plain and forceful speech, the ring of sincerity in his voice, and that terrific man-power which he put into everything he touched—all carried weight. His addresses on conservation had added a new title to his fame. Everybody wanted to hear him. The highest authorities sought his advice. The most serious causes asked the support of his approval and his name. He selected from the many invitations which reached him daily, those con-

THE LIFE OF JAMES J. HILL

nected with interests which he thought could be served by his knowledge and suggestions, and with occasions where his presence might contribute to practical results. Requests not meeting these requirements, above all those open to suspicion of catering to display, were unconditionally declined. Between 1907 and 1912, in addition to literally hundreds of talks to farmers, and casual public speeches reported in the newspapers, he made twenty-one addresses of such importance and dignity that they were afterward printed by request in pamphlet form. Copies of these were asked for from all parts of the country and from abroad in almost every mail. A supply of them had to be kept on hand to fill the demand. To put all this matter into a form more compact and more accessible to the reader, he consented to condense and connect them in ordered sequence in a single volume. His book, "Highways of Progress," published in 1910, contained the substance of all his printed addresses, along with new matter. In his preface he stated the essence of his thought and purpose: "There is great need of a broader understanding of the relation of one interest to another in the social life of man; of their interdependence as well as their separate values; of the community as an economic whole. The physical sciences have added to knowledge by applying the particular fact to the general law as explanation or corrective, and the general law to the particular fact for purposes of classification and new generalization. By this same combination of the abstract and the concrete, the general and the particular, they have thrown new light on the material world and its laws within a century. It seems to be time to apply their method to economic facts and changes. The present volume is, within the limits set by its range of subjects, an effort in that direction."

The subjects treated were Agriculture, Commerce, Combination, Irrigation, Conservation, Northwestern Development, Oriental Trade, Waterways, and Railroads. The economic gospel of Mr. Hill was that of the school in which his generation had been born and bred. He was an individualist. He subscribed to the immutable old democratic doctrine of the largest liberty for every man that is consistent with the same right for every other man. He had little faith in legislative panaceas. He believed that the State should not undertake anything that could be carried through by private initiative and effort. He did not permit these views to narrow his horizon. Big things ought, in his opinion, to be done. But this would not necessitate a paternalistic order. He had done a big thing himself. Neither state nor federal government had been called on for help. Compared with the creative and constructive effort of his own life, the handling of problems like forestry or river improvement or any one of the thousand less justifiable undertakings into which the modern state plunges, might seem a fairly simple thing.

He saw national prosperity as the product of universal industry—applied first of all to the land—of thrift, honesty, freedom, and fair dealing among men. Beyond that he found little reason to go. While his life and the acts of public and private beneficence that no man can number showed him generous without stint, while his broad sympathies responded instantly to the touch of human distress, he dissociated the world of feeling from the world of law. He disliked and distrusted projects of reform involving large and continuous expenditures of money that would have to be collected from the present generation by burdensome taxation, or saddled on its children by borrowing. He took the sane middle ground between extremists of the *laissez-faire* school and extremists of the socialistic type. His work was done with sustained literary repression; with the single purpose of making the thought clear and using the right word to hammer it home. The result is lucidity and explicitness. What he wrote he wrote well. His business letters, as scores of extracts printed in these volumes bear witness, even when written under the stress of feeling and *currente calamo*, are marvellously well phrased and to the point. Few men have been able to attract so large an audience. The public, in his case, felt less the common curiosity to see or listen to a great man than a desire to enjoy what he had to say and the way in which he said it. By its economic correctness and finality, by its substance and texture, "Highways of Progress" has title to place as a source-book to-day. Since Mr. Hill was seldom mistaken about the future, and since his economic principles run down to the bed rock of human nature, physical law and a supreme moral order in the universe, they are not likely to be overturned.

One subject often in his mind and on his lips deserves especial mention. He was an enthusiastic advocate of reciprocity between the United States and Canada. His connection with one by birth and with the other by allegiance, and the management of a railroad system that zigzagged back and forth across the international boundary for some thousands of miles, made any other doctrine unthinkable. Believing in the general theory of free trade, he thought it sheer stupidity to build a wall between these two growing communities of North America. As a plain business proposition, he could not brook the folly of obstructing commercial intercourse with a country not only a neighbour and economically in circumstances like our own, but also one of our best customers. Even when the reciprocity idea was unpopular, he proclaimed it boldly. In 1906 he urged that policy before the Merchants' Club of Chicago. Two years later he pleaded for it, as a step toward free trade between the two countries, before the Chamber of Commerce of the state of New York. He gave the same message in Winnipeg, in 1909, when the Canadian Club entertained him and Lord Strathcona. He repeated and enlarged upon it at the Canadian banquet in New York City in 1910. Probably no single cause contributed so much as did his efforts to its final acceptance by the United States and the passage of a reciprocity act during the administration of President Taft. By an ironic turn of events it was Canada that now refused to grace the wedding feast. Mr. Hill never ceased to believe that both countries would come to their senses, and that eventually trade would be as free between Manitoba and Minnesota as between Wisconsin and Michigan. He had a deep consciousness of fraternity between the United States, Canada, and Great Britain. His fealty to the English-speaking strain, wherever found, was vital and unchanging. The Dominion Government gave a banquet, June 13, 1913, to delegates attending the annual convention of the Bankers' Association at Ottawa. Mr. Hill said: "The people of the two countries, close kin by blood, inheritors of a common tradition and charged with a like mission in the world, should not misunderstand each other. There is no proper place for jealousy or hostility between them. Though we live each under his own flag, it is fitting that, in the unknown procession of human events, two countries that now dominate the interests and the progress of this continent should be the leaders of the New World in everything that stands for the prosperity and the peace of mankind." In connection with the celebration of the centenary of

288

the conclusion of peace between the United States and Great Britain, he said: "Whatever may be the fate of the general movement among the nations in favour of peace, those whose mother tongue is English will never again take up arms against one another." Most cordially was his feeling reciprocated. Canadians could scarcely have been prouder of him if the tie of citizenship had been added to that of birth. Perhaps as striking as any of the tributes paid to him in his native country was that given in 1905 by a man whose judgment certainly was not warped by partiality—Sir Thomas Shaugnessy: "James J. Hill and I may differ in some railroad matters owing to our diverse interests, but I entertain the highest regard for him as a man. He is the genius of the Northwest country, and I am confident that one hundred years from to-night his work will be much better understood in its far-reaching results than it is at present."

Nowhere was he held in higher esteem than on the North Pacific Coast. He was, in a peculiar sense, the founder of the fortunes of the state of Washington. His railroad had transformed the plucky little town of Seattle into a metropolis. His hand had multiplied transcontinental connections in that fortunate land. With the magic wand of a low rate on lumber he had lifted from its low estate what became a lordly industry. On the trade that he opened with the Orient, the Pacific Coast built great hopes. Popular admiration was universal and genuine. Even anti-railroad agitation could not embitter the kindliness that his name evoked from Bellingham Bay to San Francisco. When the Alaska-Yukon-Pacific Exposition was opened at Seattle, he was selected as the orator of the day. He lifted the occasion to a higher level than the glorification of a country growing rich out of the profusion and possibilities within it. He drew a moral from the display of a world's industry, and stamped upon it and its accessories a high thought. He said: "There are four great words that should be written upon the four cornerstones of every public building in this country with the sacredness of a religious rite. These watchwords of the republic are Equality, Simplicity, Economy, and Justice." From these he would have all men and communities begin anew. The people of Seattle desired a more permanent memorial of the great man of their affection and honour than the ceremony of a day. In February, 1909, Mr. Finn Frolich was commissioned to prepare a bust from which should be made a statue of Mr. Hill, to be cast in bronze. This was to be placed in the Exposition grounds, and afterward removed to the campus of the Washington State University. The bust was unveiled in August of the same year. It rests upon a granite base containing blocks from Japan, Canada, Minnesota, and Washington. These far four corners of the earth unite to form a pedestal of honour. Eminent men of many countries sent messages of congratulation. Long before this Mr. Hill had become, in the largest and finest sense, a citizen of the world. His fame was international. His services were cosmopolitan. This event was only part of the official confirmation of his title.

In 1910 the academic world set the seal of its approval upon the public judgment and the patent fact. In view of the great achievements of his life, his studies along economic lines and his contributions to social and ethical progress, the annual list of honorary degrees of Yale University that year contained the name of James J. Hill, as one of those on whom that ancient institution conferred the degree of Doctor of Law. Distinction from this seat of learning was naturally gratifying to him. He drew pleasure not from the empty title, which he never used, but from recognition of his work by centres of the highest culture, as well as by farmers and fellow citizens in the Northwest. In announcing the degree, Professor Perrin, of Yale, said: "Mr. Hill is the last of the generations of wilderness conquerers, the men who interpreted the constitution, fixed our foreign relations, framed the Monroe Doctrine, and blazed all the great trails which determined the nation's future. He has always been an original investigator, and we know him now as a man of infinite information. Every item of his colossal success rests upon series of facts ascertained by him before they had been noted by others, and upon the future relations which he saw in

291

those facts to human needs and national growth. He believes that no society can prosper in which intellectual training is not based upon moral and religious culture. He is a national economist on broad ethical and religious lines; but the greatest things in all his greatness are his belief in the spiritual significance of man and his longing for the perpetuation of American institutions at their highest and best."

His own thought Mr. Hill put into a short but feeling address at the Yale Alumni dinner. He had been introduced in these words: "The next speaker is Yale's youngest son. It is not his first connection with Yale. He has had two sons who took their degrees a number of years ago, and he has had three daughters that married Yale men. It may be said of James J. Hill that two of his family were born with Yale degrees, three of them have achieved Yale degrees, and one, the last and best, has had a Yale degree thrust upon him." This was his response: "Gentlemen of the Alumni of Yale: I think it is most fitting that I should express my gratitude for the honour conferred upon me to-day, and I assure you that I esteem it a very high honour if I have been able to do anything that would stand the test of what Yale has so often stood for. It gives me great pleasure to be able to say in simple words a few of the thoughts that have always helped me in my journey through life. I have never found where a lie would take the place of the truth. In nearly fifty years of rather active business experience I have never found a transaction that was worth following when it led under the shadows of a deception of any kind. So far I have tried to keep my hands clean, and I hope at my age that I am too old to learn new tricks.

"Education, in the ordinarily accepted sense of the term, we may say, means the trained mind, or the training of the mind. The mind can be trained in the university, or it can be trained in the other school of experience and discipline, in the world. There is no single asset in the possession of a nation of greater value than the trained mind; and in looking over the history of our country I am often struck with the great, over-powering value of the trained mind of Chief Justice John Marshall, who laid the foundation of our government. An incoherent paper, the Constitution, hardly understood, came to him to get an interpretation, not for the present but for the future, of its meaning and how it might be adapted to the future life of the nation. He approached the subject with great learning, and an evenly balanced mind determined to do exact justice. He said: 'That this body can never usurp authority is most true.' These are great words. While the fathers laid the foundations, he built the structure and he made it firm. The court that succeeds him depending on his courage, depending on his great wisdom, the future of this great nation will give him more honour than it does to any other single element in its creation. For behind

293

the wisdom of the Supreme Court of the United States, free government in this country will make its final stand." Many other institutions delighted to do him honour. The same degree was given to him in 1914 by Macalaster College, of St. Paul. His absence from the city at each of the three preceding Commencements had prevented until then his acceptance of an offered recognition by a home institution. Had he lived until the summer of 1916, Dartmouth, whose invitation to Commencement he had already accepted, would also have made him a Doctor of Laws. In one known instance he refused the offer by a university of a place on its honour list because he had given it large financial assistance. He could not tolerate the possibility of a suspected connection between the two in any small or envious mind. Under this rule, scores of institutions of learning were not eligible to confer the honours they would have been glad and proud to bestow upon him.

He was intensely interested in the subject of monetary reform that filled so large a place in the public mind during these years. He had fought delusion and dishonesty in currency legislation, tooth and nail, all his life. Now that a prospect appeared of some scientific reorganization of the currency and credit system of the United States, he entered the lists with as much vigour and determination as if it were a personal matter. He studied the Aldrich plan thoroughly. He objected to

294

it because it opened the way to a possible political control. After it had been sidetracked, he prepared by request a tentative but comprehensive plan of his own. It was drawn on sound principles and scientific lines. It divided the country into districts whose central banks should be conducted by men selected by all the banks of the district; but the votes were to be cast not in the ratio of capital stock, but by a system of proportional representation, so that a few large banks could never capture control. One of its best features, which nobody dared to reproduce, was the substitution of reserve notes for the greenbacks; so that this smouldering fire-brand might never again threaten a conflagration when blown upon by the breath of commercial disaster and public illusion. When the federal reserve system in its present form was adopted, though in several important respects he disapproved it, he threw the whole weight of his influence to make it a success. This was characteristic. When he fought, he put every ounce of his strength into the blow. When the fight was over, he did not sulk. He began instantly to make the best of things and to shape, with such instruments as remained, the public conduct to the public good. Exasperated equally, about this time, by the reckless extravagance and display of the big cities and their copyists, and by the persistent wail over high prices, he coined an epigram which passed from mouth to mouth everywhere and brought home unwelcome truth to unwilling minds: "The trouble with the country just now is not the high cost of living, but the cost of high living."

With the close of the Great Northern's fiscal year, 1912, five years had passed since Mr. Hill transferred its presidency to his son. During those five years, while he was Chairman of the Board of Directors, he had watched every movement and read all the signs of fair weather or foul. The experiment had been successful. The wheels moved smoothly, the property grew and prospered. Now he was ready to withdraw still further. This was part of a policy of self-denial. He was not one of those who can endure idleness, or lay down without a pang the sceptre of their power. His resignation of the chairmanship, the close of his active official participation in the conduct of the company, was an act of renunciation. Like so many of his decisions, it was inspired by a prudent care for the future. Some time, in the nature of things, entire direction of the property must pass on to others. He did not wish the transition to bring with it any shock of unpreparedness. In the letter that he addressed on his retirement to the stockholders of the system, a paper full of deep feeling and a classic of its kind, he stated his reason: "The property whose fortunes I have directed for so many years has become an organic growth. Its future will be shaped more by the forces that govern the development of the natural resources of the country than by individual initiative. The present is a favourable time for making the change. It seems wise to begin the process of adjustment to other hands at this time, when all the outlook is fair and every change may be weighed with deliberation in the light of what is for the best interest of the property. My natural regret in relaxing the closeness of a relation covering the lifetime of a generation and closely interwoven with my own is relieved by the knowledge that the property remains in competent and able hands, and is so well fortified against possible mischance that its future must be as stable as its past."

With strong, nervous touches he sketched in review the outline of his work for more than thirty years. The dramatic interest of his brief recital does not lack an underlying pathos. "A record of events still near and vivid in my memory will serve as a note of cheer and a word of farewell." The germ of his railway scheme, the purchase of the St. Paul & Pacific, the building and financing of the system, the westward push to the Pacific, the addition of the Burlington, the plan of the Northern Securities, and all the development that had raised an empire from a wilderness, are the milestones by which he marked his passage. Every page records an era. Every paragraph builds a monument. Plainly, as one would relate the incidents of an ordinary journey or the course of a simple business transaction, he recapitulated what had seemed to his contemporaries the

almost miraculous happenings of their time. All
men agree that in the world of transportation no mightier spirit ever stormed its way across a continent or
caught and held the attention of a world. To his
finished labour he had put the final touch. "The Great
Northern is now wrought so firmly into the economic
as well as the corporate body of the land as to have fitted
itself permanently into the natural frame of things. So
far as any creation of human effort can be made, it will
be proof against the attacks of time."

He had no thought of what is usually called "retiring
from business." He did not intend to withdraw himself
wholly from the Great Northern. He could not have
done so had he wished. "Not lightly," he said, "may
the relation between a man and the work in which he
has had a vital part be set aside." Nor was it to be so.
To the last moment of his life he retained all his interest, and felt all the old affection for this child of his
heart and brain and hands. Such respite as this change
might bring to him was to be devoted to other and different purposes, already present to his mind. What he
did and what he planned in the next four years forecast
the varied, busy, happy, useful life he saw stretching
before him. Yet this parting from the past, though his
hand still felt the touch of its fleeing garment, though his
eye saw other light ahead, could not take place without a wrench. This letter is a farewell to more things
than one. Mr. Hill had always lived intensely; but

lived in the present and the future. Now, with a backward look he said, making use of a phrase that will always cling close to the story of the man: "Most men who have really lived have had, in some shape, their great adventure. This railway is mine." How near he was to that other going forth, what the poet in anticipation called "my adventure strange and new," no one dreamed. It seems almost as if some subtle premonition had unconsciously charged his words with deeper meaning. But, whatever lay before, it was at the end of a more wonderful career, more sturdy battles and more glorious victories than it has been given to many men to know, that he now lowered the shield and hung the sword upon the wall.

CHAPTER   THIRTY-FIVE

LIFE'S CLOSE

MR. HILL'S formal retirement from official connection
with the railway company, like his resignation of its
presidency five years before, was a signal for larger and
livelier interest in other fields. When one considers
the scope and volume of the contributions that he had
already made to public questions, and the direction he
had given to public movements, this seems hardly
possible. Nevertheless, it is true. The last four years
of his life were abundantly fruitful. His mind and his
interest went on expanding until his latest breath.
They moved in steady progression through the world
of service. The plans that he carried out and
those that he was maturing between 1912 and 1916
express this broadening of sympathy, deepening of
understanding, and untiring generosity of purpose. At
the age of seventy-five he was a more dominant figure
in the world than ever before. What he did and what he
planned in the short period that remained before the wheel
was broken at the cistern would entitle him to grateful
remembrance by his fellow men. The affection which he
had always felt for St. Paul, the scene of so many struggles and triumphs, blurred though it had been for a little
300

time by misunderstanding of his railroad policies, re-gained its force. That city was to be either directly or indirectly a beneficiary of many generous and far-sighted plans. Three or four conceptions, wholly or partly consummated in this short period—the gift of a reference library, the building up of great financial institutions, the construction of an immense modern office building as headquarters for these and for the railroad systems with which he was allied, and his share in securing a new packing plant at South St. Paul which would make this the central stock market for the whole Northwest—are an earnest of what he meant to do.

The first of these was the fulfilment of an idea long germinating in his mind. His interest in books and libraries had grown with his growth. He knew their value as a factor in the carrying on of his educational work. It will be remembered that, in 1893, he had proposed to do away with a public celebration of the completion of his transcontinental line, and turn over the money raised for that purpose, with a gift of double the amount from himself, for the building of a public library in St. Paul. In the years that followed, especially while he was preparing and publishing economic studies on a variety of subjects, his recognition of this public need became more specialized. Books in collections for general use, when he was a young man, were mostly serious, and selected for instruction rather than amusement. He had seen all public libraries popularized, in the modern

301

sense of that word. He did not deny that the flood of juvenile, romantic, and other ephemeral publications might serve some worthy ends; but he made up his mind to construct a treasury of a different order. He had learned by personal disappointments the comparative poverty of resources of the reference departments of most public libraries. Again and again he had sought for historic relations, original authorities, and works whose value time could not impair, and had been obliged to resort to the great book collections of other cities. Not even there could he always unearth the rare and costly source books that he needed. He felt that in the average public library the average reader is well taken care of. The advanced student, the original thinker, the man engaged in investigation and research, the serious author, were relatively unprovided with proper tools. He could carry out his old idea with satisfaction to himself and benefit to the public by remedying this deficiency. He decided to endow St. Paul with a public reference library of a unique or, at least in this country, an unusual kind.

March 5, 1912, Mr. Hill announced his intention to erect and maintain a public reference library on property bounded by Third, Fourth, and Market streets in St. Paul. The site had been designated twenty years before by a library board, many of whom were Mr. Hill's friends and associates, as the most eligible in the city for library purposes. The block of which it is a part faces on one

302

side a public park, and on the other overlooks the valley of the Mississippi and the bluffs beyond. His proposition spurred on the city library board and other authorities to buy the remainder of it, complete their plans, and co-ordinate them with his own. It was most fortunate that a beginning was made at this time; for on April 27, 1915, the old library building and its contents, including the reference department, were destroyed by fire. He said that he was prepared to put three quarters of a million dollars into the project, and possibly more if necessary. The building for his collection and that for the city library constitute one architectural whole. Built of Tennessee marble, on lines of severe and classic beauty, it satisfies the aesthetic sense. A solid wall in the interior makes the Hill Reference Library a distinct institution. In both por-tions Mr. Electus D. Litchfield, a son of his old friend, W. B. Litchfield, and an architect of reputation, displayed high professional ability and a pure and accurate taste. The Hill Reference Library interior is Roman in architectural style, with the spirit of the Italian Renaissance. Great fluted pillars stretch in superimposed colonnades from end to end of the build-ing and rise, separated only by a plain entablature from those above them, to the roof. Pillars and interior wall surfaces are of Kettle River sandstone, whose perma-nent tint is that of some old marble temple warmed by the sunset glow. With a tempered light falling from the skylight and the great window at the end, the effect is that of a bit of classic architecture transported on the magic carpet of the imagination to newest America. There are separate study rooms for patrons. Mr. Hill did not expect or desire that the building should become a common resort or the collection be used in a general reading room. With the definite idea of providing for the mature and original mind and the scholarly taste, he had lists of books prepared for his future collection. He excluded law and medicine as already provided for in professional libraries. He banished juvenile books and fiction, except so far as the latter might be illustrative of permanent literature and literary history. He directed the enrolment of every work in other departments that had contributed something material and enduring to human thought, human knowledge, or human progress, and the exclusion of everything else. All fields of learning were to be represented by their greatest thinkers and discoverers. He especially desired that philosophy and religion at one end of the scale, and modern scientific accomplishment at the other, should be fully represented. He displayed, in accepting or rejecting titles, extraordinary familiarity with past and present literature. He intended that this collection should always be kept relatively small. Books that deteriorated in value because they were impaired or superseded by the progress of thought, discovery, or invention were to be weeded out. This library was destined for the *élite* among books. The working out of the plan in its entirety was one of the delights of his last years. Man could not leave a statelier monument than this exquisite building, the embodiment of a high and noble thought, which will recall him daily through all the years to come to the people of St. Paul, and to the pilgrims of learning who come there to refresh their enthusiasm and establish their faith.

The library building would distinguish St. Paul as a centre of learning and art. To the year 1912 belongs an event that would distinguish it equally as a business centre. Mr. Hill now proceeded to put into execution his matured plan for building there a great banking institution which should assure the permanent financial independence of the country in which he was so greatly interested. This story has dwelt several times upon the feudal dependence of the Northwest upon eastern sources of capital and credit. When crops had to be moved, when new interests or expansions of old ones were to be financed, money must be obtained and paper discounted in New York. In periods of depression, Mr. Hill frequently had to employ his personal influence and come forward with his personal fortune, to avert disaster. In his later years the situation had become especially irksome. The Northwest had outgrown swaddling clothes. It had to rely more than ever on its own banks. It received little help from the Government, whose surplus funds were placed there only in driblets. Mr. Hill decided to make it sufficient unto itself. The conduct of his railroad enterprises through nearly thirty years had familiarized him with every department of finance. He knew all its intricacies and understood its opportunities. Exactly as he built his railroads to develop territory and help the people, as well as to make profits for his fellow stockholders and himself, so he now set about erecting a financial institution in St. Paul that would employ profitably a part of his great fortune, help and be helped by his railroad interests, and emancipate the Northwest from a subservience which was at all times costly, and had threatened more than once to be ruinous.

He had ample personal experience in banking. He had been a director of the First National of New York, and of the Chase National, for many years. His counsel and its connection with his business interests had done much to build the latter up from a small institution to its high estate. He was also a director of the First National of Chicago, and of the Illinois Trust and Savings Company. He had been a shareholder of the First National of St. Paul since January 21, 1880, and a director since May 12 of the same year. One who looks back over his correspondence and remembers his flatly stated position, that a man had no business on a directorate unless he actually directed, and his refusal to admit men to the board of the Great Northern who would not familiarize themselves with its affairs, can understand that his connection with these financial institutions, which he had severed only when and where it was necessary in order to comply with the legal prohibition of interlocking directorates, had made him almost as familiar with banking as with railroading. Also, to a man who had financed the Dutch bond purchase, the St. Paul, Minneapolis & Manitoba, and the Great Northern, through all their changes of fortune and all the squalls of tempestuous times, the conduct of any bank could not seem a difficult undertaking. He had, as stated, been a director of the First National of St. Paul for thirty-two years; since the year after he organized his railroad company. He had at one time accepted a position as director of the Merchants' National Bank of that city, to help reorganize and build it up. By this time both the general theory and practice of banking and the financial conditions and requirements of the Northwest were familiar to him. He had them at his finger's ends when, in 1912, he made up his mind to do what he could to underwrite the financing of the Northwest.

He felt that the starting point of this enterprise should be a banking institution in St. Paul. The weight of his personal position and influence, and the business he could throw to it, would assure success in advance. The practical question was whether he should create one, or acquire one already existing and shape it to his own ideas. Naturally, as a good business man, he would prefer the latter; and equally of course his first choice would be the First National. This· was the oldest National Bank in Minnesota. It was founded by James Edgar Thompson, nearly fifty years before, December 5, 1863. Except for the first seventeen years of its life, Mr. Hill had been closely connected with it. Mr. Henry P. Upham, who became its president in 1880, had been his friend and was associated with him in gathering in some of the scattered bonds of the St. Paul & Pacific. To Mr. Hill the First National of St. Paul meant more than any other bank ever could. It had maintained its standing and traditions; and its president, Mr. E. H. Bailey, was only the fourth man who had held that office. But its stockholders were not inclined to make terms satisfactory to Mr. Hill. Preferring to begin with some institution having already "a local habitation and a name," he turned to the Second National of St. Paul. This also was an old institution. Established in 1864, it had been in continuous operation for forty-eight years. Its capital, surplus, and undivided profits were $900,000 and its deposits $3,500,000. Its president at the time, Mr. William B. Dean, was one of Mr. Hill's oldest friends. Born in the same year, sharing with him the recollections of early days in St. Paul, for many years a director of the Great Northern Railway Company, and possessing Mr. Hill's esteem and confidence, he entered readily into the plan. The stock was bought by Mr. Hill personally for $1,240,000, and formal transfer to him was made October 10. Meantime, negotiations with the directors of the First National had been reopened. A large proportion of its stock was held by heirs of estates who took little part in its management. They soon came to the conclusion that, with Mr. Hill at the head of a competing institution, they would prefer to sell. The terms offered by the purchaser were liberal; and every share of the First National was secured and delivered to Mr. Hill for a total of $3,350,000. This transaction was completed December 31, 1912, at which time he found himself possessed of the foundation that he desired for a financial institution as big as the Northwest and as energetic and enterprising as himself. The two banks were merged into one under the name of the First National Bank of St. Paul, January 1, 1913. Its capital stock afterward became $3,000,000, with a $2,000,000 surplus.

From this date began that expansion of activity and growth of resources which might be expected under the changed conditions. It is an interesting coincidence that the First National of New York, in 1893, had something more than $17,000,000 of deposits, and that the First National of St. Paul had almost exactly the same amount at the time it was purchased. In 1916 the deposits of the New York bank had been multiplied by ten, representing the growth of twenty-three years. In 1916, or three years after Mr. Hill took charge of the new First National of St. Paul, its deposits had grown, in round numbers, from $17,000,000 to $55,000,000. About the same time Mr. Hill bought for $500,000 the Northwestern Trust Company, which operated in harmony with the bank. After he had made his purchase and owned the stock personally, he qualified its directors by selling back to them stock at what it had cost him. Later on, the capital stock was increased to $1,000,000 and they received the benefits of its prosperity. He carried through his plan of remodelling his group of financial institutions in St. Paul according to his own ideas and the best methods worked out elsewhere. He put unassailable resources behind them. The deposit figures already given show abundant confidence on the part of the public. Money rolled in. Liberal and enlightened loaning policies were adopted.

For years Mr. Hill had been urging bankers to take a greater interest in farm credits and the encouragement of good agriculture. In 1909 he had pointed out to the American Bankers' Association the intimate connection between the farming industry and the banking business, and showed how they can and ought to help each other. He acted on his own advice. Loans on live stock had been placed in large amounts by the bank at the South St. Paul stockyards, and

Mr. Hill acquired control of this also. Chiefly by his influence the Armour Company decided to build a plant at South St. Paul and make it one of the principal cattle markets of the country. No one can study his work to encourage stock growing in the Northwest, his banking enterprise, and their commercial interrelation, without admiration for the mind, as scientific as practical, which conceived and carried out plans so happily coördinated, though apparently so dissimilar. All kinds of industry in the Northwest felt the stimulus. The bank stockholders were as well satisfied with returns as the stockholders of every concern managed by Mr. Hill always had been. But the public benefited as largely. Farmers, millers and stockmen could be accommodated now at home, instead of having their requests approved and sent east for acceptance. In the year before the bank was bought, the loans on grain and cattle were a million and a half. In 1915 they had risen to fifteen millions. This influence was felt clear through to the coast. Within a year and a half the European war broke out and the local banks in the Northwest, out to the Pacific, could no longer extend credit. The First National of St. Paul stood behind these institutions and, as one result only, the price of wheat in the state of Washington almost doubled. Mr. Hill associated his son, L. W. Hill, with him closely in the conduct of the bank and the trust company. Within the little over three years that the father lived after his idea was realized, he saw his utmost anticipations exceeded. The carrying out of the plan was a part of the inheritance of the son.

Mr. Hill had for a long time considered the erection of an office building which would be a suitable home for the companies in which he was interested largely and directly. The quarters occupied by the Great Northern, the Northern Pacific, the Bank, and the Trust Company were all outgrown. The financial institutions, in particular, must have greatly enlarged facilities. The railroad headquarters were to be fixed now at St. Paul for all time to come. The Great Northern Office Building Company was incorporated in 1914. Property covering more than half a block and bounded by Fourth, Fifth, and Jackson Streets, was secured, and on it was erected a massive office building of the finest modern type. It is fourteen stories high and cost $4,000,000. Its outside dimensions are 232 by 290 feet, with a court 110 by 140 feet. Its cubical contents are more than ten million cubic feet and it has a floor area of 760,000 square feet. It is as substantial and as free from ornamental excrescences as was every construction when Mr. Hill had got through with the plans. But it is provided with every convenience for work and every safeguard for life and health. There are more magnificent business buildings in other cities, but none that better please the educated taste and none more completely adapted, to its purposes. Although work on this immense structure was begun June 6, 1914, the first Great Northern office was occupied November 1, 1915. The Bank and Trust Company opened quarters there in the same month, and early in 1916 the entire building was completed. Mr. Hill had watched with perennial interest its daily progress. There was not a detail of plan or construction with which he was not familiar. Many of them were of his own origination or suggestion.

Honours and recognition continued to flow in. The management of the Panama-Pacific Exposition at San Francisco desired each state to name its greatest living citizen for a Hall of Fame. A committee of five was appointed by Governor Hammond to designate Minnesota's representative, and this body unanimously selected Mr. Hill. An event that gave him sincere and lasting pleasure was the establishment, without his previous knowledge, of the James J. Hill Professorship of Transportation at the School of Business Administration at Harvard University. Seventy-four of his friends and admirers, including men of all professions and occupations, and representing every section of the country, contributed a fund of $125,000 for its endowment. This memorial in honour of the man and his work at one of the greatest institutions of learning, this gratuitous testimony to the esteem and admiration of all sorts and conditions of men, stirred his deepest appreciation. After the fund had been turned over he added $125,000 as his personal contribution, thus doubling the efficiency of the department. He also gave personal study to the best method of making the instruction given there a part of practical railroad education. His advice and suggestions were no inconsiderable addition to the strong financial foundation. At the Commencement exercises of 1915, President Lowell said: "The chair marks an epoch in the life of the School and, by its recognition of transportation as a permanent object of systematic instruction, in the life of the nation also. It is eminently fitting that such a professorship should bear the name of Mr. Hill, who has applied scientific principles to the construction and operation of railroads to an extent and with an accuracy unknown before." Mr. Howard Elliott, for the Overseers, said in the Harvard Graduates' Magazine: "Monuments are erected to many worthy men after death. In this case it is a gratification to Mr. Hill's many friends that during his lifetime this tribute has been paid to him, and that for years to come the name of the foremost railroad constructor and operator in the United States will be linked with the leading university of the country in a work of this very great national importance."

No public event of his long life stirred him more deeply or held him by an intenser continuing interest than the outbreak and changing fortunes of the European war. There could be no question where his sympathies would lie. Approving the original position of the United States as a neutral, he was personally, heart and soul, with the cause of the Allies. His Canadian antecedents and his long and close association with many of the men foremost in the life and government of Great Britain would, of themselves, have assured this. In addition, he was wrought, as were all Americans to a white heat of indignation by the sinking of the *Lusitania* and the campaign of "frightfulness." He had a warm place in his heart for Belgium, its people and its rulers. He had often cited its industry and economic thrift in supporting a dense population, as a model to which larger and prouder states should conform. King Albert was his personal friend. He had been entertained at Mr. Hill's home in St. Paul before he came to the throne, and taken as guest over the railroad. Once, later, when congratulated on his affability toward his subjects, he said, laughingly, that he had learned this from Mr. Hill when, out on the Great Northern, he had seen the president of the company shaking hands and exchanging a pleasant word with his employees. The invasion of Belgium outraged Mr. Hill's reverence for national honour and roused his bitter wrath as a humane and kindly man. He made several large contributions to the funds collected in this country for the relief of the Belgians.

He studied intently every issue growing out of the war that might affect the fortunes of the United States.

He never showed more creative imagination or more cogent reasoning than when he discussed the probabilities of an unprecedented situation on either side of the Atlantic. He opposed a federal merchant marine, in the early stage of the war, on the ground that it would inevitably drive private enterprise out of the shipping business. On the other hand, he urged government insurance of shipping as the only policy that could meet the emergency, keep our flag upon the seas, and assure the carriage of our products destined for European markets. His greatest service in this connection, however, was the probably decisive effect of his approval of the first Anglo-French loan. So quickly do events succeed and efface each other when war is raging that people forget the doubt with which, in those first days, a new and startling proposition like this was received. Judgment in war times is almost always unbalanced. Few people can think quickly and also think straight. The proposal that this country should furnish from half a billion to a billion of cash or credit to two of the Allies brought every bizarre argument out of its hole. After time for reflection, it is amusing now to read them. The gravest censors permitted their minds to wander. On the whole, the rapid-fire opinion of the public and of a large segment of the bankers was against the plan. It was said that to make such a loan to one side would be a tacit violation of neutrality; that it would engage us in the war; that it would "take money out of the country";

that it was inspired by American manufacturers of munitions and would inure only to their benefit.

From the first instant Mr. Hill's thought rang positive and true. As always, his mind went straight to the mark. He did not concern himself with trifles or accessories, but looked at home interests and logical effects. He expressed his opinions promptly and went to New York, by request, to support this proposition with his clear ideas and decisive influence. He spoke there as simply and convincingly as he was wont to do before the Northwestern farmers. He said that England and France did not need to get this money and credit half so much as the United States needed to give it to them. Look at our own situation if we refused! We were producing food stuffs and manufactured articles, crude oil and cotton, that we must sell outside of this country. If we could not sell them, our own producers would be ruined. We could not sell them without a buyer. The financial necessities of the only countries that could take these commodities off our hands—because they alone had control of the ocean —and the growing demoralization of exchange, made it impossible for them to buy unless they could draw against cash or credit on this side.

It was as plain as a pikestaff to Mr. Hill that we should have had to offer such a loan, for our own salvation, if it had not been asked for. He pointed out that no money would go out of this country. It would stay;

317

so that drafts in payment for supplies furnished could be made against it. He insisted that the loan should not cover purchases of munitions, but only of other products. He summed up his opinion in these few convincing lines: "Only superficially is this method for the advantage of any other nation. Primarily and with much more force it applies to the maintenance of our own commerce, to the support of our own industry, to the prevention of disaster to our agriculture, to the assurance of prosperity in the United States. It is far less a favour to others than a necessity for ourselves. It means more to us just now than armies or navies or anything else. It is a measure of financial and industrial preservation. So it should appeal more powerfully to the general public, which is the real party in interest, than it has to the men who have given it their sanction already."

As soon as he had spoken, mental fog was swept away and everybody realized how true and inevitable was his conclusion. If he had not spoken, however, if he had not been there to speak, the probability is that this country would have injured permanently its own interests by wavering and hesitation, if it had not destroyed them by refusal. The representatives of Great Britain and France appreciated at its value the influence of Mr. Hill in furthering this momentous transaction. It is frankly and feelingly avowed in the following extract from a letter written to him in

October, 1915, by a member of the Anglo-French Financial Commission: "I have just been signing the contract for the Anglo-French loan and in doing so my thoughts have naturally turned direct to yourself, and I have felt very keenly how large a share of the credit for the success of our mission here is owing from my colleagues and myself to you. We owe very much to the untiring energy with which you threw yourself into the task of preparing the way and of educating public sentiment for the reception of the loan. I can say for myself that your powerful aid has been of the greatest assistance to us as representatives of the British and French governments. Your insistence upon the truth that the credit which was asked for was essential in the interests of American commerce and industry was an all-important factor in securing a favourable hearing for the loan proposal of the British and French governments." Mr. Hill's three titles to preëminence are drawn from three principalities: the railroad, the farm, finance. To an analysis of his work in each of the first two a separate chapter will be devoted. He was equally great as a financier. But this form of his genius manifested itself in so many diverse ways that its appreciation has been incorporated and its processes and results recorded in connection with the succession of events that began on the Mississippi levee and ended in the councils of the world.

From the first, he followed every development of the

319

war, on the battlefield and in the counting room, like one whose own fortune and country are at stake. He read every line of news about it. He stopped to glance at every bulletin. He would open the big atlas in his office, trace the day's operations with the point of his pencil, locate the spot in Asia Minor which the Russians had reached and the probable next stage of their advance, argue the possibility of a circuit by land from Gallipoli to Constantinople as a quick means of forcing the Dardanelles. His hopes and fears fluctuated daily with the advancing or retreating waves of the conflict. He read the black-bordered letters that came to him in increasing numbers from old friends in England with a sympathy in which the personal element was heightened by a feeling of unity in the blood, and a hope and determination that democracy and civilization should prevail. The cause of the Allies had no more devoted advocate. Here, however, as in considering the war loan, as in everything, his first thought and his final thought were for his own country.

Mr. Hill had never been more keenly alive, not only to all that concerned his immediate plans for the future but to all the portentous, untried events looming through the dissolution of the Old World that he knew and loved, than in the early months of 1916. So much of his great work was finished. So much was yet to do. As the country had turned to him for a clear knowledge of what it ought to do about the foreign loan, so it turned again

320

for some forewarning of conditions that must prevail when the wrath of heaven should cease, and humankind return once more to happier ways. He had his answer ready. To the many calls made upon him he responded with all the expected definiteness, precision, and exact adaptation of practical means to ends. He staked out like an economic engineer the right route for the nation. It was the same kind of service, though immeasurably greater, as when he mapped the location of a new railroad line by combining his photographic memory of every hill and watercourse and coulée with his mental vision of the kind and amount and direction of traffic created by millions of people yet to be. He showed what course this country ought to follow, and what fate hung upon its wisdom or its folly when the tumult and the shouting should have ceased. The last article by him printed in pamphlet form was entitled "Preparedness for Peace." This is its main conclusion: "The question of economic preparedness is, then, for us, mainly a question of capital and labour. The first and greatest need of this country in the coming era is pay rolls; pay-rolls for all those at work; for those whose occupation will be interrupted, and for those others who will come again into active competition with the men who lay down the rifle to go back to the factory, the mine, and the farm. If the black shadow which the war has cast upon the future generations of Europe is not to darken our national life also, we must be prepared to meet these new conditions not with political oratory, but with the economic weapons by which alone they can be mastered." Not by any legerdemain at Washington, not by protective tariffs or anti-dumping laws or any other hocus-pocus did he believe that we could save ourselves and keep our leadership in a remade, unpredictable world.

As it was in the beginning, so in the end it must be the plebeian virtues of industry, thrift, integrity, and enterprise that should bring us to our goal. No eye in all the world watched more keenly or with more anxious care the progress of this terrible epoch in the world's history, or pierced farther into the thick darkness that shrouded it. In letters, conversations, and printed articles he traced the path to greatness, with honour, for the country he loved so sincerely. He believed in national prosperity only when it was linked, both as antecedent and as consequent, with the success of the democratic experiment. Fifty-five years before, an unhappy chance of fate had forbidden him to bear arms that the republic might realize the hopes of its founders and bring blessing to the world. Now, in age still green with the sap of life, and ripe and wise with thought and experience, he drew a chart for battles, policies, worthy world conquests of peace, in the long future to which mysterious forces urge the nations swinging in their orbits toward some heavenly goal. Inspiration came to him as freely; thought was as fresh and true as half a century before. All his resources of knowledge, of power, of influence, were at the disposal of his country.

Over this ardent, vivid life of body, intellect, spirit, and will, suddenly a black pinion drooped. His last word to the people in their hour of wonder and doubt, of hope and tremor, reached their eyes upon the printed page only after the pen had fallen from his hand and his voice had been for ever stilled. An end sad, indeed, for those who loved him, but one such as he himself would have chosen. A fighter he had lived and fighting died, faithful to his light as a soldier and leader for the common good.

He had always been the master of his body, just as he was the "master of his fate and captain of his soul." It had served him faithfully. He had used it unsparingly. His wonderful physique had been proof for a lifetime against drains upon it, answered demands that would have emptied of vitality a weaker organism. But none can escape the slow sapping of the years. This insensible decline he could not translate into terms of the prudent self-protection which most men begin to adopt when they are fifteen or twenty years younger than he was now. All who knew him felt that for many years more his splendid natural forces would stand ordinary strain. But he would not spare himself. He had never learned the lesson, conned by weaker men through necessity and periods of invalidism, of conserving the body and taking care in time. There had been warning symptoms for a year or more. A recurring derangement of the digestive system, not dangerous in itself but bespeaking a deeper underlying cause, planted anxiety in the hearts of those closest to him. Yet even they feared no sudden collapse. He himself scouted the idea that anything serious was the matter. So, the moment that temporary relief was given, he plunged again into the thick of things. After all, he was true to himself here also. In a man who should have let drop the reins of the present and the future in order that he might take care for the morrow of his own body, no one would have recognized the James J. Hill of history. He would not and could not do it. The poison crept on and on. When it had gained the citadel, the stroke was sudden and sure. Ten days before his death he was at his office, and those about him saw little change in his appearance and none in his interest in affairs. Then it seemed wisest even to him to take a few days for rest and recuperation from an attack of more than common persistence. In a week's time his whole system had been invaded and the end was close. No remedy revealed by the medical knowledge and skill of the age was left untried, and none availed. Soon he himself was sure that life for him was over.

He met this last and greatest adventure that can rise to daunt the soul in the same spirit that he had brought to every lesser crisis of his life. No power had waned, no faculty was wanting or even dimmed by the tarnishing breath of years. Serenely he made ready for what had to be. His main work was done. Could he have had another lifetime at his disposal, there would still have been many great plans unrealized, many mighty works unfinished. But his deepest and tenderest thought now was for those he would leave behind. Except for them, their sorrow and their loneliness, the passage from time to eternity seemed to him wholly natural and little to be deplored. So, not with stoic resignation, and yet without a trace of shrinking or of fear, he passed to the ultimate test of manhood and the hour of sovereignty of the soul. He had lived, in his own inner shrine, in spiritual humility. He had sought, along with the outer ends for which all men strive, the benefit of his kind. He had given with generous hands— in his establishment of the seminary for education to the Roman Catholic priesthood in St. Paul, in his maintenance for years of institutions controlled by other denominations, in order that the youth of the land might unfold under religious influences, and in unending charities to the needy—an all-convincing proof of spiritual catholicity. Without formal acceptance of the vows or obligations of any religious body, the meditations that he sometimes, though rarely, shared with those in his most intimate confidence, the works of a lifetime, the ideals which he laboured always to set up and establish in power over men and nations, made him partaker of the life that

325

"is not far from any one of us." He died on the morning of May 29, 1916. Expressions of sorrow, tributes of admiration and of praise, such recognition as none but a kingly spirit and a life of service could command, came from high and low, and from many lands. One unbroken voice of national admiration and regret spoke through the public press. No words more eloquently simple and just were written about him than these, from an editorial in the New York *Times:* "Greatness became him, and was a condition of his errand here. Whatever he had done, it had been greatly done. He trusted democracy perhaps more than it trusts itself. He believed in its economic destiny. Giving much, he received much. We salute the memory of a great American." Two days later Rev. Thomas Gibbons, Vicar General of the Catholic Diocese of St. Paul, spoke above him the last solemn service of the Church. His body was laid at rest on a beautiful knoll at his North Oaks home, overlooking the lake and an exquisite sweep of landscape; a spot that he had greatly loved. Beautiful, simple, close to all that was dearest, having its own unique and expressive quality, uniting, by the gentle movement of leaves and waters, the soft incline of kindly skies and the silence of immobile shores, the benison of earth to that of heaven, it is a fitting sepulchre.

CHAPTER   THIRTY-SIX

THE MASTER-KEY

THE most obvious and impressive portion of Mr. Hill's
work, of course, is his unique contribution to the history
of transportation. Remarkable in many other ways as
were the contacts of his life with the world about him,
and their consequences, his were the master-mind and
the master-hand in railroad construction and operation.
Even a master-hand, however, can open no locked doors
unless it holds a master-key. He found this in knowledge of the facts and laws of commerce, with which his
mind was fairly saturated. His originality and ver-
satility as a creator and curator of traffic have illumi-
nated every stage of the progress described in preceding
chapters. The man in action was more intelligible
and infinitely more self-revealing than the man on
paper could ever be. He himself never drew up any
formal bill of rights or schedule of principles for a science
and art of railroading. His nearest approach to it was
the two chapters on this subject included in "Highways
of Progress." But he did start out from and return to
certain fundamental ideas about it which he changed
little and never abandoned. The interpretation of the
man by his own strenuous life, which these volumes

contain, should be supplemented by an interpretation a little different—more scientific and more systematically developed—of his work as the foremost railroad builder and manager of any era since first the railway was devised for the service of man. What was his master-key?

"Transportation seeks the line of least resistance." So nature speaks through every watercourse. From this original proposition, in Mr. Hill's own words, may be drawn, with almost mathematical exactness, his entire theory of railroading. It lies folded in that storehouse of meaning, the words "least resistance." From them he deduced the main laws of traffic. First let the rule be applied to construction. If he or any other wished to build a railroad, it ought to conform to nature's own physique. Granted "that there were commodities to carry or natural resources which guaranteed a future supply of commodities to carry," the first problem is topographic. He said: "The grade of a railroad is of as much importance, bearing in mind the traffic, as is the depth of water in a navigable harbour or channel, because the grade fixes the load; and many roads that were built at an early day, without keeping in mind the load that they could carry on an economic basis, have had to be rebuilt. Some of them have been rebuilt two and three times. Take the Pennsylvania road between Pittsburgh and Philadelphia; portions of it to-day are on the fourth right of way. The Lake

Shore road originally had considerable one per cent. grades. It was cut down to six tenths, and afterward rebuilt a second time and the grade reduced to three tenths, except in one or two places." This is the material aspect of the line of least resistance. Build where nature beckons with a valley, a prairie, or a mountain fissure cleft by some geological convulsion. Most railroad builders saw that far. The makers of the Santa Fe and Oregon trails, every Indian chief whose ponies dragged after him his tepee on its slanted poles, knew that. But the mere physical line of least resistance implies much more.

In this second sense, others were relatively slow to follow Mr. Hill, because they sought the lowest first cost in building. After the selection of a route along the line of least resistance, so far as is practicable, comes a method of construction obedient to the same law. He was not only the first to build a transcontinental system conforming to it, but the first in this country to adopt it as a general engineering practice. It demands low grades and abhors sharp curves. It involves expenditure greater than builders in new country are usually either able or willing to incur. They are in a hurry to get through and to begin earning money. With these earnings they can build more or better. But Mr. Hill's railroad calculations were always made as if he had a set of compound interest tables before him. Construction cheapened by climbing hills and weaving in and out around sharp corners meant more motive power, more wear and tear on track and equipment; time lost, money lost. Every day, every train load, every revolution of a wheel piled up expenses out of all proportion to the interest on the capital that would be required to build, in the first place, a line fitted for low-cost operation. Interest could be stopped by paying off principal. It could be earned by saving on operating expense. The charges of inferior or unintelligent construction are perpetual; daily, and hourly repeated, until the original defects are corrected. So he built, first and always, with a view to operating cost. He was substituting steel rails for iron, 650 or 700 pound for 300 pound wheels, steel bridges for those of wood, lowering grades, and putting in cut-offs, when other people were satisfied to collect the largest possible revenue from makeshifts. So far as the burden on traffic and the railroad's net revenue were concerned, it was mathematically the difference between paying simple interest and paying interest compounded every minute, year after year. Of course, this principle was applied with common prudence and common sense. There were many cases, such as the crossing of the Cascade Mountains, where the great first cost of putting in the permanent improvement, or the delay it would cause, was prohibitory for a new line in undeveloped country. The switchback must serve until the time should come when the tunnel could supersede it. But the original plan was made always with reference not to the temporary, but to the future permanent line. The part of the former was reduced to the minimum that circumstances seemed to require. When the time was ripe for the latter, the change could be made with least loss of time, least sacrifice of material, and lowest money cost. Analyzed to its last element, his system of construction resolves itself into a faithful following of the line of least resistance. Every successful railroad in the country has adopted his method. He was not merely a great railroad manager, but a great railroad engineer. He proved it to the most competent men on his own system. It is the dictum of the highest engineering authority. Here, as everywhere, he owed the distinction and permanence of his success to the piercing insight that gave him, before he made any move, a clear-cut apprehension of the fundamental principle involved; and courage and resolution to apply it instantly, continuously, and un-flinchingly, to the work in hand.

The law of least resistance applies with the same directness and force to operation as to construction. In any enterprise which requires large capital and must collect revenue to pay returns upon it, the difficulty of performing necessary operations, the cost of earning money, is a hill to be tunnelled or a ravine to be bridged. A level track and a straight line lessen the expense of the physical work by lowering the traction pull. Suppose the railroad line as satisfactory as

331

circumstances permit, then the method of bunching and distributing business, of making up trains, and of adjusting traffic parts to one another must be looked after with a judgment as flawless and a direction as scientific. First of all, the hauling of empty cars is a dead loss. Even if they are going in one direction in order that they may be brought back loaded, this is no excuse; for when they run loaded both ways, revenue is doubled with but a trifling addition to cost of wheelage. No need to dwell on this point. Mr. Hill's hatred of the "empty" and his hammering away at his helpers, from highest to lowest, upon the necessity of having all cars loaded have been emphasized sufficiently. This principle entered into and determined his whole plan for the development of the Pacific Coast lumber interest and of Oriental trade. It was to his mind a first condition of successful railroad operation.

The next element in the line of least resistance is density of traffic. Here are tracks and locomotives and cars. The tracks will accommodate twenty trains a day as well as two. They will carry cars loaded to capacity as readily as those only half full. They are as open to trains of seventy-five cars as to trains of fifteen. But the percentage of income that it costs to operate, technically known as "operating ratio," is vastly different in the two cases. Everywhere, in this country and abroad, increase in the density of traffic—the number of freight ton miles to each mile of track operated—decreases operating ratio and builds up net revenue. It also permits reductions of the freight charge per ton per mile. This is following the line of least resistance. Set the receipts from a million tons pushing against maintenance and operating charges on each mile of road; against payment of interest and dividends. The resistance to each ton will be a small fraction of what it is when only a hundred thousand tons are behind the push. Mr. Hill never ceased to teach this and enforce it. "I know it is difficult to get a railroad man anywhere who can load his cars, who appreciates the importance of loading a car and loading his engine with loaded cars. When we commenced, we found this: that what we call the half-loaded car from the station in St. Paul would average from 5,000 to 6,000 pounds, and the capacity of that car was 60,000 pounds; the company hauled eighteen tons of car and blocked its railway with forty feet of car to move 6,000 pounds. By paying close attention to the loading of that car we have got it up to 18,000 pounds, and I think now (1906) at the Minnesota Transfer probably higher than 18,000. We haven't handled anything like the same number of cars that we had to before, to do the same amount of business. We don't block the side tracks, we don't block the railroad."

Everywhere he sought density of traffic. He built his lines where the country was such that traffic must inevitably rise from the soil, the forest, and the

333

mine, and keep on growing. He fostered agriculture as an unfailing and ever-increasing source of traffic supply. On all the railways that he directed or influenced, the number of cars drawn and the number of tons pulled per train mile were raised steadily. Both physically and financially this was finding and following the line of least resistance. First and last he emphasized the importance of a great volume of traffic, not only in its ordinary relation to income but as a lever to which economies might be applied with surprising results. He impressed upon every superintendent, upon all who had to do with operation, the fact that a saving so small as to be disregarded commonly, a mere mill or fraction of a mill per ton, if applied to the enormous tonnage of a system would give big returns; might often make the difference between a profit and a loss. To this end a school of education was established and maintained in the Great Northern headquarters building. Men who had got results or shown promise were trained there in the meaning and value of the figures in operating sheets and reports. They were taught to dig down and discover the causes of a bad month or a poor division record. Then they knew how to remedy or, better yet, to avoid these things in practice. The idea became self-perpetuating. So conspicuous and desirable were the results that other railroad systems sought to instal his methods by employing men who had been trained to efficiency under him. A considerable number of the most successful railroad managers of the country drew their first inspiration from Mr. Hill, and received their practical discipline under his eye and command. Whatever they learned there they learned thoroughly. The Great Northern became a sort of unofficial school of American railroading.

The master-key fits the problems of capitalization, rates, and profits, as well as those of construction and operation. A sum total of stock and bonds out of proportion to the cost and value of the property, and to its earnings, is a deviation from the line of least resistance. The capitalization of the railroads under Mr. Hill's management was made and kept relatively low. He could see no permanent gain in filling a railroad's capital with water. Moreover, as his words already given state emphatically, he would have none of it because he did not think it honest. He did not want and would not touch money so obtained. Here is a public statement made by him just before he resigned the presidency of the system. It is a practical illustration of his theory of capitalization. It adjusts the master-key to this part of the lock. "No other investment in the country served by the Great Northern has received as low compensation. Now, that is on the stock and bonds issued. There would be probably thirty-five to forty million dollars more invested than is represented; some of it profits. When we reorganized the old St. Paul & Pacific we capitalized it at some ten or

335

twelve million dollars less than the judgment for the old bonds and interest. You see there was ten or twelve millions of capital wiped out. Then there is another condition there. Congress granted lands to the State of Minnesota, and those lands have been sold and used to retire bonds. I think the bonds retired were about eleven or twelve millions. If you are familiar with the history of land grants in Minnesota, you must know that most of the lands were sold and the proceeds given to the stockholders. Ours has been administered most carefully and the proceeds have been used to retire bonds, and the public is saved the interest on those bonds. I think that the actual investment in the property is thirty-five or forty millions more than it is capitalized for. That grant was to aid in the construction of the road; we used it for that purpose. It gave us a credit to begin with, and as the lands were sold the expense of taking care of them and selling them amounted to sixty or eighty thousand dollars a year, and the balance of it was used to retire bonds."

A rate unreasonably high or unreasonably low is an interference with the line of least resistance. This applies with especial force to the relation between the railroad and its best customer, the farm. Mr. Hill's conception of that, his lifelong study and service for the promotion of agriculture, will be the subject of the succeeding chapter. As it connects with his theory of railroading, he put it in a nutshell in an off-hand address in

1911, at a little town in Oregon: "The railroad, when it comes here once, is in partnership with the land upon which we live and walk. It must be poor with it, and it will only prosper when the land prospers, or the owner of the land prospers. You can sell your land and move away. If I owned the railroad—I have a great many partners, about 18,000, and about 8,000 of them are women and children, and I have to take care of their interest—with their consent I could sell the railroad, but I could not take it away. It is here, it has got to remain, and it has got to have its prosperity or its poverty with the growth of this country; and that is the reason why we are so anxious that you should grow, in order that you may make greater efforts. We know that if your efforts fail, we fail; and every dollar that we get you have got to get first; and that is the reason why we take so deep an interest in your success. We are glad now and at all times—and it has been our policy—to try to hold up the hands of the man who is cultivating the land. Imagine for a moment what the railroad would be worth if nobody lived along the line."

This is only one application of the rule, an important groove of the master-key, that a railroad should charge "what the traffic will bear." Perhaps it is impossible to rescue that phrase from the obloquy that has covered it. The public, unacquainted with railroad terminology, almost universally translated it as "*all*" the traffic will bear. It means, of course, nothing of the kind. It was coined to express graphically a conception and an economic philosophy benevolently paternalistic. It should read "no more than the traffic will bear." Every section, every locality, and many cities or little towns have some resource or possibility which can be developed only by encouragement and help. It may be a wheatfield, a mine, a bit of irrigable land, a stone quarry, a bed of clay fit for brick or tile, any one of the thousand things that invite human industry with promise of rich repayment. All depend upon access to some market. The way is barred if the full schedule rate is charged. This "infant traffic" cannot bear it. An elementary rule of transportation rate-making is that cheap and bulky commodities must pay less proportionately than costly articles, light in weight and small in volume. Another is that the same commodity cannot pay the same rate per ton per mile under all circumstances. A coal mine near a city can be worked at a profit and at the same time pay a charge to the carrier which would prevent the sale of a single ton from a mine of equally good coal if its product had to be carried so far that an equivalent rate per ton per mile ate up the whole selling price. One practical condition after another comes in to modify a strict rule of democratic equality in railway rates. They have to be and always are made such as will, under all existing conditions of distance, quality, quantity, and market management, enable each industry at least to live, preferably to

338

expand, and at the same time give to the carrier a living profit or better.

This is what is meant by rates such as the traffic will bear. No railroad manager, no railroad commission, no legislature, no court, and no individual has ever discovered or invented, or ever will, a general rule for the making of such a rate. Its elements are too many and too different. Its roots are too deep and too widely scattered. It answers to no arbitrary formula. It has always been and, so far as one can see, must continue to be fixed by rule of thumb; subject to the endless, be-cause ever-changing, correction of practical experience. The following is Mr. Hill's plain way of putting it: "Now, if we did not make the rate so as to encourage the production of wheat in a wheat country where there is nothing else, what would become of the merchandise? There would not be any. There would not be any churches or school houses or doctors or school teachers or clergymen; there would not be any town there. It would return to what it was twenty-five or thirty or forty years ago—an unoccupied wilderness. And so it is not an unfair discrimination to make the low rate for the man who is cultivating the soil, or digging in the mine, or working in the forest, because upon his product depends the growth of the entire section of the country, and you must build it up; if you do not, the railroad is not worth a cent."

Mr. Hill came back, as Congress and the Interstate

Commerce Commission and all the courts have been obliged to come back, to the principle that rates should be reasonable. A reasonable rate offers least resistance to traffic growth. But, what is a reasonable rate? He replied: "It is based entirely on the cost of operation and maintenance and its relation to the value of the property used. In this item are included the payment of interest on bonds and a fair return, in the shape of dividends, to the stockholders." This delicate problem, the fixing of a rate not too high to retard the development of the country and not too low to permit the railroad to operate successfully and meet all present and future demands upon it, has never yet submitted to any hard-and-fast solution. On no two railroads and in no two sections of the country would the conclusion be just the same. It depends on capitalization, good judgment in building and operating, the character and distribution of natural resources and, above all, on the intelligence and honour of railroad management. Here, as everywhere, the right rule benefits both sides. "It is for the public interest," he said, "that the amount to be earned should be derived from a large volume of traffic at a low rate, rather than a small volume at a high rate." He summed up fairly and truthfully the relation of his life work to railway rates before a legislative commission, after that work was practically completed: "I have tried to run a railroad without any inside ring, or anything to cover or conceal in any way, and I have tried to make it an honest institution, giving the public as fast as we could afford it the benefit of a reduced rate. And I think that a close examination of the record will show that we have lowered the rates throughout the whole West oftener and farther of our own motion than any other road, or practically all of the other roads put together."

Railroad competition is part, but only part, of the line of least resistance. On this Mr. Hill's views were extremely clear. In the main, they are stated in the chapters devoted to the history of events in 1901. Competition between railroads, in the sense that it existed fifty years ago, has gone, never to return. Nobody wants it back. The public would not endure breaking its journey at every state line or oftener; nor could business stagger through the gauntlet of several joint freight rates on every little shipment. Reckless rate wars are as economically destructive in principle as the armed clash of nations. The consolidation of rail-roads into large systems being suitable for economy in operation, and adapted to the public convenience, is a natural development of economic law and, therefore, a finality. But the sphere of this law has boundaries. Somewhere, in each individual instance, combination should stop; and competition, in the larger sense, be restored. Mr. Hill himself not only refused to stand at the head of any conglomerate aggregation of naturally unrelated lines, but announced flatly the impossibility

341

of a successful consolidation that should attempt to cover and operate over the whole country, either east and west or north and south. "Three things prevent the further organization of American railroads in systems. The first is the law. The Sherman Anti-trust Act makes it unlawful for any two railroads to effect any combination in restraint of trade; and further systematizing of railroads would be such a combination, according to the courts. The second is the determining force of commerce. Suppose a man could effect what Mr. Gould aimed to achieve—a system reaching from coast to coast, organized and operated as one road—what good would it be? The man west of the Mississippi would still ship his grain, his live stock, to Chicago, or St. Louis, and there it would change owners. Compared with such consignments to Chicago or St. Louis the amount of through shipments would be inconsiderable. Markets, geography, and commerce—these are the things that limit the development of railroad systems, and they draw the lines just about where the present systems are now. The third is the human problem of getting men to manage larger systems. Take the New York Central as it is. It has, say, 80,000 men on its rolls. That's an army. Suppose they all struck. And when a man is found big enough to carry this load and that of two or three other systems employing corresponding armies, he could not stand it."

His idea was "competition by groups." This meant

that each integral geographical and commercial section of the country, comprising states and parts of states bound together intrinsically by situation, industrial interest, and relations to markets, should have its own independent system of railroad lines, working either under one ownership or in complete community of interest. These groups of states or sections, these systems of railroads naturally concreted, will compete for business. It will be a competition between homogeneous productive areas, seaports, great through routes, and widely separated sources of supply. The evolution of the railroad interest of this country is the living proof that Mr. Hill's view was scientific as well as practical. He said: "Our Company will continue to maintain a conservative and firm position, having proper regard for the revenue of other lines, without any disposition on our part to interfere with their local rate at intermediate points." He felt all the delight of a successful general in his ability to dispose of any kind of competition that might wander his way and try a tilt with him. Before a legislative commission he said, quite seriously: "If I had a well-settled, well-built road, where the embankments had done settling and everything was up and in shape and in permanent condition, and you built a road alongside and it cost $30,000 or $40,000 a mile, and you undertook to live at the same rate, I would have your road, if I wanted it, within four or five years." And so he would. Naturally enough he was highly impatient, not so

much of the principle of public regulation of rates as of
its inevitable blundering and its susceptibility to prejudice and abuse. His experience began at a time when
railroad managements were practically a law unto themselves. He believed that he knew better than any
public authority, executive, legislative or judicial,
what would be, in any given case, a just and reasonable
rate. He meant to make such a rate if they would let
him alone. It was as much part of his theory to build
up the country by lowering rates as to maintain a paying
property by keeping them up. As in most of the serious
difficulties of all people on the face of this earth, the
trouble here is to determine exactly the content of that
word direct from the eternal heart of things, the word
"justice," with which the mortal and the finite wrestle
forever. With his knowledge of the railroads of the
country as a whole, he could not deny the desirability
of some curb somewhere upon possible individual or
corporate rapacity. But he could not see, and circumstances have failed to disclose, how the bit and the
bridle were to be fitted also to public covetousness.
"The only difference," he said, "that I can see between
a commission of five men fixing the rates on all railways
in the country and a commission operated under government ownership is a difference in name." The experience of a lifetime whose latest trial was the rate cases
just described, and the general decrepitude of the country's railway machine as proved by official statistics.

tended little to soften the harshness of this view. At the time of his death this part of the railroad question was as unsettled and as uncertain as when he began to think, and the public began to act, upon it. The perfecting of the master-key still awaited such changes in average human nature as would permit the harmonious meeting of all minds in the determination of a "just and reasonable rate."

He was disturbed and seriously anxious about the inadequacy of railroad terminal facilities. Here, indeed, the line of least resistance is broken by gullies and obstructed by landslides. Terminals, he repeated, were the hands and feet of the railroads. Nowhere was his foresight displayed more clearly than in the provision he made for his own system. He had taken thought in time for its needs in St. Paul and Minneapolis. He had built up the largest and most effective terminal facilities in the world at the head of Lake Superior. He had saved the people of Seattle from mistakes that would have hampered their terminal business for ever, and had given them a plan responsible for no small part of the city's commercial greatness. He never laid out a line without securing at every important point terminals equal to all probable needs for years to come. He saw traffic congestion recur on the main traffic arteries of the country as regularly as financial panics. One of its palpable causes was insufficient terminal facilities. If it went on increasing, the effect would be like that of clogging permanently the arteries of the human body. He said, in 1910: "This problem of terminals is the great problem of the country; the problem of transportation agencies, of financiers, of the communities directly affected and of all the industries that depend directly or indirectly upon cheap and speedy carriage for the commodities which they buy and sell. It is a problem for everybody; since probably not one business man in the whole country would fail to feel the disastrous effects if it were to be neglected for the next five years as it has for the last ten, and to blight every form of activity by paralyzing the whole of trade." In 1912 he took up the same theme at a meeting of the Railway Business Association in New York City: "No city can afford to place its trade, which is its life," he said, "on a false basis. When the commerce naturally tributary to it is handicapped by poor terminals, or overloaded with too heavy charges on account of the excessive cost of enlargement, it will go elsewhere. There are a dozen places between the Maine coast and Norfolk that could be made available for relief. A city can never grow great enough to defy safely the demands of the laws of trade and its proper accommodation. Should the decentralization plan be forced on traffic, some of our greatest cities would not merely forfeit their natural share in national growth, but they would surely decline in business, wealth, and power."

346

What he deprecated most in the general drift of railroad regulation and legislation was that, carried to its
logical conclusion, it seemed to move toward government ownership. Personally he cared little. Such a
revolution could not shake the foundations of his fortune or lessen his fame. Impersonally, it seemed to him
the ultimate calamity. As a business venture he believed it the worst step the country could make. "If
the people could let the Government have the main
lines for twenty-five years, I don't know what they
would give to get rid of them. They would be like the
man who drew an elephant in a lottery. They would
have to have another lottery to get rid of them. The
trouble would be that everything in the way of an appropriation would depend on the votes in Congress.
How would you keep the road up? One crowd, where
the population was more dense than others, would want
their road in good shape, and out here where your
population is sparse and your representation in proportion, you wouldn't have votes enough, and very soon
the road wouldn't be fit to travel over. I should be
delighted, personally, if the Government would take
the Great Northern and pay what it would cost to
reproduce it." The balance sheets of the State-owned
railroads of other countries were eloquent of incapacity.
The reports of this country's conduct of the Panama
Railroad, with its enormous rates for a service excep-
tionally easy to perform, could not be gainsaid. But,

after all, it was the forecast of political consequences that affected Mr. Hill most deeply. Sink the plummet to the depths of the railroad man, and always you would find the patriotic citizen. He believed that the taking over of the railroads by the Government, with the inevitable solidifying of the vote of two million railroad employees, "would mean the destruction of free government in the United States." In all seriousness, and with an interest, an anxiety, and a readiness for personal sacrifice such as an attack by some other country upon the United States would have evoked, he looked forward to possible federal ownership and operation of railroads as the death sentence of the American democratic experiment. The fear and the pain of that struck at the life of some of his strongest convictions and holiest hopes. Public ownership challenged in him not merely a theory or predilection, but the strong faith of a democrat and an American.

In all the ramifications of what is loosely called the "railroad problem"; in everything that touches the creation and operation of a railway line, the management of traffic, the apportionment of rates and the collection of revenue; in all the difficult domain where the interests of the individual, the railroad, and the general public come together, each wrangling with every other, and each ready to explode into elements and atoms of discord—there is but one steady interest, one guiding thought, one trustworthy clue. The complicated lock opens only

348

at the touch of one master-key. This, the following of the line of least resistance, now admits of generalized statement. That line is drawn by the highly scientific and yet plainly simple and human law of identity of interest. It travels in a circle. The moving thought comes back to a people and a transportation system reciprocally dependent. Some time, somewhere, all human activity must stoop and touch the earth to find its strength renewed. The Sons of Antaeus are the saving remnant of the past, the true progenitors of the future. The railroad must bring in the people, create the farm, build the factory, cram the warehouse with wealth, and be at once the Mentor and the Mercury of the crowd. An organized and disciplined army of productive industry must summon, sustain, and make greater, more efficient, and more helpful the railroads that shall carry it on its appointed way. The master-key is turned.

CHAPTER   THIRTY-SEVEN

THE SONS OF ANTAEUS

"LAND without population is a wilderness. Population without land is a mob." In these two pithy sentences, dating from the earliest expression of his economic ideas, Mr. Hill summed up his sociological faith.
He never recanted or modified that creed. Stripped of
non-essentials, man poses as a two-legged animal, gifted
with intelligence, standing squarely on a piece of the
earth's surface. Whatever he can make of himself and
his environment must be made with and from that
original provision. From it also stimulating reactions
arise. Take the man from the land, and it remains of no
more account in the general plan than any bit of heat-
scorched surface on Mars, or any extinct crater of the
moon. Take the land from the man, and he will drop
like a withered leaf through space. Leave him standing
room, but vest control of the land in others, and his
progeny relapse into brutish, embittered semblances of
human things, waiting only for an opportunity to repos-
sess themselves of their heritage. The wilderness is the
denial of nature's plan for the replenishment of the
earth, and its increase in products for the service of
man. The mob is the denial of nature's plan for an
350

active, friendly, coöperative association of men to subdue the earth; and, by filling it with bloom and fruit, raise their own qualities to the zenith of their power. These brief axioms are an epitome of political economy and sociology. They were absolutely fundamental to the thought of Mr. Hill. To remember this is to understand the interdependence which existed, from the first step to the last, between his work as a master of transportation and his work as a student of agricultural processes and a leader in the improvement of the farm: They were twin brothers in his conception of the business of being a man. It is possible that the world which knighted him "empire builder" may one day be in doubt whether his most lasting creations were those of the right hand or the left. Certainly he held the two in equal honour.

From the days of the achievements of Pompey and Crassus, days when caravans were on the desert, and older days when the white sails of the Phoenicians flashed in unknown seas, the service of an interchange of products of the earth drew him. Through that he realized intuitively his genius when he was dreaming of side-wheel steamers to plough the waters of Indian rivers, and when he was shouting to his dogs on the long frozen trail to Fort Garry. But his mind was logical. It never allowed the pan of either scale to kick the beam. If there were to be carriers, there must be something to carry. How could a man cover the American Northwest with railroad lines and keep them running, unless an immense volume of freight were waiting and calling for them? Of what would that consist, and whence would it come? Here, as everywhere, the man must find ground on which to stand before be could do his work. He must have more than standing room. The commodities through whose creation the people were to grow rich and wise, and by whose movement from one point to another great agencies and great abilities were to arise and be justified, would not come at call from nothing, like some prestidigitator's creatures. The builder and manager of the railroad must have wealth in abundance and variety to carry. Out of what, and by what human processes, could such abundance be summoned?

The answer to this question runs back to another favourite saying of Mr. Hill: "All wealth comes from one of four sources: the sea, the forest, the mine and the earth." It dates from the same early time as the two sentences which stand at the head of this chapter. Nobody knows when they all disentangled themselves from the complex web of social and industrial organization, and rose separate and shining to his eye. The axiomatic certainty behind them may date from his boyhood's reading; may have been hammered out on the anvil of his thought in the long nights of Minnesota winters over his books, while frost held the Mississippi ice-bound; may have disengaged itself from the packages that he handled as clerk or agent. What is sure is that this framework for constructive effort was formed and immovable within him when he first conceived the idea of controlling and extending the St. Paul & Pacific. Remember that his fulcrum was the rank growth which sprung up where the Red River carts or the gophers had exposed the rich under-soil to the kiss of sun and the thrust of seed. He visioned a railroad because he saw the raw material of what that railroad should carry. He conceived each factor strengthening the other indefinitely through the years. He was as a discoverer of perpetual motion; for the breath of life and pledge of growth for his secure ambition would be the unending energy of fertile soil and germinative potency, the genial warmth of sunshine, "the early and the latter rain." In 1907, when he was addressing the jobbers of St. Paul, and they expected him to talk about the outlook for trade and manufacture, he said, "You have just two things up here—soil and climate." In 1909, in a speech made at Minot, from which his road so many years before had made its huge drive westward, he said: "I have tried at all times not to waste energy. In the early day in travelling about the country in looking ahead to see where we might build railroads, sometimes travelling in a buck-board, and sometimes on horseback, I always carried a spade. I wanted to see what the soil was. I knew what the climate was, and with the soil and climate I was not afraid to open up the country, making it possible for people to live upon the land, cultivate it, and make homes for themselves." It was the man with the spade who conceived and created one of the greatest railway systems of modern times. If concrete symbols could represent the life of Mr. Hill, the plough and the locomotive would stand in equal honour side by side.

It has seemed worth while to drive home the prominence always given by Mr. Hill to the farm. Always his thought harked back to the land. All men are sons of Antaeus. Their wrestling bout with nature is lost unless they can touch the ground. Without that understanding, any notion of him as a railroad builder would be absurdly incomplete. Again and again glimpses of his philosophy appear through the crannies of the day's task. His railroads could grow only with the growth of the country, and the wealth of the country could grow only by the growth of his railroads. Hence, the spying out of new territory and its occupation in proportion to its ascertained fertility. Looking at a field of grain he said: "The country that will grow this kind of stuff without splicing the straw is not to be turned down." A careful student of his method summed it up many years ago in the following general rule: "Where the acres are fertile and yield large crops, there the Hill tracks radiate and cross and intermingle in a bewildering network that serves every farmer and fruit raiser and merchant and miner and lumberman wherever

354

he is; while if the soil is not capable of supporting population in large numbers, you find the Hill roads thinning down accordingly, as in the semi-arid regions, where the number of bushels to the acre and the number of cattle to the square mile are both limited. It is this wisdom in putting his railroads where they will create population and prosperity and thus secure profitable traffic that has made the success of his system." Yes, but he wanted to raise or remove the productive limit of all square miles and all acres. Almost with passion he cried out to an audience in the years after he had retired from the presidency of the railroad: "Call me anything. Call me a crank, call me anything else, but I would rather raise my voice in the direction of maintaining the fertility of the soil than in any other way, because it will do some good, not only to you but to all the generations coming hereafter."

The trouble was that the farm never kept pace with the railroad. The land was there, its quality was all that could be desired, its promise and the work of skilled immigration agents brought in people by millions. But the yield was disappointing. Everywhere settlers planted wheat because, in this rich virgin mould, it brought the largest cash return. They kept on growing wheat until the yield fell from between twenty and thirty bushels an acre to fifteen, to twelve, to eight. Then, if they had spent the winnings of the fat years, they drifted, broken, to the cities and towns, to live as best they might. If they had saved something, they moved on west or north to repeat, on rich lands yet unoccupied, the process of exhaustion. To Mr. Hill the sight of this was like the passage of one of those trains of hated empties. It was robbing these people, and their children, and him. It was impoverishing the future. It tended to defeat the great plan by which railroads should go on building farms and farms building railroads forever. He could not tolerate it. He sought and found the remedy; and continued to divide his strongest interest and his most abounding energy between the railroad and the farm. How he worked out the general principle of conservation and applied it to the land has been told in another chapter. His original interest in conservation and his study of it were both inspired by anxiety about the future of American agriculture. All the rest was only a logical corollary. Having set wheels moving for the larger purpose, he concentrated his efforts on the factor that appealed to him and on the section of the country that he knew best. Here, too, the reaction between soil and railroad would be strongest.

In 1879, when the St. Paul, Minneapolis & Manitoba was organized, and in the years immediately following, the exchange of old bonds for lands included in the grant to the St. Paul & Pacific meant to him less the extinction of a debt than the guaranty of larger and more prosperous communities, which would need more and better railroads. A previous chapter has related the beginning, in 1883, of his long campaign for more live stock of better grades upon the farm. It would, he said, break up the one-crop process. It would encourage the dairy interest, for which the Northwest was by nature so admirably fitted, but in which its farmers showed so little interest. It would, by providing a natural fertilizer, restore productivity to the soil. It would give the farmer work for the whole year, instead of intense labour during the few months of seedtime and harvest, followed by the unremunerated expenses and the demoralization of idleness during the long northern winter. So, for thirty-three years he had hammered away, in season and out of season. Such part of his crusade as is inseparable from the history of the preliminary period—his first stock distributions and their sequel—appears in its chronological setting. This is the place to take up the record and carry it to completion. The purchase and placing of high-grade stock in the Northwest continued. Although so many people failed to understand his motive or his method, he went on indefatigably. He wanted to do more and better. One of his interesting experiments, the introduction of the general-purpose cow, was well under way at the time of his death. He wanted the farmer to get, so far as possible, a maximum of dairy product and a maximum of beef product from the same animal. He worked confidently and enthusiastically to the last upon this extension of his live-stock propaganda. Professor

357

Thomas Shaw, an expert in animal husbandry who had helped in the work, furnished the following:

"For the last thirty years and more there has been no end of conflict between the breeders of cattle as to whether a place should be given on the farms of this country to the dual-purpose cow: the cow that is good for milk production and also for the production of high-class meat. In 1913 Mr. Hill authorized me to go to Great Britain and purchase a herd of milking Short-horns for his North Oaks farm, along with other pur-chases referred to later. On reaching England it was found that fully 80 per cent. of all the milk used in England came from these two-purpose cattle, an over-whelming majority of which were milking Shorthorns. Twenty-six were purchased at an average cost of about $500. These animals were all recorded in the English Shorthorn herd-book. In 1914 Mr. Hill again au-thorized me to go to England and bring out fifteen of the best cows of that class that could be obtained. Fifty young Shorthorn males were also to be purchased for free distribution to the farmers along the lines of the Great Northern Railroad. The fifteen cows were pur-chased at an average cost of $500. It would seem safe to say that fifteen cows better individually were not left in England. The fifty young Shorthorn males were all registered in the English herd-books, and when brought to America were distributed without cost to the farmers along the Great Northern Railroad in the states of

Minnesota, North Dakota, Montana, Washington, and Idaho. Twelve South Devon cattle were bought, of which two were males. These are the first South Devons ever brought to America. The demand for milking Shorthorns in the United States has gone up by leaps and bounds since these importations were made. On September 8th, 1915, the 'American Milking Shorthorn Breeders' Association' was organized in St. Paul, Minnesota, with Mr. Hill as its honorary president. There is no saying how far-reaching this movement will be. It is now believed by those competent to judge that it will become in the near future one of the most useful live-stock organizations in America."

Mr. Hill was as alive to the importance of conservation of live stock as to its introduction; as keen to establish this principle here as in the care of the soil and other natural resources. He is, indeed, primarily responsible for an important movement in this direction. The following details were obtained from Dr. Hermann M. Biggs, Health Commissioner of the State of New York: "In the summer of 1913 Mr. Hill spoke to me of the great loss from the prevalence of hog cholera in the Northwest, the economic importance of its prevention and his interest in it. He expressed strongly his belief that not only was the system of inoculation employed ineffective, but in some instances the inoculation of a herd of swine had been followed by the prompt appearance of the disease. Finally, in his characteristic way, he said: 'Do you think that the Rockefeller Institute would be willing to take up an investigation of hog cholera with a view to determining its cause and the method of prevention?' I arranged an interview with Doctor Flexner, the active director of the Institute, in which we talked the matter over; and later presented it to the executive committee of the Board of Scientific Directors. After full consideration, a recommendation was made to Mr. Rockefeller that a Division of Animal Pathology be established in connection with the Institute. A budget calling for an expenditure of about $50,000 a year having been prepared and submitted, Mr. Rockefeller later wrote saying that he had given to the trustees of the Institute securities to the amount of $1,000,000 for this purpose. Preparations for its establishment were made, and Dr. Theobald Smith was engaged as its Director. The buildings of the new division at Princeton, New Jersey have been in part completed. The Board of Scientific Directors regard this departure as one of the most important in the history of the Institute, and likely to lead to developments of the greatest value. The initiative which led to it came entirely from Mr. Hill.''

All this study and labour and expenditure, amounting to hundreds of thousands of dollars, for the introduction of improved breeds of cattle and for the conservation of live stock, was good in its way. But to Mr. Hill it was only a beginning, an accessory. His main thought was

THE SONS OF ANTAEUS

that nearly the whole industrial process of the farm must be changed. Farm yields in this country were too low. This was especially true of the West, where, as he said, comparing it with New England, you do not have "to shoot the corn out of a gun up on to the side of a hill, and shoe the calves in winter to keep them from sliding down." The acre product, as compared with that of less favourably situated land in other countries, was insignificant. There must be a general reform. He studied the history of such movements elsewhere. He went back a century to the investigations of Great Britain's Royal Commission to inquire into and recommend better agricultural methods. The records of farm yields throughout the world were laid under contribution. To the farmers of the Northwest he taught incessantly three things: a more intensive system, crop rotation, and soil maintenance by fertilization. No one outside of the Northwest, and comparatively few persons there, can appreciate, perhaps even comprehend the volume and intensity of his labours in this cause. The Great Northern sent out, in 1906, an experimental train fully equipped and accompanied by lecturers, to instruct the farmers who gathered at each stopping place in plant and animal culture, prevention of disease, and new and improved methods. This unrelenting zeal wore down prejudice and opposition. The farmers of the Northwest who, thirty years before, had looked upon Mr. Hill's invasion of their field with suspicion and without faith in his ability to guide, were becoming converted. So, too, was public opinion. At each session of Congress something was done for the extension of agricultural education. In the states, the wheels of agricultural colleges began to revolve more rapidly.

He spoke, wrote, encouraged, lent a hand everywhere. But the Government and the states did not move fast enough or far enough for him. What he wanted was to get into the minds of the men on the land the practical knowledge required to extract from any farm its greatest possible product, while sustaining or even increasing its fertility. They could not all go to the agricultural school. The agricultural school could not come to all of them. Even the county agent system, which may be said to be one of the indirect results of his campaign, could reach a comparatively small number. "We cannot wait," he said, "until all the old farmers die off and the younger generation that has been educated at farm schools comes into control." As always, when he saw that a thing was good he wanted it realized—turned into fact—at once. So he did it himself. In 1912 the Great Northern formed its organization for agronomic inquiry, demonstration work, and the education of the farmer on his own land. Mr. F. R. Crane, who had twelve years' experience in responsible positions in the University of Illinois and the Special Agricultural School of Menominee, Wisconsin, was

THE SONS OF ANTAEUS

placed in charge of the work. The remarkable results obtained under his superintendence owed much not only to the original plan of Mr. Hill, but to his minute and continuous examination, suggestion, and surveillance. The first year a tract of five acres was selected on each of 152 farms in Minnesota and Dakota. The owner agreed to plough, plant, and cultivate the five acres exactly as directed. Selected seed was furnished to him. He received the product of these acres as his own, being paid in addition for his labour. There was a great gain in the quality as well as the quantity of the yield. The record of these Great Northern plots as compared with the average yield of the state, measured by the acre product in bushels, was as follows:

	Minne-sota	Average for State
Wheat	29.86	15.8
Barley	44.65	28.2
Oats	67.09	41.7
	North Dakota	
Wheat	31.47	18.
Barley	49.71	29.7
Oats	78.64	41.6

It was also shown in practice that better methods would not of themselves completely restore soils that had been abused. Such improvement, unaided, was too slow. The plan was enlarged to include soil analysis,

363

disclosing soil defects; communication of this information directly to the man on the farm himself; demonstration of its value, and advice and assistance in supplying the elements necessary to high productivity. Mohammed had not come to the mountain, so the mountain went to Mohammed. Early and late Mr. Hill repeated his slogan: "We must get the facts direct to the man on the land." No facilities being within reach at that time equal to the scientific analysis of soil samples from hundreds of farms, he turned over to the work the extensive greenhouses attached to his residence in St. Paul. There soils were analyzed. There experiments were conducted, by growing plants in pots filled with earth specimens taken from different farms and treated in different ways. The results pointed out scientifically the nature and amount of the addition to each kind of soil required to bring it up to high fertility. These pot cultures made the diagnoses from which prescriptions were ordered for all these separate ailing or anaemic soils over the Northwest. Mr. Hill knew many happy moments in this laboratory of living things; passing between long lines of sturdy witnesses to a better agriculture, watching the growing grain, measuring relative improvement, seeing in fancy the new wealth incubating here, forecasting effects along the lines of his own system and anticipating their repetition, by force of example, all over the country. Most of the soils were found deficient in phosphorus. Acid phosphate was

364

added, in combination with barnyard manure. The farmer tried out the remedy on the demonstration plot on his own holding, following instructions literally. It was proved that there was a net gain in the market value of the product of from $2.65 to $3.00 per acre over the cost of the fertilizer. Every farmer who harvested and garnered these crops was a convert. Every neighbour saw or heard of the results. Letters of approval testified to the rise in favour of the new methods. The work more than justified itself. Mr. Crane gave the following summary of what had been done down to the year of Mr. Hill's death:

"In the past five years we have operated, under contract, with ten hundred and sixty-five farmers at different points in Minnesota, North and South Dakota. We have, in several specific instances, done work in Montana. We have put in thousands of acres of alfalfa with no agreements drawn up. We have averaged each year a little over three cars of pure seed grains which we have distributed free of charge. We have averaged each year a distribution of about five hundred tons of commercial plant foods, which were made up principally of acid phosphate. The work has now advanced to the point where we are establishing permanent twenty-acre rotation plots upon different farms located in the states through which the Great Northern Railway passes. These plots will be continued upon the same farm for a period of ten or fifteen years. This plan received the official approval of Mr. Hill. These points serve as centres where we bring the farmers together each year to talk over the advance being made in agricultural methods. The increase in yields, from a percentage standpoint, will run from 25 to 33 per cent., in many cases more than doubling the yields upon the rest of the farm. There are, of course, a few failures, but these are running less than 1 per cent. In every case we can satisfy ourselves that it is largely the fault of the farmer where a failure takes place."

Mr. Hill's plan contemplated a system of agriculture regenerated in its fundamental principles. The railroad would get its reward from the larger volume of business contributed, field by field, from each rejuvenated farm. "You may think it strange," said Mr. Hill to a gathering of merchants, "that I would rather see butter and cheese and cattle raised, where five bushels of corn would be concentrated in the weight of one bushel in the steer. We will not be short of tonnage. We will have all we can carry, and more. No trouble about that." His thought was true and living: If the land pays a higher return for labour, more labour will seek the land. If farming becomes a business of profits as closely calculable in advance as those of merchandising, it will attract capital and men as powerfully. If the farm is a better place to live, a healthier, happier, more profitable, more comfortable place than it ever was before, the drift of population

366

from country to city, swelling urban communities at the expense of acres lying fallow and lost to the world's uses, may be checked. Wealth may accumulate and men not decay. All this was included in his purpose and his hope. "See to it," he said at a meeting of farmers, "that the children of the farm go where they will not be taught to despise the soil or long,for a future freed from its labours, but will learn the fact, now being fully understood, that the right kind of farming offers scope for the keenest intelligence, occupation for the most active brain, and opportunity and reward for the highest ambition." In answer to a request to write an article for one of the papers published at Yale University, and give practical suggestions, his message to the collegian was that, in the new life and with the new ideas of the day, there is a fitting place for the University man on the farm. His propaganda in this country was noted and rightly valued abroad. Between him and Sir Horace Plunkett, thinking and working along the same lines for the uplifting of agricultural Ireland, there was reciprocal interest and appreciation. A letter from Sir Horace in 1914 contains this passage: "I write to you now to say that, largely owing to your own writings, the problems of rural reconstruction are not only obtaining far more attention than formerly in the United States, but there are an endless large number of very effective philanthropic organizations and many big thinkers and

367

social workers doing fine practical work upon the problems. There are many things and people I should like to show you in Ireland, where I am certain you would be immensely interested in the working out of ideas which you have favoured in the United States."

The agricultural interest of the United States owes a lasting debt to the enthusiasm and the life-long labours of James J. Hill. It was inextricably linked with his chosen work in life. He saw railroading and agriculture as twin agencies in the conquest of the world's fair future. There should be no more wilderness, and no more mob. On the land would be room and work and a competence for all. If, in the work of Mr. Hill for agricultural improvement and instruction, there was a strain of self-interest—and assuredly there was—it was woven there by the nature of things. If he took toll, he also gave service in heaped measure to the material progress of his time. None of it was more willing or loyal than that which he offered to the toilers of the earth. If his scheme dug deep to make new piers for wealth and give new scope to power, it rose also, not merely by implication but by virtue of his wide prevision and his real and deep solicitude for his country and his kind, to the height of statesmanship.

He became now, himself, the head of his own peripatetic agricultural university. He was always on call. His voice carried farthest. Old settlers, who had found him staunch for a lifetime, flocked to hear him and

LORD MOUNT STEPHEN
As president of the Bank of Montreal, an associate of Mr. Hill's in the financing of
his earlier railroad ventures, and a life-long friend

brought the newer comers with them. Every year he undertook voluntarily labour comparable to that of a candidate for high public office. Invitations to address farmers' meetings and county fairs came in by scores. Wherever he went, his audience numbered thousands. He made out, long in advance, itineraries for these addresses on farm needs and methods. Only the most imperative call of larger interests under his care was allowed to interfere. He travelled from one county to another, speaking in rural centres, seldom in large towns, at meetings in the open air, under a big tent, in a close and sometimes chilly auditorium, in all weathers, regardless of his own health or the strain upon it, and often making two or three of these addresses in a single day. This was pure missionary work. By this time his railroad did not need such efforts on his part. It was the people on the farms that he cared for and wanted to help. His talks were always extempore; simple, full of homely argument, crowded with apt metaphors drawn from the life about him, enlivened by humour and by sallies at the expense of some of the old acquaintances whom he saw everywhere. Strange and inspiring spectacle! A man well past the threescore years and ten that bring at least surcease of labour, a man of such achievement, such wealth, such power, whose presence was sought for eagerly at meetings of renowned and powerful associations all over the country, setting aside their invitations in order that he might be free to preach the gospel of better farming at some country crossroads. To the end of his life he maintained this custom, become now both duty and delight. Had he lived, the autumn of 1916 would have found him, as did that of the year before, lending the momentum of his knowledge, his experience, and his personality to the betterment of farm conditions; which implied for him universal prosperity, the rise of the average individual character, and the security of national institutions.

One hundred and thirty years before the opening of the Christian era a wise old thinker, without our light to guide him, wrote compassionate words, at the same time pitiful and proud, which run parallel with Mr. Hill's larger and deeper purpose and his inarticulate thought. These are the words of the Son of Sirach, caught here and there as he muses upon "The Wisdom of Business": "The wisdom of a scribe cometh by opportunity of leisure; and he that hath little business shall become wise. How shall he become wise that holdeth the plough, that driveth the oxen, and whose discourse is of the stock of bulls? He will set his heart upon turning his furrows. So is every artificer and workmaster. So is the smith sitting by the anvil, and considering the unwrought iron. So is the potter sitting at his work, and turning the wheel about with his feet. All these put their trust in their hands; and each becometh wise in his own work. Without these shall not a city be inhabited, and men shall not sojourn nor walk up and down therein. They shall not be sought for in the council of the people, and in the assembly they shall not mount on high. But they will maintain the fabric of the world; and in the handiwork of their craft is their prayer."

CHAPTER   THIRTY-EIGHT
TEMPERAMENT AND PERSONALITY

IN EXTERNAL appearance James J. Hill was a man
to hold the eye of any stranger who met him on the
street or saw him in a gathering of men. He gave
at the first glance an impression of immense reserves of
power, and of the custom of command. There was
about him a natural distinction which made it impossible that any one should fail to recognize in him, though
still unknown, the unusual. "Who is that man?" would
be the inevitable question that instinctively singled him
out in a crowd.

Physically he was rather below the middle height,
but powerfully built. His great shoulders and body
to match were part of the equipment that had enabled
him to brave the hardships of the frontier, and to under-
go a lifetime of labours such as few men could sustain.
Although he always drew relentlessly upon these physical
resources and did not know the meaning of overwork or
fag of brain or body, he did not squander them uselessly.
Notwithstanding his impetuosity he was a temperate
man. He smoked a good deal. He was not a teeto-
taler, but his habit was abstemious. One of the com-
panions of his early days in St. Paul, when he shared
372

the escapades indulged in by the youth of the unlicked little community, said that when the fun was over and the drinking bouts began, into which such occasions often insensibly merged, he quietly vanished. He had too serious a view of himself and the work he believed to be before him to invite either physical or moral deterioration. He was a vigorous man to the end of his days. In his fishing vacations on his salmon river in Labrador, he tired out men younger than he by a good many years. He was fond of hunting, and walked when most men would ride. His innumerable journeys through rough country during the location and construction of the railroad, his pilgrimages among the farmers, and his personal supervision of experiments in farm methods and stock raising, carried on upon his own large properties, hardened his frame to iron. No severe illness had ever weakened him. Body was equal to the demand of even such a brain and such phenomenal activity. It never failed and never seemed even to decline until just at the last.

One who stepped into a hall where Mr. Hill was sitting on the platform with others, even though well behind them, would notice him instantly. The great domed head, set firmly on a torso longer than it seemed because so broad and muscular, rose above all others. In such a setting, one word alone—the one so often used—would describe him. His attitude, his air, were leonine. He sat there as if unconscious of the lordship that the whole man proclaimed. At closer range you felt the piercing eye. His look had the quality found in all great leaders of men. It saw into and down and through. When he was roused to anger, his glance could smite without a word. There were few who cared or dared to face it then. The short, close beard that he always wore half hid the expression of the mouth. About the full lips there was the imprint of the open heart, understanding, and sympathy. Here, too, was the stamp of that strong sense of humour which saved intensity of conviction from becoming fanaticism, and earnestness from hardening into intolerance. The mouth, like the deepest nature of the man, was kindly.

His mode of speaking was all his own. Like his garb, like everything about him that he could fashion to his will, it was simplicity reduced almost to an extreme. If, as many eulogists have said truly, he "made two blades of grass grow where only one grew before," he also made only one word grow where two words grew before. He sought them as short and simple as could be found, provided they were adequate and true in the expression of an idea. He often spoke of "The Pilgrim's Progress" as a model of style. He preferred a word of Saxon family to one of Latin race. His speech and his writing went straight to the point. Ruthlessly he cut away from his work everything that did not seem indispensable to plain expression of the thought. He hated an unnecessary adjective as

374

much as he would have despised the painting of a fine picture on the side of a freight car. Informally, he could at need express himself with a vigour and directness that did not need explanation or invite repetition.

Almost all genius, every man without exception who has dominated other men and mastered opposing circumstances and forces, has been both helped and hindered by a capacity for mighty wrath. It is part of the equipment of success. Passion goes with power. Mr. Hill was no exception to this rule; and when his anger broke restraints, men ran to cover. He was the opposite of what is described by the term "ill-tempered." His normal attitude toward men, toward life, toward work, was expectant and appreciative. But he had tasks that would brook no trifling. The lion would have become entangled in the net if he had not broken its meshes at the first approach. He was impatient with incompetence. The mediocre must stand aside. He chose his helpers as the surgeon does his implements. The best would be none too good for his major operations. Relax the standards, let personal pity perpetuate the unfit in places of responsibility, and the stronghold would be turned into an asylum for incapables. His wrath broke on incompetence repeated; on the slack, on the unintelligent, above all on the dishonest or unfaithful. These cowered quickly away from the destroying blast that stripped them to the buff of cheap or impotent natures. He was troubled by them no more. But he was gentleness and kindness itself to men who did their best and in whose best there was a promise of the superlative he sought. He would give one more trial, and yet one more opportunity. He wished that his helpers might make good. Not a few who served him in difficult and trying places for more than a score of years, occasionally surpassing his expectation and sometimes falling below it, but always doing their honest best, never had to meet the whirlwind of his anger, and never heard addressed to them a single unkind word from his lips.

To all who were capable and faithful he showed a beautiful loyalty. ' They never needed to give explanation or defence. They had not to fear the secret whisper of envy or jealousy or hate. Sometimes a letter containing direct attack or plausible innuendo designed to discredit a subordinate would be turned over to the man himself, with the remark: "That fool doesn't know what he is talking about." In the opposite direction his opinion was just as final. The employee who deceived him, who was caught "soldiering," who was guilty of any form of dishonesty, was struck out of his books. He could readily forgive; but his forgetting was also so complete that it was useless ever to mention the name of that stranger to him again. In one respect his temper was peculiar. It soared and broke and burned most fiercely when it clashed with little men and little things. He had no use and no time for them. They were wasters of life, every moment and effort of which were needed for great designs. After a crisis, in a time of hope dispelled and opportunity destroyed, he was calm and self-possessed. When, for example, the unexpected decision was rendered in the Northern Securities case, and others were gloomy and inclined to wonder if they might not have done better or differently, he was in his gayest and serenest mood. He had not a word of blame for any one. He said that it was all over, and things would come out all right. That kind of temper can make its possessor a man, but cannot break him. It also develops affectionate loyalty in others. Many thought that in order to get on well with Mr. Hill it was necessary to humour him; that, if you dared to express your own opinion or question his, you needed to have a cyclone cellar handy. This was true enough if your facts limped or your logic stammered. It was just as true, it was inevitable that, determined as he was to get to the heart of all matters, he wanted to hear anything sound and well put. He would not squander time and effort in mental boxing feats. But if you thought differently from him about some serious question, and told him quietly and clearly how and why, no bombs burst about you. The man who dared to do this, because he believed it important that he should, found himself liked and trusted. Mr. Hill might not alter his views or his policy about the disputable matter one iota, but he marked that man as worthy of his esteem and confidence.

Average human opinion clings as obstinately to faith in some magic talisman that will assure success as voodoo does to its tar baby. Articles are written and magazines are published about it. The plodder and the beginner are firmly convinced that if they could get the key to this spell "of woven paces and of waving hands," glory and honour and wealth would come out with banners to meet them. So Mr. Hill, like every other conspicuously successful man, was greatly pestered by people who besought him for his recipe. These believers in chance and luck and witches' broth and the philosopher's stone asked him to tell them how to succeed. His best answer was this: "As far as rules go, I would say that those that have helped me to succeed are, 'Work, hard work, intelligent work, and then some more work.'" Opportunity, as he often freely acknowledged, had favoured him. But it had waited for six years, in those old days, upon others as faithfully as upon him, and they had despised it. It is as young and generous and insistent to-day as ever it was. The difference is only in its mask, which continually changes. Wealth, oftener a hindrance than a help to success at the beginning, he and a thousand others have proved to be not necessary. These two conditioning circumstances, money and opportunity, are external, and neither is particularly important. The real sources of success lie within: knowledge, foresight, courage, honesty, labour. Without these, an Olympian genius would decline to mediocrity. Take this prize list of qualities from the biography of Mr. Hill, and nothing would be left but some scraps of disfigured paper. Take them from his life, and no success would have been possible. His sympathy with young men of worthy ambitions made him willing occasionally to answer eager, childish questions. He did set down for them some rules drawn from personal experience that ought to be written where every boy might read them:

"A young man has always had to help make his opportunities, and he must do that to-day, as ever. But young men fail more nowadays than they used to, because they expect to reap almost as soon as they sow. That is the very great trouble with the young men of the present. They expect opportunities to come to them without application, or proper shaping of things so that opportunities will drift their way. You have to keep your eyes open and catch hold of things; they'll not catch hold of you, as a rule.

"If a young fellow doggedly bucks the world and circumstances without sense or reason all the time, he is liable to get nothing more than a sore head. He must know how to take advantage of opportunities, to use his brains; in short, a young man who has no brains ought at least to have enough animal sense to find it out, and learn to depend upon and get what benefits he can from the brains of others.

"The working days and the working hours are those in which there is necessary work to be done, whatever time that may require. Spare hours are well spent upon the study of history, literature, and art. Whatever any able mind of great genius has given for the instruction or enjoyment of the world is worth while. Ample and accurate information is the best step toward success for every one; and the world of historic fact, economic fact, and scientific fact, with the bearing of each upon the probable future of human effort, is now so large that a man will find all his leisure too little for his desire to equip himself with knowledge. In books and pictures, as in practical things, only the best are worth any one's time and attention."

Here is his final word to young men: "The best advice to a young man, as it appears to me, is old and simple. Get knowledge and understanding. Determine to make the most possible of yourself by doing to the best of your power useful work as it comes your way. There are no new receipts for success in life. A good aim, diligence in learning every detail of your business, honest hard work and a determination to succeed, win out every time, unless crossed by some exceptional accident or misfortune. Many opportunities come to every man. It depends upon himself, and upon what he shall make of himself, what he makes of opportuni-
380

ties and what they will make of him." What he said to the young man and to the individual he urged upon every man and upon the community. He had sunk a shaft to the bedrock of human nature. Finding it everywhere essentially the same, he built upon it. To the members of a savings bank association who had invited him to speak at a dinner, he sent this brief but comprehensive letter: "Whatever encourages thrift in a people builds a sure foundation for their prosperity, security, and honour. Economically, the saving of some portion of earning or income raises barbarism to civilization. Morally, it leads to self-mastery and the wholesome pride that accompanies the sense of independence. Politically, it strengthens civic interest and virtue by giving men a stake in the state. The wonderful qualities shown by the French in the present war could be displayed only by a people that had raised thrift to the rank of a distinctive national virtue. More, perhaps, than any other, the need and the value of it should be impressed upon the people of the United States."

The divinity that shapes our ends—very often by shaping our beginnings—had sent him into the thick of life. One rule above all others he followed there. "Success with honour" was his motto. He would have no other kind. He was prouder of that unsullied escutcheon than of anything else in the world outside of his own home. Look back at the signal lights along the chapters that have led up to this point. Remember how he had won wealth by serving his stockholders, his refusal to profit personally by anything they could not share, his "stand without hitching" promise made good in the fight over Northern Pacific, his proud word in the presence of culture as represented by one of America's great universities: "I never earned a dishonest dollar. I have never seen the place where a lie would take the place of truth." No man could go through his experience without having reason many times to doubt and distrust other men. It did not corrode his judgment. In 1907 he said in a public address: "If you listen to some, and occasionally the daily press, you would think that there was not an honest man doing business in the United States. And the bigger business a man did the bigger sinner he was held to be. In my opinion there are good and bad men in all walks of life. No great business can prosper permanently that is not built on principle and carried on along straightforward lines." On the same occasion he expressed his own code of action in words so modest that it is not easy to realize how noble is the profession of faith they imply: "I have got to stand by my record. If I have been able to do any good, I am glad. If I have made any mistakes, it has not been intentionally. If I have injured any one, I am sorry."

At different times in his life, Mr. Hill had a financial interest in one or more newspapers. In every case except one, this was similar to his interest in a New York or Chicago bank, or in any of the numerous industrial enterprises that came to him with a sound business statement and a request for a loan. A paper, on changing hands, might need new capital; and, if he knew the country and the men, and believed both to be a guaranty of financial success, he would help to place a bond issue. Beyond that he would not go. He made no private use of the connection, and asked nothing except that interest and principal should be paid when due. The exceptional relation is his ownership of the St. Paul *Daily Globe*. The question has often been asked why Mr. Hill bought this paper and why, ten years later, he discontinued its publication. The true answer ought to be given, because it helps to explain the fine sincerity of the man. Perhaps I may be pardoned here for the use of the first person singular, because I was editor and manager of the *Globe* for two years after Mr. Hill purchased it and also for the last two years of its life. Mr. Hill bought it in the early part of 1896, primarily in order to keep it from becoming an organ of the advocates of the free coinage of silver. The *Globe* had passed through bankruptcy two years before. It had not got upon its feet when those who controlled it fell into the same plight. Before this time they had been approached by a wealthy owner of silver mines in Montana with a proposition to buy at any reasonable price. The big fight between the gold standard and the silver standard was on, and would be decided definitely in the election of that year. The zeal with which Mr. Hill had thrown himself into the cause of sound money has been described. The *Globe* was then the only daily Democratic paper published in the Northwest. It was an institution of his own city. He did not want this or any other newspaper. He bought its entire capital stock to keep it from falling into the outstretched hands of the free silver people. Having bought it, he desired it to become a success. His only requirement of those who managed it was the publication of a clean and able newspaper, faithful to the Democratic traditions of Grover Cleveland's time.

Ten years of trial proved that the *Globe* could not be made a paying proposition. Mr. Hill did not drop it on account of pique, or for any other than a strictly business reason. The balance sheet which caused him to approve my recommendation that the *Globe* be discontinued showed, for the preceding month, under no exceptional conditions, an increase of $1,100 in circulation receipts and a decrease in advertising receipts of $1,500. This abnormal relation had become chronic, and resisted all attempts to change it. Circulation being rather a financial liability than an asset, unless advertising space and rates conform to it, to continue the business would have been absurd. Exactly as Mr. Hill bought the *Globe* because he did not wish a paper published in St. Paul to fall into hands that he might

384

not approve, so, now, for a similar reason, strengthened by the fact that his name had been connected with it, he directed that it cease publication at a given date, killed the news franchise, and ordered the plant broken up and sold. These are the facts of a transaction that cost Mr. Hill real disappointment as well as a considerable sum of money. During his ownership of the paper he said repeatedly that, if it could be made a paying property, he did not want and would not take a dollar from it.

It would be natural to suppose that a man of strong will and extensive business interests, especially when these were subject to almost continual public criticism or assault, should use his own daily newspaper to defend and promote his other properties and purposes. As a fact, this was furthest from his thought. During the four years when I controlled and decided the editorial and business conduct of the *Globe*, Mr. Hill gave me but one instruction. He told me to "make it a good newspaper and a credit to the town." Never, either directly or indirectly, did there come an order, a suggestion, even a hint, of any other thing that Mr. Hill would like the newspaper to do or not to do. His proud refusal was carried so far as to be embarrassing. A public question arose in which the public interest might, according to one's honest judgment, lean one way or the other. The policy of the paper and my own convictions were still unsettled. I knew that Mr. Hill's

385

financial interest in the matters affected by the proposed action ran into six figures, but did not know on which side it was to be found. I thought that he was entitled to be consulted before his own newspaper took its stand. So, for the first and only time during my connection with the *Globe*, I went to Mr. Hill to ask for his advice in a matter of newspaper policy. I stated the case to him just as it is stated here. This was his reply: "Mr. Pyle, when I put you in charge of the *Globe*, I told you to make it a good newspaper and a credit to the town. I have had no reason to think that you cannot follow that rule. You must go ahead and use your own judgment." I did so; but I did not know then and I never knew whether the position which the *Globe* took in that important matter was favourable or hostile to Mr. Hill's own interest. This is a fair sample of the man. Nobody knew the fact; some would not have believed it if they had been told. "Men are never at heart's ease while they behold a greater than themselves." But such was his idea of the proper relation between the business end and the editorial end of a newspaper. He would have hated a press influenced for him against its will just as much as he despised one prejudiced against him. He did not believe that any newspaper had a right to live or to wield the baton of publicity unless it could be absolutely fair, fearless, and free.

Personal publicity he sincerely disliked. He would do what he thought proper for the success of an idea or a cause close to his heart. But he detested anything that turned the limelight on himself. There was not one atom of personal vanity in the man. In 1886 he was still new to power, and newer yet to the Eastern public. His railroad was racing across Montana, and its Pacific extension was yet to be financed. A little judicious personal advertising might have helped a lot. An important financial journal in New York wrote for his picture. He answered: "While I appreciate the courtesy of your request, I have no desire to have my portrait published; and your president will therefore, I hope, kindly excuse me if I do not send my photograph." In 1891 a writer of national reputation, who was also a personal acquaintance, requested material for a sketch. He refused, with this gracious palliative of the blow: "It is much more pleasant to have our friends think well of us than to have our acts published." The collector for an educational institution had the bad judgment to suggest in his letter that the names of subscribers would be published, and the denomination and nationality most concerned would take notice. The reply to this was delivered without gloves: "I note what you say in regard to its being of some personal advantage to me through the publication of names. I beg to say that anything contributed by me would do as much good without publication of my name as with it; and for myself, I do not seek preferment among any class of citizens." Needless to add that no check accompanied the biting comment. Whenever any concern was unwise enough to make a suggestion like this, it went permanently on the blacklist.

Mr. Hill had a keen sense of wit and humour. What lightened the rude days of his youthful life with practical jokes and ready repartee became, with years and mature taste, a lively appreciation of the humorous. He was always ready to listen to a good story and to tell one, with that merry twinkle of the eye that changed him from a ruler of men to a comrade. He could repeat pages from Bon Gaultier or Father Prout. He saw the funny side even of serious things; and, if they became too serious, could pass easily to sarcasm that bit and stung. It is a pity that comparatively so few of the tart and amusing anecdotes and illustrations with which he sprinkled his offhand talks to farmers and others have been preserved. No one knew better how to make a point and clinch it with some homely reference to the daily life of those about him; some story about the people who had come in Minnesota's early days in such numbers from the state of Maine that he said he knew any man who had not come from East Machias must have come from South Machias. But the finest flavour of these things is lost when they are not accompanied with the cock of the eye, the wrinkle of laughter about the mouth, and its hearty rumble in the voice. When the friends of the president of the Santa Fe railroad system were getting up a birthday book for him, they sent to Mr. Hill asking for a suitable quotation. Here is what he gave them from the old delight of his boyhood; an extract from Plutarch's "Life of Caius Gracchus": "His most especial exertions were given to constructing the roads, which he was careful to make beautiful and pleasant, as well as convenient. . . . When he met with any valleys or deep watercourses crossing the line, he either caused these to be filled up with rubbish, or bridges to be built over them, so well levelled that, all being of an equal height on both sides, the work presented one uniform and beautiful prospect. . . . For these reasons, the people highly extolled him, and were ready upon all occasions to express their affection toward him." A charitable woman sent to a large number of the most prominent men in the country, asking each to send her a fable, or a limerick, all of which were to be published and sold, and the proceeds to be used for pure milk and nursing for sick babies. To this cause Mr. Hill contributed the following. They connect delightfully with his two central ideas of the railroad and the farm:

The Equine and His Equal

A Lean Horse once Looked over the Fence into the Next Field, and saw a Lean and Rag-ged Man Spad-ing the ground. "Let Me in There," he said; "I will Work the Soil for you while you Feed Me, and we will both grow Fat and Sleek."

"You're On," said the Man; and He and the Horse were Prosper-ous and Hap-py until they both Waxed Fat and Saucy. Then they Got Mad at each other, and the Boss said he would Show that

Plug that a Man can Kick Hard-er than a Horse. He put a Muz-zle on the Poor Beast and Gave him Oats at the Rate of One Grain a Day, and the Neigh-bours Sat up Nights to keep him off the Grass.

Soon the Horse was too Weak to Work any More. So the Field was Ne-glect-ed, and he and the Man both Starved to Death. Before he died, the Wise Guy said to the Weep-ing Crowd: "This is Your Fu-ner-al too, my Fool Friends. Let me Hand you this Mor-al to Frame and Hang over your Emp-ty Din-ner Tables: 'The Mare Makes Money Come Just As Fast As Money Makes the Mare Go.'"

And here is his double-barrelled limerick:

The Farm

"There was a young farm in the West,
    So much over-worked and hard-pressed
        That it wearily said:
        'I'll just take to my bed
    And drop through to China to rest.'

"But alas! when the roots of the trees
    Caught the eye of the frugal Chinese,
        They proceeded to pounce,
        And to plant every ounce
    Of that Farm to Potatoes and Peas."

When he presented to the authorities of the Roman Catholic Church the seminary in St. Paul, he asserted, in words already given, his belief in the necessity of religious education for the highest development of the individual and the safety and security of the state. That belief included all varieties of faith and all kinds of institutions. In an address at the dedication of a building of the North Star College at Warren, Minnesota, he said: "No nation can exist without a true religious spirit behind it. Laws that forbid teaching Christianity are the weakest things in our government. I hope to see the Decalogue in every schoolroom. The Bible will be the measure of the mental growth of this republic and of the prosperity of our nation." On a similar occasion, in 1910, at the University of North Dakota, in which he took a great interest, he amplified his thought: "I was glad to hear the President of the University of Illinois speak so kindly of those other institutions of learning, the denominational colleges. They have their place. Nobody has greater interest in the young men or the young women than the mothers and fathers who send them out to get their education. I can realize the anxiety of that mother at whose knee they have been taught from early childhood to repeat their morning and evening prayer, when she sends them away to build up mind and character, if character is to be built up away from that personal influence, and from the influence and support of Christianity. It will not be strange if some of them come back with their minds filled with doubt. I do not care what the denomination may be. If they are true to their own profession they will do a great deal of good, and never will do any harm to any other denominational institution. I feel a deep interest in this matter because there has been a tendency at times for young people to go astray, not because they have more knowledge but because of their want of knowledge. Truth will never conflict with

391

truth. You can magnify it and add to it and it will always be harmonious. There will never be a real conflict; and all natural law can be applied as far as we have the intelligence to apply it. All scientific investigation can be carried to a limit beyond our comprehension if we pursue it far enough. But when we come to the spiritual, it is limited, as far as we are concerned, to what is given us through revelation. There is no conflict, there can be none between the state university and what are sometimes called fresh water denominational colleges." Struggling colleges from all over the Northwest came to him for help. They did not come in vain, provided they were conducted under the auspices of some religious denomination. Most of the pupils of these institutions, he said, came from country districts and had been brought up under religious influences. The time of first leaving home is one of upheaval for boy or girl. If, in addition to home associations, the religious influence is withdrawn, there is great danger. Mr. Hill had a profound sense of the value of religious experience, not only to the individual but to the state. No government, he often repeated, has ever been stable unless there was some strong religious conviction in its people. So his interest in education that should not be divorced from faith was threefold: for the soul, for the nation, for the spread and permanence of divine truth itself.

Behind the life of activity in the world, and the preparation that he deemed most suitable for it, stands the home. He saw in it the only human force that can create and maintain character. He paid to it this fine tribute: "The home is the centre and anchor of life both for children and parents. It gives happiness to one and forms the character of the other. All after life is built upon the home life; from it the first and best and most lasting education is drawn. A boy or girl who is taught there to be obedient and affectionate and considerate of others, to look forward to making the best use of whatever opportunity life may bring and who receives, after leaving the home, such education as the best schools and universities have to offer, has all the preparation for after life that there is to give, and one that should not often fail. This is a method many years old, but I do not know that it has ever been improved upon." No wonder that he felt this strongly. The essence of his native qualities came from that little house near Guelph, where stern yet kindly influences had shaped him for what he was to become. His own home, which had surrounded him for almost fifty years with ideal happiness, expanded and completed the character and conviction of the man. He had brought up his big family in tender intimacy with him. Two of his sons have been mentioned in their association with his labours and their own independent achievement. The third, Walter, abounding in natural energy and enthusiasm, was more attracted by his father's work for the farm than for the railroad. He engaged in farming on a large scale in the Red River Valley, taking especial interest in the growth and improvement of live stock. One of Mr. Hill's seven daughters died in infancy. Of the six who survived him, Mary married Samuel Hill, of Seattle; Ruth became the wife of Anson McCook Beard, of New York City; Charlotte, the wife of George Theron Slade, vice-president of the Northern Pacific, residing in St. Paul; Gertrude, the wife of Michael Gavin, II, of New York City; Clara has not married; and Rachel is the wife of Dr. Egil Boeckmann, a St. Paul specialist.

Away back in the years when he was building into Montana a railroad which jeering critics told him could carry nothing but buffalo bones, and when even those who supported him had to "walk by faith and not by sight," he said to one of his close friends: "To the support and loving patience of my wife I owe more of my success than to anything else in the world." He repeated that without the change of a word to the end of his life, on those rare occasions when he was moved to give a glimpse of that withdrawn self which very few were privileged to see. Most intimate and greatest of his traits was his intense devotion to his family and the life of the home. Here, on ground too sacred for intrusion, it is fitting to mention only things known, spoken, openly lived through long and happy years. No other interest on earth could for a moment compare with that he felt in those closest to him by the family tie. He could listen like a stoic to news of some great financial or industrial disturbance that presaged a war of giants, but the suffering or danger of one in his own household would wreck his firmness and change his imperturbable self-confidence to doubt and fear. Whenever you could not find him in his office or elsewhere that business called him, you knew that he was to be reached in his home. There struck strong and deep the roots of his being. There was the inspiration and support of his wonderful career. Great souls are, by their very quality of greatness, often doomed to loneliness. It was not the fate of Mr. Hill. Understanding, sympathy, companionship were the return given to his life-long devotion by those who were dearest to him. Did he have a clear mind, clean hands, and a pure heart? There was a shrine there before which the light burned always.

Mr. Hill was the simplest and most democratic of mortals. He hated all ostentation. He would rather wear a suit of old clothes than new ones. Democracy in him was not merely a matter of indifference to external show, it was of the mind and heart. He never made his own position or power unpleasantly felt, except in the presence of presumption or inefficiency. In his heart he delighted to find in any man with whom he came necessarily into contact some quality to which his own nature responded. He passed his judgments, sometimes unsparing and always keen as a sword, more readily on those in high places than on those of low estate. He fraternized with the men whom he had learned to appreciate and who, in their turn, had learned to value and love him. He was freely accessible. Unless his day were already apportioned to business necessities, anybody might see him. He would walk in upon a subordinate at any hour and chat with the familiarity of a business partner and a personal friend.

Reference was made in its proper chronological place to Mr. Hill's knowledge and love of pictures, and to the collection of paintings that he gathered through the years. This did not represent a passing attraction; but the gratifying, so soon as it became possible, of a side of his nature as pronounced and characteristic as its more familiar and practical forms of expression. He was a born artist. He had that unerring appreciation of artistic values and that inner responsiveness to the appeal of the beautiful and the true upon which the kingdom of art must be built. As soon as he had a home, Mr. Hill began to adorn it with pictures of the best-accepted standards of the time. They helped him to gratify and express a feeling which had found little to feed upon in the crude atmosphere of the frontier and the circumstances of his strenuous life. In the eighties of the last century, he got hold of a Corot and a Rousseau, brought them from the East and placed them in the small collection he already possessed. It was like the opening of new

396

doors that let in abundant light. More remarkable than his self-education by books and reading was this silent self-education in the lore of art, through contemplation of its best examples and comparison of painter with painter and school with school. These two new pictures gave him new enthusiasm, delight, and inspiration. He himself said, expressively, that they "drove the others out" of his gallery. From this time he set his standard. He chose what appealed to him; not to the moment's fancy, but to the artist who stood critically back of the man, and was satisfied with nothing but the best. To the end of his life he would pass hours in study and enjoyment of his masterpieces. If any of them failed under the test of such scrutiny and personal interpretation, it was banished. He cared for nothing but the superlatively good; and though his knowledge ripened, it would scarcely be true to say that his taste in pictures changed materially after the revolution of that first revealing flash. For it was less a product of education than a part of the man himself. During the last weeks of his life he spent several hours of each day among the pictures that were still, as they had always been to him, a source of deep delight.

This is a matter upon which the expert should be heard. One of the best judges of art in this country, who knew Mr. Hill well, expressed in a letter, written after his death, this opinion: "In 1886 Mr. Hill already had a miscellaneous collection of rather old-fashioned pictures, the only ones he had had a chance of seeing, good in their way and, though not first class, superior to all those in the collections made near him. At that time subject and composition made the strongest appeal to him, but he already had an eye for colour and quality. A number of pictures then unknown to him, works of the 1830 school, were shown to him. As soon as he saw them, he became an admirer of the works of Corot, Delacroix, Millet, Rousseau, Diaz, Daubigny, Dupré, Decamps, and others. He bought with taste and discrimination and in a few years made what is certainly the finest and most complete collection of that school in this country. What was remarkable were the facility and readiness of Mr. Hill in art matters. Had he had more time, he would have been a great art expert. He could talk most interestingly about everything pertaining to art and to the artists whom he knew and admired. His perspicacity was really great. Although his collection was composed of works of the older men, all anterior to 1870, he understood from the first the greatness of the modern so-called Impressionist School. As far back as the eighties he acquired some works of Monet, Renoir, Jongkind, and others, and often complained that he could not place them with his other pictures unless he built a new gallery. He fully understood Puvis de Chavannes, and gave that artist an order for a large decoration for his St. Paul home. It was not carried

398

out because of the artist's death. Altogether, Mr. Hill was as brilliant in the world of art as in that of practical affairs."

That is the testimony of a man whose business was to know pictures thoroughly, and to view critically works of art, schools, methods, and purchasers. Equally emphatic are the words of a collector, a personal friend, one of the few whose knowledge and taste were equal to Mr. Hill's own. This friend said this of him: "America had no more intelligent connoisseur of modern art than Mr. James J. Hill. He was born with that absolutely indispensable qualification of any art collector, a sense of quality. This was highly cultivated and enlarged as the result of keen observation, study, and experience. To an extraordinary degree he appreciated and loved what was beautiful, with a very unusual ability to discriminate between what might and what really ought to please. His examples of the Barbizon school were unsurpassable. Not one of them was bought because a dealer recommended. All were acquired upon his own judgment, because of their appeal to his refined taste. Whenever he found himself the owner of a work which matured judgment taught him was not of the best, he parted with it. No matter how the burdens of business pressed upon him, he always turned with pleasure to the contemplation of works of art. The fact that a painting was the work of an artist of great reputation was nothing to him. It was not the reputation of the painter, but the painting itself which must make its appeal. The works of the men once thought great, which encumbered and disfigured too long many of the most important collections of the country, had no welcome from him and found no home with him. An enthusiastic love of art was an essential part of himself, all the more admirable because of the gigantic business undertakings which occupied him so greatly and incessantly. While he will always be remembered by the nation at large for his great constructive genius and successes, those who care for art will always remember him as one of the few great collectors who relied, and were able to rely, upon their own judgment."

These expressions of authoritative opinion place in a clear light the side of Mr. Hill's character related to art, as the term is used ordinarily. But the whole truth is broader and deeper. Not only was he a born judge and lover of fine pictures, but he responded in all things to the appeal of the beautiful. This is the artistic temperament in its completest expression. It was Mr. Hill's inheritance. It gave him secure touch in many fields. Keats's words are more practical than we dream; kinship with beauty in the abstract is a talisman even in the search for concrete truth. Mr. Hill loved jewels, and knew them as he did pictures. It was cause for wonder that he, who had suffered all his life from the handicap of sight through one eye only, should be so absolute a judge of pictures, should be able to take

400

two pearls or sapphires in his hand, not distinguishable from each other to the untrained vision, and with scarcely a moment's delay accept one as satisfactory and reject the other. Yet minute examination would show that the almost imperceptible departure from the perfect in form or colour or lustre was actually there. He loved fine rugs, and knew them as perhaps few persons in this country did. He had a feeling for beautiful china; and whenever a set or a piece that he admired appeared on the table he noticed it and remarked upon it. The essential thing is that in all these so different lines of artistic expression he had his gift from nature. His comprehension of art was very little acquired, almost wholly intuitive. He felt the beautiful before he could explain it. He responded to the spirit of beauty wherever he found it embodied. This was a great and wonderful gift; without an understanding of which any appreciation of the temperament and personality of the man would lose much of his native vitality, warmth, and charm.

Perhaps this gift was identified with the Celtic quality in him that showed itself in many other ways. He had a passion for things characteristically Scotch. A copy of Burns furnished reading for his early youth. He knew the poems from beginning to end; could repeat pages of them offhand. The pibroch and the kilts always brought a gleam to his eye and a smile to his lips. With an intimate friend, whose blood came from

401

the land of the thistle, he would spend an entire evening capping quotations, repeating ballads, and singing snatches of them one after another. Whenever at an entertainment his hosts wanted to give him especial pleasure, they arranged for a skirl of the pipes and a Highland fling in national costume by Scottish performers. He never forgot a Scotch face or friend. He had something also of the Celtic feeling about intimate places and natural objects. He felt this way about the Mississippi River. Up it he had voyaged to St. Paul. On its banks his early business life had been spent; up and down it went the commerce by which he lived; from it he learned the lessons that were to bring ample repayment. That old life was magically and almost mystically dear to him. He knew the original name of every place on the river's banks, of all the old boats, of spots which the vagaries of the current had stranded miles inland or buried under invading waters. It made him happy to follow the banks of the stream on his trips between St. Paul and Chicago, as if he were accompanied each time by this old friend. His love for the freshwater pearl was no doubt partly due to the fact that so many specimens came from the shallows of theMississippi. Here are different sides of a strangely complex being: disciple of the beautiful and of the practical; full of powerful and generous emotion, while accepting every conclusion of a stern logic; master and director of multitudes of men, yet as full of sport and jest and laughter-raising inventions in his home as a boy just out of school. Of such is the kingdom of the artistic temperament; which on one side reaches out to ineffable and blinding mysteries, and on the other touches homeland in the heart of a child.

He was one of the most universally informed men of his time. Not only had he expert knowledge of pictures, but he had also studied architecture carefully. He was a connoisseur of precious stones. His acquaintance with literature was both wide and thorough. He knew the best book on almost every subject under the sun, and could name it to you offhand. He had a large number of them in his private library. This collection covered not only the useful arts, the fine arts, the sciences and human records, but pure literature as well. He knew the great masters without exception. Like many people, he had little appreciation of Browning. But of other rulers in the realm of poetry and prose he could repeat pages at will, and did so with relish. His taste and his selective judgment were as marked as was his ability in the so different line of his daily activities. He would ask if you had read such and such a work on some subject—history, economics, philosophy, psychology—perhaps when it had barely reached the reviewers, perhaps when the foreign publisher had not yet put it on the American market. You did him a favour if you recommended to him some book of which he had not heard and which made an actual contribution to human knowledge. He would suck it dry in a few hours, and henceforth everything worth while that it held was his possession for ever.

Mr. Hill was a most companionable man. He loved the society of old friends, who always were welcomed. No man could be more gracious in the reception of a visitor. It pleased him to recall, in company with others, things that were a part of his past and theirs. He was eager to discuss current events, new ideas in science and industry, tendencies in the thought and action of the time. What a man of the ancient world said of himself could be said of him: that nothing pertaining to humanity was alien to him. His penetrating analysis sought out and his intelligence grasped the meaning of these things just as it attacked the ordinary work of his life. He would, in a leisure space, spend two or three hours in such discussion; passing from theme to theme, wasting no words, rounding a principle with its historical support or disproof, anticipating its probable operation in the future. He gave to such moments the same earnestness and delight that others give to their amusements; and, in the same way, they seemed to give him relaxation. His mind was absolutely tireless, and its edge always undulled.

He was an enthusiastic admirer of Napoleon. Genius is intimately allied only to itself. When it can be forgotten that the spheres in which these two men worked and the ultimate purposes they put before themselves

404

were as far apart as the antipodes, striking correspondences of quality and of method appear. Taine, in his "Origines de la France Contemporaine," gives a marvellous analysis of Napoleon, much of which might be transferred to these pages, so apropos is it of their subject. The man himself, too, speaks: "I," said Napoleon to Rœderer, "I work always. I ponder things deeply. If I seem always ready to reply to anything, to confront anything, it is because, before undertaking anything, I have thought it over for a long time; I have foreseen everything that can happen. It is not genius that reveals to me suddenly what I must say or do on occasions which take others by surprise, it is reflection; meditation. I work all the time." Mr. Hill, in his way, obeyed the same law for overcoming; spoke words identical in their purport with these. They give a verbal portrait of him as exact as if drawn from life. He measures up to this colossal standard in achievement. In moral perception and spiritual fidelity he passes immeasurably beyond. He gave a life and a labour like this to the great human experiment, in its entirety, upon this planet. Since that experience, the "great adventure" of humanity itself, goes on unfolding endlessly, he is sure of the only earthly immortality.

The inmost nature of such a man must find its true expression and interpretation in the acts of his life taken as a whole. That is the law by whose light it has been studied and all these pages written. If it has been difficult to analyze his work as a railroad man or an agricultural reformer or a financier or an economist, and state the abstract conclusion in a few clear terms, how supremely difficult to apply the same process to the man himself! Essentially, it cannot be done. He was too many-sided. His thought caught and held too many far-off things; reflected from too many facets the light of tallow candles in cottage windows and of fixed stars and nebulæ away in uttermost space. Yet whoever has followed sympathetically and would bring together the separate threads of this extraordinary life can find a clue. One broad generalization, complete and true, speaks the final word.

James J. Hill was temperamentally one of the greatest educators that the world has seen. He had all the intellectual and spiritual qualities for it. He had the vocation. He had a passion for imparting knowledge. His norm was truth. He wanted to know the exact facts, all the facts, about everything. When he had them, scientifically ascertained and classified, he drew from them their laws by the inductive method to which science owes its all. Then he cast a horoscope. Next, knowing precisely what the individuals and communities that these laws would exalt or destroy ought to do to find one fate rather than the other, he must tell them. He was burdened with the duty, as a physician feels that he must warn his patients what their symptoms mean; open before them the two highways that

406

lead to life and death. According to one or another of many different series of circumstances that might conceivably have wrought upon his boyhood and youth, he would have become a great scientific investigator, a great soldier, a great discoverer, a great priest or missionary, great in almost anything involving research and leadership and service. But in any of these avocations he would still have been a great educator. And such he was where life actually did call him. Read almost any of his letters or speeches, take the concrete facts of his life, listen to him as he talked to railroad men or farmers or congressmen or financiers, and you will perceive, through all and first of all, the man who has got hold of a bit of the truth, worked it out until it is all certitude, and now flames with the inextinguishable desire to pass it on to others. The possession of accurate knowledge, the determination rising to a sense of duty that others should know as well, and the kindly and catholic sympathy which alone can keep the torch alight as it is carried from mind to mind and from soul to soul—by these the born educator enters into his kingdom. They picture, feature for feature, the character, the temperament, the abiding individuality of James J. Hill.

APPENDIX ONE

FIRST PROPOSITION MADE TO DUTCH
BONDHOLDERS BY HILL AND KITTSON

St. Paul, January 29, 1877.

JOHAN CARP, ESQ., % Messrs. J. S. Kennedy & Co., New York.

DEAR SIR: Referring to our interview with you in regard to the purchase of the First Division of the St. Paul & Pacific R. R., with its railway, equipment, property and franchises, we are now prepared to make and do make you the following proposition, viz.:

We will purchase the Main and Branch lines of the First Division of the St. Paul & Pacific R. R. Co., together with the equipments, franchises, and all other property and privileges now owned by that corporation, and will pay therefor, on delivery to us of a perfect title, vesting in us, under such corporate name as we may adopt, said railroad and its franchises, and all other property, clear of incumbrance, the sum of ($3,500,000) three million five hundred thousand dollars in cash, and will also, as a part of the purchase, deliver to you a release of all the unsold lands covered by the land grants to said company (amounting at present, we believe, to about 1,100,000 acres), and also of all balances unpaid on lands of the company heretofore sold and now outstanding, we retaining all other properties of all kinds, franchises, equipments, etc., now owned by or belonging to said R. R. Co.

It is understood that if this proposition is accepted by you, that the foreclosure proceedings now pending against said R. R. Co. shall be pressed to a completion and sale without delay, and the title to the railroad, franchises, etc., made and possession delivered to us with as little delay as possible, and at the earliest practicable day.

A land department, or such other organization as your committee

408

shall deem best, and to be controlled and managed by the committee at its expense and charge, shall be continued by the new corporation as a part of its organization, for the purpose of enabling the committee to make sale of said lands, and a land scrip issued, bearing no interest, to be used in payment for said lands; or such other plan for selling the same may be adopted as your committee shall deem most expedient.

A fair and equitable running arrangement and connection shall be entered into, at the time of completing the sale hereby provided for, between the lines of the First Division R. R. Co. and the committee representing the Brainerd and St. Vincent lines of the St. Paul & Pac. Co., as now situated, or as they shall be hereafter completed.

Should this proposition be accepted, it is desirable that we should be informed thereof at an early day, in order that we may be prepared to make promptly all necessary arrangements for the execution and performance of the contract to be entered into between us.

We have suggested the plan of a land scrip, for the reason that we believe it would be the most convenient way to handle it, as the lands now unsold could be classified and valued, and scrip issued to the amount of the valuations so made. This would also have the advantage of making the balance now unpaid on lands already sold (about $400,000) payable in cash. The average price of lands sold by the R. R. Co. during the past year would make the amount of scrip to be issued over $7,000,000.

We expected when we saw you to make an offer for the St. Vincent & Brainerd extension lines, but the affairs of that company are so complicated that we are unable to learn what the property fully consists of; and again, the bonded indebtedness is so very heavy that any offer we would be likely to make would look very small to those who have put so much money into the enterprise. We believe that the location of the portion which lies in the Red River Valley is the very worst that could have been made, being located for over two thirds of the distance on the very lowest ground, and subject to overflow almost every spring upon the melting of the deep snows of that latitude. The writer has seen

409

the greater part of the distance from say ten miles north of Crookston to within 12 miles of Pembina or St. Vincent covered with water from two to six feet in depth, and this in the spring of 1870.

We refer you to the fact that although there was 104 miles of that road built in 1872, there have been no settlements made or farms opened outside of a narrow strip on the Red Lake River, up to the present time, and the road has earned nothing from its local business. During the time since 1872 the country on the west side of the Red River, which then had no settlers whatever, has become comparatively well settled, and one county has the past season raised 100,000 bushels of wheat to sell.

You may think that the contest over the land grant has kept settlers from making homes alongside the railroad. Such is not the case, however, as the land grant covers only half the lands, leaving the other half open to settlement or free homesteads; but the land on the west side of the river is much higher and not subject to overflow, and the consequence has been that settlers have gone from 20 to 50 miles away from the railroad in preference to opening their farms alongside of it. These facts lead us to the conclusion that the only business the St. Vincent line will have to depend upon is the Manitoba trade, for which steamers on the Red River will always compete, no matter who owns the road; while the rich and rapidly growing country on the west side of the river will eventually demand another railroad, and thus make another competitor for the through business.

If we owned the St. Vincent extension to-day, we would cross the Red River between Moorhead and a point 25 miles south of the Red Lake River, and build every mile of new road on the west side, and thus secure the commerce of the west side for a local traffic.

As to the Brainerd line, we beg to say that we think its completion would only benefit the Nor. Pacific R. R., and would injure the Main line by taking the business which would go to and from St. Paul via Glyndon if a proper connection were made; and would injure the Branch line by opening a competing line for trade from the Sauk Valley to Lake Superior; and as it would have to depend on the Nor. Pacific for business, it would have to carry at very low

410

rates as against the line from Duluth to St. Paul now used by the Nor. Pacific for that business.

You will pardon us for saying so many things against the St. Vincent and Brainerd lines, but our excuse is that they are all true; and while it may not be the kind of information which led your people to invest in the bonds of that line, we sincerely hope that you will employ some disinterested party, in whom your committee have full confidence, and let him quietly examine the country in all bearings on both sides of the river, having in view the fairness of our statement, and when he has reported we will make you an offer for those lines. Or, for the purpose of obtaining a fair valuation of the property, you might select a professional engineer, whose reputation and knowledge would entitle him to confidence, and we would do likewise, and they two could select a third, to constitute a board to examine and report the facts and value of the road as it now stands; and we are inclined to think we would be satisfied with their valuation.

Should our proposal to purchase the First Division be accepted, we would be ready to build a short line to connect the Main line with the St. Vincent track south of Glyndon, and make any fair and equitable arrangement for running connection or joint operation, so as to make the entire through rate from St. Paul by rail to Fisher's Landing or even through to Manitoba one interest, believing as we do that there are at the present time all the facilities by rail and river that the business will call for, or that can be profitably operated, for the next ten years.

However, if your committee desire to make an offer at which they will sell the railroad of the St. Vincent and Brainerd line, they retaining the lands, etc., we will be glad to do what we can to meet their views consistent with our ability to pay interest on the purchase, and we think an arrangement might possibly be made whereby the committee would get the benefit of local sympathy to secure whatever legislation would be necessary.

In other words, we do not wish to misrepresent your property in any manner whatever, but we submit that its true value has never been fully understood by your committee, and for that reason we again ask that your committee take steps, either for yourself or

411

jointly with us, to determine the present value of the property and its probable future.

We only desire to arrive at what is fair, and will be ready to act at all times on that basis and aid you to a settlement of the whole matter.

If there is anything in this proposal that would have to be modified without materially changing its terms, we would be ready to make such change or modification.

Your early reply will oblige,

Yours very truly,

N. W. KITTSON,

JAMES J. HILL.

APPENDIX   TWO

OFFER FOR OPTION CONSTRUED AS OFFER TO PURCHASE

Saint Paul, May 26, 1877.

JOHAN CARP, ESQ., Attorney and Agent, Bondholders' Committee, Utrecht, Holland.

SIR: I cabled you from Montreal on Monday last, the 21st inst., as follows: "Finances arranged. Letter on Friday."
I now beg to inform you that I have made arrangements with George Stephen, Esq., president of the Bank of Montreal, and the Honorable Donald A. Smith, commissioner of the Hudson's Bay Company, representing Canadian and English capital, who have agreed to furnish the money in case we shall conclude a contract with you for the purchase of the bonds of the Main and Branch lines of the First Div. of the St. Paul & Pac. Railroad Co., and the Extension lines of the St. Paul & Pac. Co., held by your committee, as per your letter bearing date New York, February 28, 1877, that is to say—

$ 675,250.00 of the   1,200,000 issue Branch Line.
    796,000.00 "   "   2,800,000   "   "   "
  1,264,000.00 "   "   3,000,000   "   Main   "
  4,057,000.00 "   "   6,000,000   "   "   "
12,000,000.00 "   "   15,000,000   "   Extension"

After a careful examination of the property, we have determined upon a valuation of the whole, on the basis of which we are prepared to purchase the several issues of bonds (with all unpaid cou-

413

pons attached) held by your committee as above specified, at the following prices—

For the	1,200,000	issue	80	cents on the dollar of face of bond.
"	"	2,800,000	"	20	"	"	"	"	"	"	"	"
"	"	3,000,000	"	35	"	"	"	"	"	"	"	"
"	"	6,000,000	"	40	"	"	"	"	"	"	"	"
"	"	15,000,000	"	11	"	"	"	"	"	"	"	"

While we consider the above prices an equitable valuation for the respective classes of bonds, your committee may make such changes in prices as they think best, provided such change in prices does not increase the aggregate amount to be paid by us.

If the purchase is made, the bonds are to be delivered in London, England, at such banking house as we may select, and to be paid for on such delivery.

As the amount required for the above purchase is large, and is to be furnished by our friends, we desire that as short a time as possible should elapse between closing the contract and the time fixed for the delivery of and payment for the bonds, in order to avoid contingencies which might happen during that period.

In case, therefore, your committee is prepared to sell us the bonds on the terms above mentioned, we shall require 60 or 90 days (the latter if possible) after receipt of advices from you to that effect, in which to take the necessary steps for completing the transaction by closing the bargain and obtaining the necessary funds to pay for the bonds.

Upon receipt of this we ask that your committee shall advise us by cable as soon as possible if they are willing to dispose of their bonds on the above terms, also naming the time for closing the transaction.

We hereby beg to withdraw our former offer for the First Div. lines. I have the honor to be

Very respectfully,

N. W. KITTSON.

JAS. J. HILL.

APPENDIX   THREE

MR. HILL'S ESTIMATE OF THE COST AND THE VALUE OF THE ST. PAUL & PACIFIC

A

Saint Paul, September 1, 1877.

DESCRIPTION OF ROAD AND PERSONAL PROPERTY

Branch Line . . . . St. Paul to Sauk Rapids   76   Miles
Main   "   . . . . St. Anthony to Breckenridge 207   "
Extension "   . . . . St. Cloud to Melrose . . . . 35½   "
   "   "   . . . . Brainerd South . . . .   4½   "
   "   "   . . . . Red River Valley Portion 104   "

                        Total Miles Completed Road   . . .   427
                        Add Total Miles of Side Track   . .   28¼

                        Total Miles of Track 455¼

Red River Valley R. R. . Crookston to Fisher's Landing (Completed line, iron owned by Extention Co.) . . . . 10⁶₁₀ Miles
Breckenridge Cut-off . . . . Breckenridge to end of track south of Glyndon, now building by Bondholders' Committee, to be completed October 20, 1877   34   "

Lines of which the grading is nearly complete
{
   End of track north of Crookston to St. Vincent . . . . about   67   "
   Melrose to Glyndon . . . . about 102   "
   Sauk Rapids to end of track, South of Brainerd . . . . about   51½   "
   Grading nearly completed   . . . . 220½   "
}

415

APPENDIX

Rolling Stock,
Main & Branch Lines
{
26 Locomotives
12 First Class Pass. Cars
5 Second "   "   "
14 Baggage and Express Cars
217 Box Freight and Stock "
156 Flat Lumber and Coal "
10 Caboose Pay and Other "
}

Total Cost of Rolling Stock as per Company's books...... $821,088.90
All in good order and repair and estimated to be worth at
    least 50% of cost.............................. 410,544.45

Trustees' Valuation and Inventory made October 10, 1876, of which the
supply of Lumber, Wood, Ties, etc. has been increased.

Main & Branch Lines.. Machinery, Tools, etc., in Shops not
            including Supplies of any kind.. $61,022.04
            Stock on hand in charge of Machin-
            ery and Road Dept. Supplies,
            Lumber, Ties, Wood, etc...... 228,152.48

Extension Line........ 2,800 tons new Iron at Glyndon
            at $40.00.................. $112,000.00
            1,700 tons new Iron at Duluth at
            $35.00 .... 59,500.00
            Ties, Switches, Frogs, Spikes, Fish
            Plates, etc., Est.............. 40,000.00
                                        211,500.00
            Less for duties unpaid Iron at
            Duluth.................... 28,000.00
                                     $183,500.00

Main & Branch Lines.. 850 tons old Iron partly worn out at
            $20.00..................... $17,000.00

REAL ESTATE OUTSIDE OF LAND GRANT

Branch Line.......... St. Paul Depot Yards Shops, etc.,
            at very low estimate......... $400,000.00
            St. Anthony and St. Anthony Junc-
            tion...................... 15,000.00

416

APPENDIX

Main Line. . . . . Minneapolis. 75,000.00
Townsites—Waverly 5/M, Dassel
5/M, Darwin 5/M, Howard Lake
5/M, Smith Lake 5/M, Cokato
5/M, Litchfield 30/M, Swede
Grove 5/M, Atwater 5/M, Kan-
diyohi 5/M, Willmar 30/M, De
Graff 10/M, Benson 30/M, Clon-
tarf 5/M, Morris 20/M, Herman
5/M, Doran 5/M, Campbell
5/M, Tintah, 5/M, Brecken-
ridge 10/M. 200,000.00

$690,000.00

NET EARNINGS FIRST DIVISION COMPANY

YEAR ENDING JUNE 30TH	MAIN LINE	BRANCH LINE	TOTAL
1871	$100,974.90	$159,432.32	$260,407.22
1872	9,227.55	103,518.13	112,745.68
1873	32,685.87	133,278.04	165,963.91
1874	77,038.84	139,036.78	216,075.62
1875	35,607.14	120,730.88	156,338.02
1876	220,324.43	143,965.71	364,290.14
1877	135,855.35	128,287.07	264,142.42

During the year ending June 30, 1877, the following material was purchased and work done and charged to operating expenses instead of Construction and Equipment:

1,000 Tons Steel Rails laid. . . . . @ $60. . . . . $60,000.00
1,150 " Reheated Iron Rails, laid, " 45. . . . .   51,750.00
170,000 New Ties . . . . " 26. . . . .   44,200.00
New Bridges and Stone Culverts.   14,500.00
New Passenger Depot, Minneapolis 6,500.00
6 New Flat Cars. 2,100.00
Rebuilding 20 Box Cars. 6,000.00
" 4 Passenger Coaches. 3,200.00

$188,250.00

St. Paul, Minn., September 6, 1877.

417

APPENDIX

	BRANCH		MAIN	
	ACRES	AMOUNT	ACRES	AMOUNT
No. of Acres sold up to Dec. 31, 1874.....	44,208.97	$271,592.98	49,352.79	$694,750.95
No. of Acres sold during year 1875....	2,386.80	14,213.78	52,243.10	498,134.12
No. of Acres sold during year 1876....	11,726.45	59,900.00	225,316.78	1,470,238.08
Total	58,322.22	$345,706.76	326,912.67	$2,663,123.15

```
Total No. of Acres in Grant: Branch...................   425,756.00
                             Main.................... 1,313,961.43
                                                      ------------
                                                      1,739,717.43

Less No. of Acres sold, up to
   date of December 31, 1876: Branch........    58,322.22
                              Main.........   326,912.67    385,234.89
No. of Acres unsold January 1, 1877 ....................  1,354,482.54

St. Vincent Lands
   No. of Acres received from State........   750,000
   "    "    "   earned but not deeded......   146,000    896,000.00


No. of Acres to accrue
   End of track to St. Vincent............    384,000
   Melrose to Glyndon..................      652,800
   Brainerd Line.......................      358,400    1,395,200.00
                                                        ------------
      Total.....................................        3,645,682.54

Average price per acre of lands sold to date, Branch ............ $5.92
   "    "    "    "   "    "    "    "   " Main............   8.15
```

St. Paul, Minn., September, 1877.

418

APPENDIX

B

STATEMENT OF BONDED INDEBTEDNESS

Branch Line—Mortgages

	Original Amt. of Mortgage	Amt. Outstanding Dec. 1/76
St. Paul to St. Anthony—Railway......	$ 120,000	$ 120,000
" " " Sauk Rapids "	700,000	366,000
" " " " " Real Estate....	1,200,000	1,058,250
" " " " " Consolidated...	2,800,000	1,112,000

Main Line—Mortgages

	Original Amt. of Mortgage	Amt. Outstanding Dec. 1/76
St. Anthony to Morris (150 Miles)......	$ 1,500,000	
Real Estate " " "	3,000,000	$ 1,749,500
" " Breckenridge...........	6,000,000	5,336,000
Extension Lines.....................	15,000,000	15,000,000

.The 1,500,000 mortgage is held by the Trustees as Collateral Security to the 6,000,000 Bonds.

There is a subsequent mortgage of 1,000,000 St. Paul to Breckenridge on record, but the Bonds are in the hands of the Company having never been sold and consequently the amount is no claim against the property; if, however, they had been sold the 6,000,000—and 3,000,000 loans are both prior mortgages and would have to be paid in full principal and interest before anything would be due to the 1,000,000 mortgage.

The respective amounts of outstanding Bonds are held as follows:

120,000	outstanding all held in U. S.
366,000	" " " " "
1,058,250	"	697,250 in hands of Dutch Committee
1,112,000	"	813,000 " " " " "
1,749,000	"	1,280,000 " " " " "
5,336,000	"	4,162,000 " " " " "
15,000,000	"	12,663,000 " " " " "

APPENDIX

Of the five classes of bonds partly held by the Dutch Committee the balance of the bonds are scattered through France, Belgium, Holland, Germany and Austria, except about $200,000 of the 1,200,000 issue which are held in St. Paul.

The amount of outstanding bonds is given of date December 1, 1876, since which time a considerable amount of the 3,000,000 and 6,000,000 bonds have been retired for lands.

The 120,000 issue is a first mortgage on the Railroad from St. Paul to St. Anthony, the 366,000 outstanding is a second mortgage on Railroad from St. Paul to St. Anthony and first mortgage St. Anthony to Sauk Rapids on railroad only.

The 1,058,250 outstanding covers the railroad and lands to a distance of six miles each side of track St. Paul to Sauk Rapids subject to the 120,000 and 366,000 on the railroad—the 1,112,000 outstanding is a first mortgage on the lands outside of the six-mile limit on each side of the railroad and subsequent to the three foregoing mortgages on the property covered by them.

The 5,336,000 outstanding is by virtue of its owning the 1,500,000 mortgage a first mortgage on the railroad to the amount of $10,000 per mile for the first 150 miles west from St. Anthony and second on the lands, and the only mortgage on both lands and railroad west of the 150 Mile Post to Breckenridge.

The 1,749,500 outstanding is a first mortgage on the lands west of St. Anthony to 150 Mile Post and subject to the $10,000 per mile on the road.

Amount required to purchase bonds in the hands of Dutch Committee;

CLASS	OUTSTANDING	PRICE	AMOUNT
1,200,000	697,250	80 c.	$ 557,800
2,800,000	813,000	20 c.	162,600
3,000,000	1,280,000	35 c.	448,000
6,000,000	4,162,000	42½c.	1,768,850
15,000,000	12,663,000	11 c.	1,392,930
		Total.....	$4,330,180

420

Amount required to foreclose mortgages and pay balance of outstanding bonds not held by Dutch Committee. Estimate of our Attorney...................... $300,000

Amount required to complete and equip portions of railroad from Breckenridge to Glyndon and end of track to St. Vincent............................... 910,000

$1,210,000

Add above amount. 4,330,180

Total amount required to buy the property as it now stands, and complete the system as far as at present desirable..................................... $5,540,180

After the purchase is made on the foregoing basis, and the Breckenridge to Glyndon and end of track to St. Vincent portions are completed and equipped, all in good condition for business the property will consist of:

570 Miles track worth say 20/M................		11,400,000
Present equipment...............	$410,544.45	
Added for new equipment..........	100,000.00	
Shops and Tools..................	61,022.04	
Material Supplies, etc.............	228,152.48	
Old Rails.......................	17,000.00	816,718

$12,216,718

Surplus property St. Paul & St. Anthony Junction not required for use of Company.......................... $400,000.00

Townsites Main Line. Estimate........ 200,000.00 600,000

Land Grant 2,634,482 Acres of land lying for the most part in well-settled counties and of a quality much above the average of western land worth at least the U. S. Government minimum price for lands within the limit of railroad grant, $2.50 per Acre 6,586,205

Total Valuation...................... $19,402,923

In addition to the foregoing the Trustees for the Bonds have in their hands *Cash* $210,000 and we are informed by the present Manager of the property that of the above lands there are sold about 68,000 Acres,

APPENDIX

upon which there is due secured by mortgage on the lands, and bearing interest at 7% per annum, $750,000.

The mortgages of the 1,200,000, 2,800,000, 3,000,000, and 6,000,000 issues have by reason of their failure to pay interest, been declared due, principal and interest, and the Trustees are now in possession.

Suits have been commenced and an order of Court for the sale of property may be had during the present fall; while on the other hand it may be delayed for a year longer; in the meantime the Trustees will hold the property as at present for the benefit of the Bondholders.

A majority of the outstanding bonds can at their pleasure change the Trustees, and it is the duty of the Trustees to use the revenue of the property solely for the benefit of the Bondholders in accordance, with the priority of the respective mortgages. (See Trust, Deed, etc.)

The net earnings of the property for the year ending July 1/77, as per statement, should read $452,392.42 for the reason that the sum $188,250 was paid on account of new rails, rolling stock, etc., and added to the value of the property that amount those portions of Minnesota and Manitoba which would be solely tributary to the parts of the line it is proposed to complete, it is difficult to estimate the increase of earnings from that source, however, we believe that $600,000 per year would be a low estimate and with fair average crops the net earnings would undoubtedly reach $700,000 or $800,000, which amount will increase from year to year as the country is settled up. Mr. Farley, the present Manager of the property, estimates the future earnings much higher than we do but we have endeavoured to make all of our figures on the safe side.

In making the calculations for amount necessary to finish and equip the unfinished portions as above we have intended to make use of all the rails, fish plates, spikes, ties, and other suitable material on hand, the property of the Company.

We have estimated the cost of cancelling outstanding bonds other than those held by the Dutch Committee in case of foreclosure upon the advice of our Attorney based upon similar foreclosures of other roads, with a liberal allowance for contingencies.

422

APPENDIX   FOUR

MEMORANDUM PREPARED BY MR. HILL AS BASIS OF AGREEMENT WITH THE DUTCH BONDHOLDERS

In view of the impossibility of negotiating a loan for an amount sufficient to purchase the bonds which acceded to the terms of our letter of May 26, 1877, viz.:

1,200,000 issue	625,000 at 75c.
2,800,000 "	708,000 " 28c.
3,000,000 "	907,000 " 30c.
6,000,000 "	3,400,000 " 35c,
15,000,000 "	11,200,000 " 13¾c.

It is proposed to modify the terms of above letter of May 26th as follows (which may include all outstanding bonds of the foregoing issues, except the $15,000,000 issue, outside of the amount above named).

We propose to purchase the foregoing bonds at the prices above named, and pay for the same in the following manner, i. e.: To pay to the holders of said bonds, during the pendency of the suits to foreclose the mortgages securing the respective issues of bonds, interest on the amount of purchase money at the rate of 7 per cent. per annum, payable semi-annually, and to pay the principal of said purchase within six months after the completion of said foreclosure proceedings, by issuing and delivering to said bondholders bonds of the company to be organized upon the sale under said foreclosure and reorganization, bearing interest at the rate of 6 per cent., gold, payable semi-annually, for their respective holdings; and, in addition thereto, to issue and deliver, upon such reorganization being completed, 6 per cent. preferred stock to the respective bondholders assenting hereto, at the rate of $250 for each $1,000 bond of said new issue.

We further propose to pay the holders of the special stock the amount expended by them in building the Breckenridge-Barnes link, so called, and also to advance the necessary means to complete the Extension line from end of track north to Crookston to St. Vincent, and from Melrose to Alexandria, and also to obtain the exclusive connection with the Canada Pacific R. R. from St. Vincent to Winnipeg, it being understood, in this connection, that the Red River Transportation Company will so coöperate as to best serve the interests of this enterprise, if carried out as herein proposed.

The new issue of bonds and stock above named, to be issued after said foreclosures, shall cover, in addition to the purchase money for said bonds, the cost of purchase of said Breckenridge-Barnes link, and completing the extension lines as above mentioned, and such bonds and stock shall be issued in payment therefor; we to have the option, if we so prefer, to pay the purchase money of said bonds in cash, in lieu of said bonds and stock.

During the pendency of said foreclosure suits, and the reorganization of the new company, the bonds to be purchased as above provided shall be placed in the hands of J. S. Kennedy & Co., or such other trustees as may be selected, to be delivered upon a full compliance with the terms herein set forth, it being understood that such trustees shall, at the time of each semi-annual payment of interest upon the purchase money of said bonds, deliver to said purchasers one coupon from each bond held by them in trust.

The purchasers to have, from the date of acceptance hereof, full control and management of said foreclosure proceedings, and the same shall be prosecuted under their direction. And it is expressly agreed that the custody of said bonds shall not be changed during the pendency of this agreement, without the consent of said purchasers; and the purchasers shall be hereby empowered to repre-

424

sent and use said bonds for all purposes which they may deem necessary in the management of the foreclosure proceedings.

There shall be no special or preferred stock issued except what shall be required to carry out the foregoing arrangement.

If the above proposal is acceptable to bondholders, articles of agreement in accordance therewith shall be made and entered into as soon as may be.

APPENDIX   FIVE

AGREEMENTS BETWEEN THE ASSOCIATES

A

Preliminary Form of Agreement of January 21, 1878

Whereas the undersigned did, on the 5th day of January, 1878, at the city of New York, make an offer to the committee of Dutch bondholders in Holland to purchase their holding of the bonds of the St. Paul & Pacific Railroad Company and of the 1st Division of the St. Paul & Pacific Railroad Company, upon certain terms and conditions stated in said offer—the ultimate object in making said offer being to obtain possession of said railroads and all the property belonging thereto, with the intention of reorganizing said companies, after completing the pending foreclosures thereon as soon as practicable after the sales under said foreclosures, upon the basis of an issue of common stock of such reorganized company amounting to $5,000,000.00, a bonded indebtedness of not exceeding $12,000.00 per mile of finished road, and a 6 per cent. preferred stock not exceeding $3,000.00 per mile of finished road:

Now, in case our said offer of purchase shall be accepted by said Dutch Committee, and said purchase concluded, it is understood and hereby agreed between us that the interests acquired under said purchase and in said reorganized company, and the profits and losses accruing from said enterprise, shall be held and borne by us in the following proportions, viz.:

George Stephen, two-fifths (2-5)

Donald A. Smith, one-fifth (1-5)

Norman W. Kittson, one-fifth (1-5)

James J. Hill, one-fifth (1-5)

It being, however, understood and agreed that one-half of the said two-fifths so held by said George Stephen, as above, is

426

APPENDIX

held by him for the purposes of securing the coöperation of an associate or associates in said enterprise, through whom the financial aid necessary to enable us to complete such purchase may be obtained, as understood between us in New York at the time of making our said offer of purchase.

It is expected that the said one-fifth interest so to be disposed of by said Stephen will be sufficient for the purpose of securing such associate or associates, and that, upon the completion of such purchase and the reorganization of said company, the interest of each of the undersigned in said enterprise, and in said new company, shall be an equal one-fifth interest therein, subject only to said bonded debt and said preferred stock.

Having full confidence in each other and in the success of said enterprise, we hereby mutually agree to become responsible for the repayment of all moneys required to be advanced to us in carrying out said purchase (if said offer be accepted), and to join in the execution of any papers or securities which may be required in obtaining such advances.

Witness our hands and seals this 21st day of January, 1878.

> GEO. STEPHEN.
> DON. A. SMITH. (SEAL.)
> N. W. KITTSON. (SEAL.)
> JAMES J. HILL. (SEAL.)

In presence of
>R. B. Galusha,
>as to Kittson & Hill,
>also to Stephen & Smith.

B

Final Form of "Montreal" Agreement of March 27, 1878.

Whereas, the undersigned have, under their agreement dated the 13th day of March, one thousand eight hundred and seventy-eight, executed by them in the city of New York, purchased of the committee of the Dutch bondholders in Holland the holding of the said Dutch Committee in the bonds of the St. Paul & Pacific Railroad Company, and in the First Division of the said St. Paul & Pacific

427

Railroad Company, and other property in said agreement named, the ultimate object in making said purchase being to obtain the possession and ownership of said railroads and all land grants and other property pertaining thereto, and of reorganizing said companies on completion of the foreclosures now pending in the courts in Minnesota, as soon as practicable after the sales can be made under said foreclosures, upon the basis of an issue of common stock of such reorganized company of five million dollars or any amount hereafter agreed upon, a bonded indebtedness not to exceed twelve thousand dollars per mile of finished road, and a 6 per cent. preferred stock not exceeding three thousand dollars per mile of finished road:

Now it is understood and agreed by and between the undersigned, for the purpose of carrying out the above object and of complying with the terms and conditions specified and contained in our said agreement with said Dutch Committee for the purchase of said bonds and other property, that the interests acquired in the properties purchased by us under said agreement with said Dutch Committee, and in the railroad company to be reorganized by us in pursuance of said agreement, and in the profits and losses which may accrue from said enterprise, shall be apportioned between us in the following proportions, viz., the said George Stephen, two fifths; Donald A. Smith, one fifth; Norman W. Kittson, one fifth; and James J. Hill, one fifth; it being, however, understood and agreed between us that one half of the said two fifths interest so set off to the said George Stephen as above shall be held by him for the purpose of securing the necessary means to carry out and complete our said agreement with said Dutch Committee, through the bringing in and securing the coöperation of an associate or associates, if necessary for that purpose, it being expected that said one fifth interest so to be disposed of by said George Stephen will be sufficient for the purpose of securing said moneys and the bringing in of such other associate or associates, if necessary, to fully carry out and complete our said agreement with said Dutch Committee according to its terms and conditions; and that upon the reorganization of said railroads, as provided in said agreement, the interest of each of the undersigned in said reorganized company

428

shall be equal, subject only to the prior liens of the bonded debt
of said railroads, and the preferred stock named in said agreement,
or to such amount thereof as shall be required to fully comply with
all the terms and conditions of our said agreement with said committee, and to pay in full all moneys borrowed or advanced for payment of interest or debts incurred in completing said railroads and
in fully carrying out our said enterprise.

And we further agree to become jointly and severally, and we do
hereby become jointly and severally responsible for the payment
of all moneys required to be advanced at any time in the prosecution of said enterprise, and for the full and entire performance of
our agreement with said Dutch Committee according to its terms
and conditions, and that we will jointly and severally execute and
deliver all notes, bonds, or other securities which it may be necessary to execute from time to time, to procure any loans or advances
required to be obtained in the prosecution and completion of said
enterprise, it being understood that as between ourselves we are
liable in equal shares.

It is further agreed by the parties hereto that in case of the death
of either of said parties pending the reorganization of said railroad
companies under said foreclosures, then the legal representatives
of such party so dying shall be entitled to demand and receive of
the surviving parties hereto all sums of money which such deceased
party shall have advanced during the prosecution of this enterprise
in aid thereof, including personal expenses, and for which he may
not have been reimbursed, together with interest thereon at the
rate of 12 per cent. per annum from the date at which such
advances shall have been paid, a statement of which advances
shall be furnished to said survivors; and said survivors shall have
the option of paying to the legal representatives of such deceased
party, as and for the value of his full and entire interest in and
under this agreement, a further sum of seventy-five thousand dollars; and upon such payment being made to the legal representatives of said deceased party, all interest or claim of any and every
kind, in and under this agreement or said agreement with said
Dutch Committee, of such deceased party or his estate, shall be held
and thereby be wholly discharged, satisfied, and determined; and

the representatives of said deceased party shall thereupon be entitled to demand and receive all securities of every kind which he may have pledged as collateral or otherwise in obtaining loans or advances; and all obligations of all kinds under said agreements from and after the death of said party shall be assumed and paid by the surviving parties hereto, and the estate of such deceased party shall thereupon be forever released and discharged from all obligations under said agreements, or upon any note, bond, or other obligation executed in carrying out the same for any purpose.

And it is further agreed between the parties hereto that if from any cause either of said parties shall desire to transfer or dispose of his interest in said enterprise, at any time before its final completion, he may do so: *provided, however,* that no such transfer or disposal of his said interest shall be made except by and with the express consent, first obtained, of all the other parties to this agreement, and then only to such person or persons as shall be acceptable to all the other parties hereto; *and further provided,* that the party so desiring to dispose of his said interest shall first offer the same to the other parties hereto jointly, at such price as he shall be actually offered in cash therefor; and should such joint purchase be declined, then such offer shall be made to each of the other parties hereto; and if severally declined by them, then such transfer or sale may be made to another person or persons, who shall, however, be acceptable to the other parties hereto.

It is also understood that the Red River Valley Railroad, upon payment of its actual cost (amounting to about twenty thousand dollars) to the parties entitled to receive payment therefor, shall, upon the reorganization of said railroad companies as specified in said agreement with said Dutch Committee, become a part of the property covered by and included in our said enterprise.

And in order that there shall be no conflict of interest between our said enterprise and the Red River Transportation Company, it is further understood and agreed that in so far as any of the parties hereto now hold or shall hereafter acquire any of the stock of said Red River Transportation Company, the said stock now held or so hereafter acquired by either of said parties shall be paid for and become and be the joint property of the parties hereto

APPENDIX

in equal shares; and for this purpose the value of such stock now
held by either party hereto shall be taken to be of the value of
60 per cent. of the par value thereof, and all such stock as shall
be hereafter purchased shall, for the purposes hereof, be held and
taken at its actual cost, and shall stand upon the same footing as is
herein provided for all the advances made in this enterprise.

In witness, whereof, we have hereunto set our hands and seals
this twenty-seventh day of March, one thousand eight hundred
and seventy-eight.

GEO. STEPHEN (Seal)
DON. A. SMITH (Seal)
N. W. KITTSON (Seal)
JAS. J. HILL (Seal)

Signed sealed and delivered in presence of
Thos. W. Ritchie.
R. B. Galusha.
(Endorsed:)
Syndicate St. P. & P. Ry.
Montreal Agreement,
27 Mch., 1878.

APPENDIX   SIX
AGREEMENT WITH DUTCH COM-
MITTEE FOR PURCHASE OF BONDS

THIS AGREEMENT, made and entered into this thirteenth day of March, A.D. eighteen hundred and seventy-eight, by and between GEORGE STEPHEN, DONALD A. SMITH, NORMAN W. KITTSON and JAMES J. HILL, parties of the first part, and CHEMET & WEETJEN, KERKHOVEN & CO., LIPPMANN, ROSENTHAL & CO., WURFBAIN & SON, TUTEIN, NOLTHENIUS & DE HAAN, of Amsterdam, H. C. VOORHOEVE & CO., of Rotterdam, and JOHAN CARP, of Utrecht, the Committee of the Dutch Bondholders of the SAINT PAUL AND PACIFIC RAILROAD COMPANY and of the FIRST DIVISION OF THE SAINT PAUL AND PACIFIC RAILROAD COMPANY, parties of the second part, WITNESSETH:

ARTICLE I

That the said parties of the first part do hereby agree to and with said parties of the second part to purchase, and the said parties of the second part do hereby agree to sell to said parties of the first part, the following amounts of the bonds of said companies respectively, of the various issues now held by said parties of the second part, as such Committee, for the following prices, and upon the following terms, namely: Of the one million, two hundred thousand dollars ($1,200,000) Branch Line Issue, of the second of June, 1862, six hundred and twenty-five thousand dollars ($625,000) at seventy-five (75) per cent. of the par value of said bonds; of the two millions, eight hundred thousand dollars ($2,800,000) Branch Line Issue of October 1, 1865, seven hundred and sixty thousand dollars ($760,000) at twenty-eight (28) per cent. of the par value of said bonds; of the three million dollars ($3,000,000) Main Line

432

Issue of March 1, 1864, nine hundred and seven thousand dollars ($907,000) at thirty (30) per cent. of the par value of said bonds; of the six million dollars ($6,000,000) Main Line Issue of July 1, 1868, three million, five hundred and twenty thousand dollars ($3,520,000) at thirty-five (35) per cent. of the par value of said bonds; of the fifteen million dollars ($15,000,000) issue so-called Extension Mortgage of April 1, 1871, eleven million, four hundred thousand dollars ($11,400,000) at thirteen and three quarters (13¾) per cent. of the par value of said bonds. Said purchase prices to include all unpaid coupons belonging to said several classes of bonds, which shall pass with said bonds.

ARTICLE II

Said bonds of said various issues are to be placed in the hands of John S. Kennedy and John S. Barnes (composing the firm of J. S. Kennedy & Co., of the city of New York), as joint and several trustees named in this agreement, to be held by them as such trustees, and to be delivered by them to the parties of the first part, as such purchasers, upon payment of the purchase price thereof in cash, as hereinafter mentioned. But if said payment shall be made in bonds and stock, as hereinafter provided, said bonds shall be held and controlled by said Trustees, until such final payment is made, for the purposes and uses and for the furtherance and completion of this agreement, and for the purpose of completing the foreclosures herein contemplated.

ARTICLE III

Said purchase price is to be paid on or before the expiration of six months from the date of sale of the mortgaged premises described in the various mortgages securing said various issues of bonds, respectively, under the decree of foreclosure which shall be last obtained in the various suits now pending in the district court of the county of Ramsey, state of Minnesota, and in the circuit court of the United States of the district of Minnesota, for the foreclosure of said several mortgages.

433

APPENDIX

ARTICLE IV

During the pendency of said foreclosure suits, and until the payment of the full contract price of the bonds purchased and sold under this agreement, the said parties of the first part shall pay to the said J. S. Kennedy & Co., agents for said Committee, at the city of New York, upon the (22d) twenty-second days of June and December, in each year, a sum in gold coin equal to the semi-annual interest upon the gross purchase price of said bonds, as specified to be paid in cash, computed at the rate of 7 per cent. per annum thereon, said interest to commence to accrue upon said purchase price from the twenty-second day of December, one thousand eight hundred and seventy-seven.

ARTICLE V

The principal of said purchase money is to be paid as hereinafter provided, either in gold or in first mortgage gold bonds of the company to be organized by said parties of the first part, under said foreclosure sales, pursuant to the laws of the state of Minnesota in such case made and provided. Said first mortgage gold bonds shall bear interest at the rate of 7 per cent. per annum, payable semi-annually in gold coin at the city of New York, or, at the option of the holder, in the city of London, at the rate of four shillings sterling to the dollar.

ARTICLE VI

Said bonds are to be received at par, except as hereinafter specially provided; and if such purchase price is paid in bonds at par as aforesaid, said parties of the first part further agree to cause to be issued and to be delivered to the said parties of the second part, or to their said agents, preferred full paid stock of said new company at the rate of two hundred and fifty dollars ($250) for each and every one thousand dollars ($1,000) bond of said new company delivered in payment of said purchase price, as a bonus; which preferred stock shall bear a dividend not exceeding six (6) per cent. per annum in currency; to be payable, however, only in case the earnings of said new company for each year shall be sufficient for that purpose, after payment of all proper expenses,

434

and interest on the bonds issued as herein provided; and said interest shall not be cumulative. *And it is expressly understood,* that no liens or incumbrances shall be placed upon the said reorganized road, except the mortgage hereinafter mentioned, at the rate of not exceeding twelve thousand dollars ($12,000) per mile of completed road. The total amount of said preferred stock shall be limited to twenty-five (25) per cent. of the total bond issue herein provided for.

ARTICLE VII

The option, as to the payment of the purchase price of said bonds in cash, or in bonds and stock as aforesaid, shall be as follows: In the first instance, said parties of the first part shall have the option of making such payment in cash, or in the bonds and stock of said reorganized company as aforesaid, at their election; provided, however, that if said parties of the first part shall elect to make such payment in cash, any holder of the certificates issued by the said Committee, parties of the second part, for bonds purchased under this agreement, shall have the option of demanding payment for the bonds for which he holds the receipt or certificate of said Committee, either in cash, or in said new bonds and preferred stock, at the rate above provided, at his election.

ARTICLE VIII

Any holder of the said Committee's receipts or certificates, for bonds purchased under this agreement, shall have the right to demand and receive the said new bonds at ninety (90) per cent. of their par value, in payment for the bonds for which he may hold the said certificate or receipt; but in the event of his electing to do so, he shall not be entitled to receive preferred stock as above provided. The options to the holders of the certificates of said Committee, as contained in this and the preceding articles, shall be exercised and declared by said Committee, acting for said certificate holders, within sixty days after written notice to said Committee, or to the said J. S. Kennedy & Co., from said parties of the first part, stating their election in regard to the form of payment, as above provided.

435

APPENDIX

Article IX

Said parties of the first part further agree to build and complete the *Extension* line of said St. Paul and Pacific Railroad from its present terminus near Snake River to St. Vincent; the work thereon to be commenced as soon as practicable, and prosecuted with the utmost despatch, with a view to the completion of the said extension during the year 1878, if possible. In order to secure the completion of said extension, the said parties of the first part hereby agree to make and execute their joint and several personal bond, in the penalty of one hundred thousand dollars ($100,000) as liquidated damages, conditioned for the completion of said St. Vincent Extension within two years from the date of this contract.

Article X

It is further agreed that said parties of the first part shall pay to said J. S. Kennedy & Co., as the agents of said Committee, in gold coin, at the city of New York, the cost of the Red River and Manitoba Railroad (known as the Breckenridge-Barnes link), at the same time as is provided for the payment for the said bonds hereby agreed to be purchased (of which cost, in gold, satisfactory evidence is to be furnished to said parties of the first part), with interest thereon, at the rate of 7 per cent. per annum, up to December 22, 1877; which cost and interest is to be taken as the cost of said railroad on that day; and said parties of the first part hereby agree to pay the interest upon said last-mentioned amount, at the rate of seven (7) per cent. per annum, semi-annually in gold coin, on the twenty-second days of June and December of each year, to the said J. S. Kennedy & Co., agents of said Committee, at the city of New York, until the final payment therefor is made as aforesaid.

Article XI

The bonds and stock of said Red River and Manitoba Railroad Company are to be deposited with said J. S. Kennedy & Co., together with a proxy or proxies, in favour of said parties of the first part, and held by them as trustees under this agreement, pending

436

the fulfilment thereof. Said parties of the first part shall have the right of representing and voting on said stock, through said proxy or proxies, at all meetings of said company, and of using the same, so far as shall be necessary to the control, management, and operation by them of said Red River and Manitoba Railroad, and shall also be entitled to receive and expend all incomes derived therefrom, pending the final completion of this agreement.

ARTICLE XII

Said parties of the first part having deposited, in the Bank of Montreal, in the city of New York, the sum of two hundred and eighty thousand dollars ($280,000) in gold coin of the United States as a guarantee and security for the fulfilment of the obligations on their part expressed in this contract (as appears by a certain letter addressed to J. S. Kennedy & Co., by said Bank, dated February 9, 1878), said amount shall be paid over, and the said Bank of Montreal is hereby directed and authorized to pay over the same, to the said J. S. Kennedy & Co., as agents for said Committee as aforesaid, without further or other order or directions from said parties of the first part, upon delivery to the said George Stephen (of the parties of the first part), at the Bank of Montreal in the city of New York, of this agreement duly executed by said party of the second part, together with a declaration in writing by John S. Kennedy and John S. Barnes, composing said firm of J. S. Kennedy & Co., in the form subjoined to this agreement, stating that they hold in their hands, as joint and several trustees named in said agreement, the bonds and stock purchased hereunder, upon the terms, conditions, and trusts herein expressed; and it is understood and agreed that this payment is received by said Committee in full satisfaction of all expenses, disbursements, and liabilities heretofore incurred by them in behalf of said Dutch Bondholders; it being the intent of the parties to this agreement that the purchasers of said bonds are not, in any manner, to be held in any further or other sum for any expenses or liabilities incurred by said Committee in behalf of the holders of said bonds, or of said Committee's certificates.

437

APPENDIX

ARTICLE XIII

Said parties of the first part further agree that in case they shall elect to pay for said purchase in bonds and stock as aforesaid, or in case any of said bondholders shall elect to receive payments in said bonds and stock as aforesaid, the issue of bonds proposed under this agreement upon the line of said railroads, as reorganized, shall not exceed twelve thousand dollars ($12,000) per mile of finished road.

ARTICLE XIV

It is further understood that the six (6) pending foreclosure suits in the district court of the county of Ramsey, Minnesota, and in the circuit court of the United States for the district of Minnesota, in the names of Edmund Rice and others, Trustees; of Horace Thompson and others, Trustees; of Jacob S. Wetmore and others, Trustees; and of John S. Kennedy and others, plaintiffs; and the suit of the First Division of the Saint Paul and Pacific Railroad Company against Edmund Rice, Horace Thompson, John S. Kennedy, Jesse P. Farley and John S. Barnes, commenced in June, 1877, in the district court of Ramsey County, Minnesota— shall be controlled and conducted by the said parties of the second part, or their agents, in concert with and under the advice and instructions of the said parties of the first part, as purchasers of said bonds, free from all expense to said parties of the second part from and after the said 22d day of December, 1877: *provided*, that nothing shall be done to delay the prosecution of said suits to their final ending.

ARTICLE XV

It is further understood that, in case the trustees now in possession of said First Division of the Saint Paul and Pacific Railroads shall hereafter make any division of the earnings of said railroads now in, or hereafter to come into, their hands, the share of such earnings belonging to the bonds so purchased by said parties of the first part, as aforesaid, shall be paid to them by said trustees, at the time of making such division.

438

APPENDIX

ARTICLE XVI

It is further agreed that said parties of the first part shall have the right, at any time during the pendency of this agreement, to demand and receive from said John S. Kennedy and John S. Barnes, the trustees holding said bonds, such amounts thereof as they may call for, upon payment in cash to said J. S. Kennedy & Co., as agents of said Committee, of the purchase prices aforesaid for the bonds so withdrawn by them: *provided, however*, that such withdrawal shall not affect the option of the owner or owners of the certificates issued by said Committee, representing the bond or bonds so withdrawn, to the payment therefor in bonds and stock as above provided, and that the amounts of bonds remaining in the hands of said trustees pending said foreclosures shall not at any time be reduced by such withdrawal below sixty (60) per cent. of the total amount of the outstanding bonds of each respective issue, at the time of such withdrawal; and the bonds so withdrawn shall be retired by exchange for the lands of the companies, as provided in the several mortgages, and shall be withdrawn and used only for that purpose.

ARTICLE XVII

In case any bonds are withdrawn from the trust deposit, as hereinbefore provided, the cash paid in to said agents of said committee, in lieu of the bonds so withdrawn, shall be held by them until the final payments are made as herein provided; when said sum and its accumulations shall be paid over to the trustees to be named in the first mortgage of the new company herein provided to be organized, and said sum shall be held by said trustees as a sinking fund, to be applied to the payment of the bonds to be issued under said new mortgage, according to the terms thereof; which shall provide for the application of said trust fund to the purchase of said bonds at the lowest market price, or by lot, at a premium of 5 per cent. on the par thereof.

ARTICLE XVIII

It is further agreed that any mortgage which shall be executed ᵛupon said proposed reorganized railroads, and the bonds secured by

439

APPENDIX

said mortgage (in case any of said bonds shall be used in carrying out this agreement), shall be satisfactory to said J. S. Kennedy & Co., and shall before execution be approved by them, as to substance and form, as to the trusts created, and as to the trustees appointed in and by said mortgage, and shall cover all the property of every kind belonging to said new company at the time of the execution thereof, including its land grants; and shall provide that said bonds shall be receivable at par in payment for the lands of said company.

ARTICLE XIX

It is further agreed, that in the event of the loss or destruction of any of said bonds by fire or shipwreck, during their transit from Europe to the city of New York, the said parties of the first part will accept, as proof of said loss a notarial certificate, in usual form, attested by an United States consul, setting forth the numbers of the bonds so shipped; the amounts thereof; and the numbers and amounts of the coupons thereto attached; together with satisfactory proof of the destruction by fire, or loss at sea, of any steamer upon which the same shall have been shipped; and, upon receipt of such certificate and proof of loss, will accept the bonds actually delivered under this contract, and will make the payments herein provided to be made, as though no such loss had occurred, and such lost bonds had actually been delivered: *provided*, that said committee shall indemnify the said parties of the first part against the production of said lost bonds at any time thereafter.

ARTICLE XX

It is further agreed that should it be necessary to produce any of the bonds deposited under this agreement, in court, for the purpose of proof in any of the foreclosure suits now pending in Minnesota, as above stated, or for any other purpose connected with the said suits, said bonds may be removed from the place of deposit hereinafter mentioned, by said trustees, or either of them, for such purposes; and if said bonds should be required to be used in the purchase of the railroads and properties covered by the mortgages securing said respective series of bonds, or any of the

440

same, or in completing any of the said foreclosures or the sales thereon, or for the purpose of carrying out this agreement in any manner, or of reorganizing said railroad companies, or of issuing the new bonds contemplated by this agreement, the said trustees are hereby authorized, jointly or severally, to make any use of said bonds that may be necessary for said purposes; and to buy in said railroads and properties at any sale or sales thereof under the said foreclosures, or any of the same; and to use said bonds in making payments therefor; and shall thereupon take title to said railroads and properties in their own names or name, as such trustees, and hold the same until the delivery to them of the cash or the bonds and stock of said new company, as provided by this agreement; which delivery, being duly made or secured to be made, said trustees or trustee so holding title shall convey the said railroads and properties to the said newly-organized company.

Article XXI

And it is further agreed that said trustees shall deposit said bonds and stock certificates, hereinbefore referred to, in the vaults of the Mercantile Safe Deposit Company of the city of New York, in their names as trustees jointly and severally; and there keep the same in iron safes, rented for that purpose, pending the full and final payment of the purchase price of said bonds and stock, as stipulated in this agreement; except in so far as may be necessary to remove or use the same, or any part thereof, as above provided.

Article XXII

It is also understood that either party to this contract shall have the right at any time, to verify the amounts of bonds so deposited, by counting and examining the same in the presence of either of the said trustees, under such rules and regulations as shall be made by said trustees for the safe keeping thereof.

Article XXIII

It is further agreed that in case of any failure on the part of said parties of the first part to pay the full amounts of said semi-annual interest, at the times and in the manner aforesaid, and of the con-

441

tinuance of such default for thirty days thereafter, or in case of the failure of said parties of the first part to make the final payment of the purchase price of the said bonds and stocks, as hereinbefore stipulated, within six months after the sale under the decree last obtained in said foreclosure suits as hereinbefore provided, any and all sums of money which shall have been paid by said parties of the first part under this contract, including said sum of two hundred and eighty thousand dollars ($280,000) and all payments made on account of interest as herein provided, shall be forfeited to said parties of the second part; and thereupon said trustees shall immediately return and restore to said parties of the second part the ownership, possession, and control of the bonds and stocks deposited with said trustees under this agreement; and all rights which said parties of the first part may have acquired under this agreement shall absolutely cease and determine, and the bonds and stock deposited with said trustees under this agreement shall be held by them solely for the benefit of said party of the second part, and subject to their exclusive orders, disposition, and control.

Article XXIV

It is further agreed that all expenses in the said foreclosures and other suits, incurred since the 22d day of December, 1877, and all expenses connected with the custody of said bonds and attending the making and full execution of this agreement and said trust, (including the proper remuneration of said trustees), shall be borne by said parties of the first part.

Article XXV

It is further agreed that while this agreement shall remain un-completed in any respect, in case any vacancy shall occur in the office of either of the trustees named in this agreement, or any successor in the trust hereby created, by death, resignation, or otherwise, the vacancy so arising shall be filled by the appoint-ment of some suitable and competent person to be selected and appointed for that purpose by the surviving or remaining trustee.

442

ARTICLE XXVI

It is further agreed that until a dividend of six (6) per cent. shall have been paid upon the preferred stock, for any one year, the said parties of the second part, as such committee, shall have the right to nominate two (2) directors in the new company which may be hereafter organized by said parties of the first part, at the time of such organization after foreclosure of said trust deeds, and at each election for directors thereafter; such persons so nominated to be acceptable to said parties of the first part; at least two (2) months' notice shall be given of, and prior to, any election for directors; and thereupon the said Committee may name the persons selected by them to said parties of the first part; who, having accepted the said nomination, shall elect the parties so named, at the same time and place as other members of the board of directors.

ARTICLE XXVII

And it is further agreed by the said parties of the first part that they will proceed to, and duly organize the said new company hereinbefore referred to, within six months from the date of the sale under the decree last obtained in the said several foreclosure suits hereinbefore referred to; and so that the said bonds and stock herein provided to be used in making the payments under this agreement shall be duly executed and ready for delivery on or before the termination of said period of six months above specified.

IN WITNESS WHEREOF the said parties have hereunto set their hands and seals the day and year first above written.

Signed, sealed, and delivered in the presence of

As to George Stephen and Donald A. Smith ⎰ R. B. Angus.   GEO. STEPHEN   (Seal)
⎱ Lenox Smith.   DON. A. SMITH   (Seal)

As to Norman W. Kittson and James J. Hill ⎰ Lenox Smith.   NORMAN W. KITTSON   (Seal)
⎱ Edw. T. Nichols, Jr.

By R. B. GALUSHA, his Atty. in fact.

443

APPENDIX

JAMES J. HILL	(Seal)
CHEMET & WEETJEN	(Seal)
KERKHOVEN & CO.	(Seal)
LIPPMANN, ROSENTHAL & CO.	(Seal)
LEO LIPPMANN, GEO. ROSENTHAL.	
WURFBAIN & SON	(Seal)
TUTEIN NOLTHENIUS & DE HAAN	(Seal)
H. C. VOORHOEVE & CO.	(Seal)
J. CARP	(Seal)

WE, JOHN S. KENNEDY and JOHN S. BARNES, composing the firm of J. S. Kennedy & Co., of the city of New York, being the parties named as trustees in the foregoing agreement, *do hereby* jointly and severally accept the trusts therein created, and do acknowledge to have received from the said parties of the second part to said agreement, the bonds mentioned in said agreement, to the amounts, of the numbers, and with the coupons thereto attached, particularly specified and stated in the schedule hereto attached marked A. B. C. D. & E.

Also the stock of the Red River and Manitoba Railroad Company, mentioned in said agreement (called the Breckenridge and Barnes link) with the proxies thereto attached, as per memorandum hereto subjoined.

To have and to hold the same upon the trusts, and with the powers in said agreement particularly set forth.

JOHN S. KENNEDY.
JOHN S. BARNES.

The word "*first*" in seventh line erased, and the word "*second*" interlined, before signing.

444

COMPARATIVE SHOWING OF ST. PAUL & PACIFIC AND ST. PAUL, MINNEAPOLIS & MANITOBA

Report of St. Paul & Pacific Main Line for year ending June 30, 1878:

Gross earnings	$595,286.54
Operating expenses	359,217.45
Net earnings	236,009.09
Payments other than operating expenses	244,875.64

These last included $143,793 for equipment, $20,625 for construction, and $53,160 for interest on bonds.

Report of St. Paul & Pacific Branch Line for year ending June 30, 1878:

Gross earnings	$351,395.57
Operating expenses	167,832.21
Net earnings	183,563.36
Payments in addition	90,897.15

Report of St. Paul & Pacific Line St. Cloud to Melrose, year ending June 30, 1878:

Gross earnings	$36,433.72
Operating expenses	28,394.70
Net earnings	8,039.02

First report of the St. Paul, Minneapolis & Manitoba Company to the Railroad Commission of Minnesota, for year ending June 30, 1880:

Gross earnings	$2,933,108.24
Operating expenses	1,300,512.00
Net earnings	1,632,595.42

Other payments: Construction, $226,097; reorganization expenses, $47,865; additional real estate, $131,088; taxes $86,560; interest on bonds, $947,227.

APPENDIX

Land statement:

	ACRES
Received of grant........................	2,296,802
Yet to inure............................	1,551,198
Obtained from old organization by purchase of road...............................	1,477,569
Sold and contracted year ending June 30, 1880 .	268,741
Sold and contracted all years to June 30, 1880.	739,737
Receipts for year........................	$ 306,864
Receipts for lands, all years...............	4,784,959

APPENDIX   EIGHT

COMPARATIVE SHOWING BY SYSTEMS

	St.P.M. & M. June 30, 1883	C. & N. W. May 31, 1883	C.M. & St.P. Dec. 31, 1882	C.R.I. & P. Apr. 1, 1883
Av. Miles Operated	1,203	3,464	4,296	1,381
Gross Earnings, Per Mile......	$7,604.75	$6,950.63	$4,745.51	$8,826.87
Operating Expenses, Per Mile......	3,610.13	4,061.69	2,836.61	5,148.31
Net Earnings, Per Mile......	3,994.62	2,888.94	1,908.90	3,678.56
To Capital Stock Ratio Net Earnings..........	24.03	25.55	18.49	12.11
Fixed Charges, Per Mile......	$1,050.94	$1,311.56	$1,303.21	$796.52

GROWTH OF SYSTEM IN TWENTY-FIVE YEARS

	1882	1907
Gross Earnings		
Passenger	$1,587,180	$10,605,597
Freight	4,773,005	41,270,191
Total	6,629,694	55,144,402
Operating Expenses	3,320,776	32,562,775
Net Earnings	3,308,917	22,581,626
Taxes	195,001	2,050,923
Operating Expenses per cent. of Gross Earnings	50.08	59.05
(In 1906....50.42)		
Gross Earnings Per Mile	$7,159	$9,217
Operating Expenses per Mile	3,586	5,443
Net Earnings Per Mile	3,573	3,774
Total Miles of Road Operated (All in Minnesota and Dakota; Including Lines Operated Independently)	1,057	6,498
Total Miles of Single Track (All in Minnesota and Dakota; Including Lines Operated Independently)	1,191	8,141
Locomotives	137	943
Passenger Equipment Cars	121	668
Freight " "	3,787	40,043
Bonded Debt	$18,646,000	$99,904,939
Capital Stock	15,000,000	149,915,500

INDEX

References to Vol. II are indicated by the character ² preceding the figure or figures

Adams, Charles Francis, president of Union Pacific, forms alliance with Mr. Hill, 336; agreement with Great Northern for trackage rights over Union Pacific, ²33

Adams, E. D., representative of Deutsche Bank in Northern Pacific reorganization, ²11; letter to, regarding Oregon lines, 37

Agriculture, Mr. Hill's interest in, 361; plans for better farming, 374; farm demonstration, train and lecture service inaugurated by Great Northern, ²361; extensive research work, 361; Mr. Hill's greenhouses given up to experimental work, 364

Allouez Bay Dock Company, incorporated, ²226

Amalgamated Copper Company litigation in Montana field, ²206

American Milking, Shorthorn Breeders' Association organized, ²359

Ancestors of Mr. Hill, 3

Anglo-French Loan, advocacy of, ²316

Angus, R. B., accompanies George Stephen on inspection of St. Paul & Pacific Railroad, 205; Mr. Hill's letters to, 300, 304; with Messrs. Stephen, Hill and Smith in Canadian Pacific syndicate, 310; letters to, on building of Canadian Pacific, 313; letter from Mr. Hill on Canadian Pacific, 322; resigns from Board of Directors of St. Paul, Minneapolis & Manitoba, 323

Armstrong, ——, business arrangement with, 90

Art collection of Mr. Hill and his artistic discrimination, 359, ²396

Astoria & Columbia River Railroad, purchase of, ²258

Bacon, Robert, on conference committee on building a line from Pasco to Portland, ²254

Baker, George, helps determine plan of Northern Securities Co., ²164

Banking institution founded in St. Paul, ²305

Baring Brothers' failure, influence on money market, 470

Baring & Co., letter to, on condition of Great Northern, ²92

Barnes, John S., representing attorneys for Dutch Committee of bondholders, attends meeting with Messrs Stephen, Hill, Smith, and Kittson in Montreal, 207; letter regarding offer made to Dutch Committee, 213; letter from J. P. Farley regarding transfer, 214; representing J. S. Kennedy, at organization of St. Paul, Minneapolis & Manitoba Railroad Co., 287

Barth, T., report on causes of Northern Pacific failure, 444

Bass & Co., J. W., first employers of Mr. Hill in St. Paul, 32

Beaupre & Kelly, business competitors in St. Paul, 90

Becker, General George L., President First Division Company, extracts from report, 159; statement as to value of stock of St. Paul & Pacific, 186

Begg, in History of Canada, quoted, 280

Biggs, Dr. Hermann M., statement of Mr. Hill's initiative in hog cholera investigations and prevention, ²359

Birth of James Jerome Hill, 5, 9

Blanchard & Wellington, partnership with, 57, 80

Blindness, partial, of Mr. Hill, 17

"Bonanza farming," rise and decline, ²191

Borup & Champlin, Mr. Hill's connection with, 32

Bradstreet's *Journal* article on Mr. Hill's ᶠ experiments, 369

Brunson, Lewis & White, Mr. Hill's employers in St. Paul, 32

Bryan, Wm. Jennings, opposed by Mr. Hill, 496

449

INDEX

450

INDEX

INDEX

452

INDEX

Kittson, Norman W., forwarding agent to the Red River country, 70; history, 74; consolidation with in steamboat business, 100, 111; agent Hudson Bay Company at St. Paul, 111; joins in acquiring control of St. Paul & Pacific, 168; proportion of stock held with Mr. Hill in Red River transportation business, 187; becomes interested in acquiring St. Paul & Pacific, 187; attends meeting in Montreal with Messrs. Stephen, Hill, Smith, and Barnes, attorney for bondholders, 207; with associates organize St. Paul, Minneapolis, and Manitoba Railroad Co., 287

La Cross & Minnesota steamboat line organized, 47
Lake Superior & Southwestern acquired by the Manitoba, 415
Lake Superior & Mississippi Railroad built from St. Paul to Duluth, 146
Lake Superior Company, Ltd., organized, ²222; stock transferred to Great Northern shareholders, 228
Lee, Higginson & Co., letter to, 473; letter to, on Oriental trade, ²92
Legislation injurious to railroad, ²260
Letters to boyhood friends, 34, 41
Library presented to St. Paul, ²302
Limerick by Mr. Hill, ²390
Litchfield, Edwin C., owner of stock in First Division Company, 157; Mr. Hill's negotiations, 216
Litchfield, E. B., forms "The First Division of the St. Paul & Pacific," 155
Litchfield, E. D., sells First Division Company of St. Paul & Pacific to Northern Pacific Railroad Company, 157, 158; receives back stock of First Division Company, 166; attempts reorganization of St. Paul & Pacific, 193, 196; stock in St. Paul & Pacific purchased by Hill's associates, 249; settlement with, for Branch Line stock, 284
Litchfield, Egbert S., partnership with, 88, 89, 157
Litchfield, Electus, D., architect Hill Reference Library, ²303
Live stock, Mr. Hill's aid in improving, 363, 365; his stock farms, 364; blooded stock imported and distributed to farmers, 365, 366, 375, 376
"London Agreement," text of, ²14
Lord Mountstephen. See Stephen, George.

Lord Strathcona and Mount Royal. See Smith, Donald A.
Lowell, President of Harvard University, remarks on James J. Hill, Professorship of Transportation, ²314
Lumber, low rate from Pacific Coast points, ²51

McCormack, M. L., reminiscent letter to Mr. Hill, 115
McDougal, Hon. William, turned back by Louis Riel, 101
McMillan, W. J., reminiscences of, 19
MacVeagh, Hon. Franklin, early associated with Mr. Hill, 80
Marriage of Mr. Hill, 60
Maternal ancestors, 4
Mehegan, Mary Theresa, bride of Mr. Hill, 60
Merchants' Club of Chicago, excerpt from Mr. Hill's address before, ²263
Mesaba iron mines, Great Northern acquires railroad to, 464
Mesaba ranges, ²225
Meyer, B. H., author, "A History of the Northern Securities Case," ²163
Military experiences in Minnesota, 43
Milwaukee & Prairie du Chien Railroad, Mr. Hill secures forwarding agency of, 53
Minneapolis milling industry, growth of, 97
Minneapolis & Cedar Valley Railroad receives land grant and aid, 135
Minneapolis & St. Cloud Railroad charter purchased by St. Paul, Minneapolis & Manitoba, 331; used as basis for Great Northern, 461
Minneapolis Union Railway Co., incorporated, 392
Minnesota, exhibits at World's Fair, New York, 1853, 25; early settlements in, 25; conditions in early days, 27; first shipment of wheat and flour, 42; first railroad, 46; peat deposits of, 94; railroad land grants, 133; territorial legislature grants charter to Minnesota & Pacific Railroad Co., 134; ground broken for first railroad, 1858, 136; rapid growth of cities, 137; railroad land grants revert to government, 152; first railroad between St. Paul and Minneapolis, 154; bad crops and grasshopper invasion of 1873, 177; first Railroad Commission created, and its report, 177; act passed enabling foreclosure of mortgage on land grant railroad without destroying its immunity from taxation, 197; agricultural developments and immigration, 241,

455

INDEX

THE COUNTRY LIFE PRESS
GARDEN CITY, N. Y.